Bitcoin

Your Off-Ramp
from the Corrupt Political System
and Protection from Economic Collapse

A Beginner's Guide

Benjamin Hart

Ripple Lake
Publishing

Fort Lauderdale, Florida

Stay in Touch with Ben!

Sign up for Ben's <u>FREE</u> *Bitcoin Weekly Report* at

BitcoinInstitute.Net

For my wife Wanda,
who escaped Communism with nothing
but one dress and her sandals, so
understands why Bitcoin is important for
freedom's survival.

When all Hell breaks loose, Bitcoin allows
you to escape with your assets quickly to
where civilization might still exist.

Contents

CHAPTER 1

What Is Bitcoin?

B itcoin was created by a pseudonymous computer scientist named Satoshi Nakamoto as a way to send money securely over the internet.

We still don't know who Satoshi Nakamoto is or was.

He might have been one person or a group of software engineers and cryptographers who had been working together and sharing information on this project for decades. Bitcoin was officially launched on January 3, 2009, with the mining of the first block – the Genesis Block (Block Zero).

Not knowing who invented Bitcoin remains one of the world's most intriguing mysteries.

The first use of Bitcoin to purchase a commercial product occurred on May 22, 2010.

A computer programmer from Jacksonville, Florida, named Laszlo Hanyecz bought two Papa John's pizzas for 10,000 bitcoins.

He did not actually buy the pizzas directly from Papa John's. He made the request on May 18, 2010, in an online forum called bitcointalk.org.

"I'll pay 10,000 bitcoins for a couple of pizzas, like maybe 2 large ones so I have some leftover for the next day," he wrote. "I like having leftover pizza to nibble on later." [1]

A 19-year-old California software engineering student named Jeremy Sturdivant answered the request and had Papa John's deliver the pizzas to Hanyecz.

On that day, the value of one bitcoin was about one-third of one penny. Sadly for Sturdivant, he quickly spent the 10,000 bitcoins he received for the two pizzas. Hanyecz says he mined and spent approximately 100,000 bitcoins in the early days of Bitcoin.

Neither regrets their decision.

---

[1] bitcointalk.org/index.php?topic=137.0

"I think it's great that I got to be part of the early history of Bitcoin in that way," Hanyecz told *Coin Telegraph* in 2018. "I like to think that what I did helped." [2]

By the way, when Bitcoin is used to describe the system or idea, we capitalize the "B."

When it's used to describe use of the currency as units, the "b" is written in lower case. If we are talking about a specific transaction involving more than one bitcoin, we add an "s" to show the plural, as in "She bought 3.2 bitcoins."

If we are talking about bitcoin as money in a general way, we'll drop the "s" – as in "She has a lot of bitcoin" or "Her private key was stolen, so she lost all her bitcoin."

So what exactly is Bitcoin?

Bitcoin is the most successful attempt to use decentralized blockchain cryptography to create digital money. It's a set of software protocols and processes. Your bitcoin is secured by military-grade SHA-256 cryptography.

Cryptography is the science of creating and sending secure messages that only the intended receiver of the message can understand.

Bitcoin has inspired thousands of other cryptocurrencies. Bitcoin continues to be by far the largest in terms of market cap. It's also the most decentralized of all the cryptocurrencies and assets. We'll get into why this is important in a moment.

Ethereum is the second biggest crypto asset in terms of market cap. It's about half the size of Bitcoin. Ethereum is not actually a cryptocurrency, though it utilizes a cryptocurrency as part of its ecosystem. Ethereum's currency is called ether (ETH).

Ethereum is trying to be a decentralized internet for decentralized applications. We'll talk about Ethereum later.

Bitcoin wants to be one thing – incorruptible decentralized digital money. Bitcoin's two most important properties are:

1) There will never be more than 21 million bitcoins.

2) What makes Bitcoin different from all other cryptocurrencies is it's the most decentralized.

---

[2] Molly Jane Zuckerman, *Coin Telegraph*, May 27, 2018.

Why is "Decentralization" Important?

What does "decentralized" mean? And why is this important?

"Decentralized" means no one person or group of people owns or controls Bitcoin. There is no agent between you and who you are transacting with, no intermediary, no central authority – no bank, no credit card company, no government agency. All transactions are directly peer-to-peer.

An analogy is when you are shaking hands with someone. If you want to shake hands with another person, you just put your hand out and shake hands.

There's no middleman or intermediary shaking hands for you. You are shaking hands "peer-to-peer."

That's what Bitcoin is. No middleman, no intermediary.

Transactions are done "peer-to-peer."

This means no one can confiscate your money. No one can intercept your money. No one can freeze your Bitcoin account. No one can interfere with your transactions.

Also, no one can dilute the value of your Bitcoin by creating more than 21 million.

Bitcoin is governed by math and algorithmic protocols, not by people. So Bitcoin can never fall victim to political corruption or greed.

Bitcoin is not stored or housed on a central server under someone else's control. This makes Bitcoin very different from a bank or a credit card company, which people control.

This is what makes Bitcoin "trustless." It's a "Zero Trust" system.

This is in contrast to your bank, which you must trust with your money. If your money is in a bank, the government or a third party can easily seize your money or freeze your account with a court order. The IRS can take your money without a court order.

That can't happen with Bitcoin. So again, what exactly is Bitcoin?

The Bitcoin "blockchain" is a public ledger of all transactions distributed live and in real-time across a worldwide network of more than 1,000,000 computers (miners and nodes) who protect the system.

This might sound complicated, and it is. But Bitcoin is just a ledger – a way to track transactions, like when you balance your checkbook or use QuickBooks.

How Bitcoin's Decentralized Ledger Works

A ledger is a list or history of transactions – of who paid who what amount and on what date.

In the Bitcoin system, instead of a single person or one central authority having this ledger, the ledger is public and is distributed to anyone who wants it. The identities of the transactors are concealed by cryptography. The amounts sent are public and broadcast live to everyone in the network.

All transactions can be viewed live, as they occur, by anyone who has the Bitcoin software. This blockchain ledger is constantly updated and refreshed as new blocks of transactions are added.

Each refresh to the ledger contains every Bitcoin transaction that has ever occurred. Computers on the Bitcoin network are called nodes and miners. There are approximately 1,000,000 nodes and miners on the Bitcoin network spread out around the world.

Miners are specialized nodes who mine for bitcoin by racing to solve complex math problems.

Bitcoin mining is crucial to securing the Bitcoin network for reasons I'll detail later.

This network of nodes and miners verifies transactions and protects the network.

Every node on the Bitcoin network always possesses a complete, up-to-date copy of the blockchain ledger going back to the first Bitcoin transaction, which occurred on January 12, 2009.

What makes blockchain different from Microsoft Excel is that Bitcoin's blockchain ledger is not editable. It can never be changed. The only change possible is when a new block of transactions is added to the chain about every 10 minutes.

The Bitcoin ledger on every node (computer) must always be identical. If one user were to tamper with Bitcoin's history of transactions, all other nodes in the network would cross-reference each other and instantly identify the node that has the incorrect information.

A miner or node who attempts to broadcast a ledger that is not an exact copy of the ledger that the rest of the network has will be ignored and treated as spam. This policing function is accomplished automatically by the software on each node (computer).

We'll examine the many layers of Bitcoin's security as we

progress through this book.

The security structure of Bitcoin is brilliant – will be seen by historians one day as one of the world's great wonders.

Blockchain technology is also used in a centralized way by banks and financial institutions.

Bitcoin is governed by math, protocols, and algorithms, not by people. Because it's so decentralized, no one owns Bitcoin. No one controls Bitcoin.

This is what makes Bitcoin so different from all other cryptocurrencies and monetary systems. Using this technology, participants can send and receive bitcoin without any central clearing authority.

Decentralization Protects Bitcoin from Government Attack.

Because Bitcoin is protected by a network of 1,000,000 nodes and miners dispersed around the world, a hostile government would have great difficulty destroying Bitcoin. This probably isn't even possible at this point.

If Bitcoin were controlled by a central authority, it would be easy for a government to attack Bitcoin. It could attack the person or small group that controlled Bitcoin.

If Bitcoin were under the control of a person or small group, the government (whether the United States, the European Union, or China) would have taken out Bitcoin by now because governments do not want competitors to their own fiat currency.

For example, China banned bitcoin mining and bitcoin transactions in the summer of 2021. Bitcoin's price then dropped about 50 percent as China's miners moved their mining operations to Kazakhstan, the United States, and more hospitable countries to start mining again.

Within three months, Bitcoin's price had returned to where it was. Bitcoin transactions never skipped a beat during China's crackdown on bitcoin miners.

The bigger the Bitcoin network grows, the more nodes and miners are added to the network, the more decentralized Bitcoin becomes, and the less susceptible Bitcoin is to government attack.

Bitcoin was certainly vulnerable to a government attack in its early days when the network of nodes was small. Bitcoin appears to have grown beyond the point where government can destroy Bitcoin.

Bitcoin is a guerilla army of 1,000,000 nodes and miners spread out across the globe. A government would need to destroy every computer, every copy of the ledger, to destroy Bitcoin.

That's the power of decentralization. There's no one target to hit.

Humans are inherently corrupt and have an unquenchable thirst for power. Whenever humans are involved, corruption follows. Bitcoin requires zero trust in humans. This is what makes Bitcoin trustworthy.

No other cryptocurrency or crypto asset is anywhere near as decentralized as Bitcoin. Satoshi's vision was to develop a "zero trust" decentralized monetary system and network where the money could never be debased by politicians. This system would be governed by math, not people, and would be protected by a decentralized network of nodes and miners.

Satoshi wanted to give the world a system of honest money – an alternative to the government's money printing press. More on "The Big Problem Bitcoin Solves" in a moment.

But first, let's get into how to access Bitcoin and start using it.

Just head on over to Bitcoin.org and follow the instructions. There are a number of good wallets to choose from. Just choose one that Bitcoin.org recommends. Two of the most popular are Electrum and BlueWallet. They only support Bitcoin.

Bitcoin from a User's Perspective

The best way to learn how to transact with Bitcoin is to buy a small amount and start using it.

Here's a summary of what using Bitcoin looks like for the user:

1) Two people decide to make a transaction. Let's say Jim is in the United States and needs to send money to his daughter Jill, who is in Nigeria. Both have gone to Bitcoin.org and downloaded a Bitcoin wallet on their phones.

2) Jim has used his debit card to buy and load some bitcoin into his wallet to send to Jill. He's not sending her an entire bitcoin.

He's just sending her a fraction of a single bitcoin, called "satoshis."

3) Bitcoin wallets have a private key and a public key. A public key is like a slot in a vault where people can drop in money. The slot only goes in one direction. You can email your public key code to people or publish it on your website so people can send you satoshis.

4) Never let anyone get hold of your private key code, unless you want them to have it, such as a family member. Your private key allows you to send money to any Bitcoin wallet on earth instantly or almost instantly. As long as you keep your private key code a secret, your bitcoin is secure.

5) Jim initiates the payment to his daughter Jill in Nigeria. The software broadcasts a message to the Bitcoin network saying something like "I, Jim, am sending 0.05 bitcoin to Jill, and whoever mines this transaction will earn a 0.0001 bitcoin transaction fee." Bitcoin miners receive this transaction and add it to their list of pending unconfirmed transactions called the "mempool."

6) Miners take transactions from the "mempool" and bundle them into "blocks" that can hold around 3,000 transactions per block. You can choose the transaction fee you want to pay. There's a default amount that will vary depending on how busy the network is. If speed is important, you can pay a bit more. You can even transact for free if you don't mind waiting. The reason you can transact for free is that miners are competing for block rewards. More on this later. It's recommended you pay the default transaction fee or a bit more because miners prioritize transactions that will pay the highest transaction fees. Bitcoin fees average about $2 per transaction.

8) A worldwide network of nodes and miners (computers and their operators) use algorithms and military-grade cryptography to verify the status of the users, whether Jim has the bitcoin to spend, and to make sure Jim's bitcoin gets to Jill's wallet in Nigeria and is deducted from Jim's wallet.

9) Once the block of transactions is verified by a consensus of nodes and miners and inserted into the blockchain, Jill can get her money from Jim.

Bitcoin is sometimes criticized as being too slow. Whenever you initiate a transaction, you must wait for your transaction to be approved by a consensus of nodes and miners spread around the world.

Bitcoin was built for security, not so much for speed.

Bitcoin is not an optimal choice for buying a cup of coffee, grocery shopping, or conducting routine daily transactions.

Bitcoin is best suited for larger transactions of $500 or more.

Bitcoin is more like gold – a store of value. Bitcoin is often described as "digital gold."

Gold is not great for conducting daily transactions either. If you go to the grocery store, it won't work well to shave a sliver off your gold bar and give it to the cashier.

Fiat cash or a conventional credit card will work best at the grocery store, most of which are not yet set up for accepting Bitcoin payments. That's coming.

A network called Lightning is being built on top of Bitcoin that is designed to make small transactions both instant and nearly free. Bitcoin is the base layer, much like gold used to be the base layer for the dollar.

Lightning is built for speed and convenience more than for security. You would only want to keep a small amount in the Lightning Network – enough for your routine daily transactions. Lightning is secure enough for small transactions. But its emphasis is speed, not military-grade security.

If you want security, you lose speed. If you want speed and super-cheap transactions, you give up some security.

Your physical wallet is not that secure either. I've lost my wallet many times. But I only keep enough cash in my physical wallet to get me through the day, so it's not a big disaster if I lose it.

It's more just a nuisance.

The Lightning Network is for speed and is almost free.

You can also buy bitcoin on Square's Cash App and PayPal's Venmo. Your transactions are instant on these Apps, but your bitcoin remains under their custodial control. You lose decentralization and lose control of your Bitcoin. You are in the position of having to trust Cash App or Venmo with your money.

This might not seem like a big deal. But if your bitcoin is sitting in a bank or wallet under someone else's control, the government will be able to seize your money at any time without notice. Or your money can be frozen by a legal action.

This happens all the time.

Centralized control allows for more speed. Decentralization is part of what makes Bitcoin so secure. With Bitcoin, you are your own bank. No one can freeze your account, seize your money, or stop your transactions.

Bitcoin is unfreezeable, unconfiscatable, uninterceptable money. No one can access your bitcoin but you.

Decentralization is just one element of Bitcoin's security. There are many layers of Bitcoin security. We'll get into some of the more intriguing details in the pages ahead.

CHAPTER 2

The Big Problem Bitcoin Solves

Whenever I consider investing in an emerging technology, I always ask this question: What big problem is this new technology solving?

The primary problem Bitcoin addresses is dishonest money, the endless and massive money printing by the central banks – often called "fiat money."

Fiat money is government-issued currency that is not backed by a hard asset, such as gold. Its value comes simply because the government decrees its value and has established its fiat currency as legal tender.

There will never be more than 21 million bitcoins. But there will always be more fiat money printing.

Until 1971, the value of the dollar was pegged to gold. At that time, one ounce of gold cost $35.

Then on August 15, 1971, Richard Nixon announced that the U.S. dollar would no longer be pegged to the price of gold.

Why did the U.S. go off the gold standard?

The simple answer is the government wanted more money, wanted no limits on the quantity of money it could print.

Increasing taxes is never politically popular. It's also difficult under the U.S. system to raise taxes because tax increases must be passed by both chambers of Congress, including a three-fifths super-majority of 60 votes in the U.S. Senate, and then signed into law by the President.

So tax increases are both politically unpopular and difficult to enact. It's much easier for the government to simply print money, which produces a hidden tax called inflation.

Inflation is a way for politicians to increase taxes without going to the trouble of passing legislation and going on record with their vote in favor of tax increases.

Inflation is like termites eating your house. Termites are difficult to detect. You don't notice them right away. But termites will destroy your home over time. Inflation does the same to the value of your money.

Since the dollar went off the gold standard in 1971, the price of one troy ounce of gold has gone from $35 to about $1,800.

This means that the dollar has lost 98 percent of its value relative to the value of gold since 1971.

This loss in value has occurred because of massive fiat money printing by the U.S. Federal Reserve ("The Fed").

If we think of money as representing your time, labor, and ingenuity, this means the U.S. Government has stolen 98 percent of what citizens were paid for their work back in 1971.

Your savings represent your life's work and the energy you expended to create value. The government is literally stealing your life with its massive money printing operation.

That's the problem Bitcoin solves – replaces dishonest central-bank-issued fiat money with honest money.

Important properties of honest money include a fixed supply and a fixed set of rules.

About 19 million bitcoins have been "mined" (created) so far. The final 21 millionth bitcoin will be mined in the spring of 2140.

6.25 new bitcoins are mined and put into circulation every 10 minutes on average.

Starting in April of 2024, the number of bitcoins entering circulation will be cut in half to 3.125 new bitcoins every 10 minutes.

These newly mined bitcoins are paid to miners for the work they do to verify transactions and guard the Bitcoin network. Mining for bitcoins is how new bitcoins enter the system, much like mining for gold puts new gold into the system.

Each year, gold mining increases the world's supply of gold by about 1.5 percent.

With Bitcoin, Satoshi Nakamoto sought to approximate gold mining in the digital realm.

About every four years, the Bitcoin algorithm cuts the supply of new bitcoins entering the system in half until the 21 millionth bitcoin is mined in 2140. Then no more bitcoins will ever enter the system.

CHAPTER 3

How Bitcoin Began

A group of pro-freedom software engineers and cryptographers in the 1980s and 1990s began looking at ways to create digital money as an alternative to fiat central bank-issued currency.

Cryptography is the science of creating and solving codes. It's a way of creating secure communications, where only the sender and receiver of a communication can understand what's being said. The word comes from the Greek word "Kryptos," which means hidden.

Before the 1970s, cryptography was primarily practiced in secret by the military and by spy agencies.

Then in the 1980s, an American computer scientist named Dr. David Chaum started writing about how cryptography could be used to create digital money and allow anonymous transactions.

Chaum earned his Ph.D. in Computer Engineering from Berkely in 1982. He went on to become a professor at New York University and later at the University of California.

In October of 1985, Chaum published a paper titled "Security Without Identification: Transaction Systems to Make Big Brother Obsolete." [3]

Chaum is a libertarian.

Chaum developed an electronic cash system called "ecash" that was designed to protect the anonymity of users. He also invented blind digital signatures, mixed networks, and other cryptographic protocols.

In 1981, Chaum published a second paper titled "Untraceable Electronic Mail, Return Addresses, and Digital Pseudonyms."

Chaum's 1982 Berkeley Ph.D. dissertation proposed a digital vault system that includes all the key elements in Bitcoin except "proof of work." His thesis outlines a decentralized distributed system for achieving consensus among nodes, chaining the ledger

---

[3] chaum.com/publications

history into blocks, and time-stamping blocks. Chaum's dissertation even provides the code for his system.

In 1983, Chaum outlined a proposal for digital cash, which introduced blind cryptographic signatures.

The concept was to allow participants to deposit money from a bank into the system, then use that money in ways that could not be traced by any bank, government, or third party. His system could also detect double-spending – meaning money inputs and outputs can only be used once.

Digital files are easy to copy. When you forward an email, you are forwarding a copy of an email. You can forward copies of emails infinitely. A challenge in the digital world is to prevent users from copying their digital tokens and spending them repeatedly.

Chaum's dedication to protecting digital privacy stemmed in part from his observation that the digital world, while potentially a great force for human progress, could also be used to enslave people.

Computerization and digitalization allow government and big tech companies to track a person's every keystroke, internet search, movement, and thought.

In 1985, Chaum wrote that "Computerization is robbing individuals of the ability to monitor and control the way information about them are used. Already, public and private sector organizations acquire extensive personal information and exchange it amongst themselves." [4]

Chaum predicted that digital dossiers would eventually be collected on every individual, and that this would lead to the development of a digital prison with total surveillance.

Chaum's prediction in the 1980s probably sounded alarmist and far-fetched back then, but it's turned out to be dead-on accurate.

Google and today's big tech companies track and catalog your every keystroke, every movement, every Google search, every communication –all stored in the cloud and constantly combed by artificial intelligence (AI) to create profiles on you and your life and predict your next move, like in the movie *Minority Report*.

Chaum believed that digitalization, far from being a force for freedom, was more likely to lead to enslavement – a high-tech

---

[4] Craig Jarvis (2021). "Cypherpunk ideology: Objectives, Profiles, and Influences" (1992–1998), Internet Histories, DOI: 10.1080/24701475.2021.1935547

totalitarianism that would be even more sinister than the nightmare totalitarian society envisioned by George Orwell in his classic novel *Nineteen Eighty-Four*. Chaum believed that all money would ultimately become digital. He wrote that the trend toward a cashless society would then become a form of digital surveillance – allowing AI-powered government to track your every purchase and movement of every dollar in and out of your bank account.

The IRS (or any government entity) could then just seize all your money and assets with a push of a button. Chaum predicted all this in the early 1980s.

So Chaum dedicated himself to finding ways to protect people from this push-button totalitarianism that was ever-growing and expanding in the emerging digital world.

Chaum is widely credited with being the father of decentralized digital currency.

Some believe David Chaum might be Satoshi Nakamoto – since he is credited with developing most of the key pillars of the Bitcoin system architecture – with the exception of Bitcoin's "proof of pork" mining system.

But he denies being Satoshi.

In addition to inventing e-cash, Chaum also outlined a system for using blockchain technology to secure voting systems that would be verifiable and auditable end-to-end, without revealing how people voted – thereby protecting the secret ballot.

Chaum's work inspired a movement some called the "cypherpunks," who dedicated themselves to destroying corrupt central-bank-issued fiat money.

In late 1992, cryptographers Eric Hughes, Timothy May, and John Gilmore founded a small group that met monthly in the San Francisco Bay Area. This informal club developed into a worldwide emailing list of about 700 software engineers who were interested in these ideas so they could share information on the project.

The term "cypherpunks" was coined by a female computer engineer named Judith Milhon.

She was a self-taught computer programmer and civil rights activist who was part of this early group of cryptographers who were meeting in the San Francisco Bay area.

Her friends called her "Saint Jude."

The Origin of Bitcoin's "Proof of Work" Mining

A key cornerstone of Bitcoin's security is the aforementioned "proof of work" system. This is the primary activity of bitcoin miners when they mine for new bitcoins and protect the network. Mining for coins is how new coins enter circulation.

Proof-of-work was originally developed in 1993 by Cynthia Dwork and Moni Naor as a system that deters spam and malicious uses of computing power. Proof-of-work (PoW) is a form of cryptographic algorithmic proof that requires the email sender to prove to others (verifiers) that a certain amount of specific computational effort was used to send the email or other communication through the network.

Verifiers can confirm the amount of computational power with minimal effort (an automated algorithm and proof-of-work code) that tips the balance of power against the spammer, attacker, and malicious computer network actor.

This proof-of-work involves computers solving a math puzzle and then sharing a code to prove the puzzle has been solved. The code is included in the header of the communication where it's checked by the software algorithm.

In 1997, a British software engineer named Adam Back created Hashcash, which has a structure similar to Bitcoin. It utilizes proof-of-work and includes mechanisms to prevent double-spending. Back holds a Ph.D. in computer science and a degree in Distributed Systems.

Back was one of the first two people on the Cypherpunks mailing list to receive an email from Satoshi Nakamoto. Some have speculated that Back is Satoshi, but he denies it.

In 1998, a reclusive Chinese computer engineer named Wei Dai published a proposal for launching B-money. In his proposal, Dai outlined a protocol where a copy of a ledger is distributed to everyone on the network. This ledger tracks how much money each user has and who is paying who. Each time this ledger is updated with a new block of transactions, a copy is distributed to the entire network.

B-money was never launched.

Also in 1998, a cryptographer named Nick Szabo published a proposal for Bit Gold.

Bit Gold was also never launched. Szabo's proposal combined decentralization, different elements of cryptography, time-stamped blocks stored in a title registry (similar to blockchain) and generated by using proof-of-work math puzzles.

Bit Gold's structure is so similar to Bitcoin that some speculate Szabo is Satoshi Nakamoto. Elon Musk speculates that Szabo is Satoshi

But Szabo denies it.

In 2004, a computer engineer named Hal Finney created what is called "reusable proof-of-work" that produced unique cryptographic tokens that could only be used once, much like unspent transaction outputs in the Bitcoin system.

Finney outlined how "reusable proof-of-work" (RPoW) using a SHA-256 hashing algorithm could be used to secure digital money. But validation and protection against double-spending were still performed by a central server under Finney's system, so was missing decentralization.

Decentralization is a key pillar of Bitcoin's security and makes Bitcoin unique in the world of crypto. No other cryptocurrency or asset has been able to achieve Bitcoin's level of decentralization, or come close.

Few crypto assets even try to be decentralized.

Ethereum claims to be decentralized, but isn't – as we'll see later.

On August 18, 2008, Satoshi Nakamoto registered the domain name of bitcoin.org and created a website, or perhaps his associates created the site.

On October 31, 2008, Satoshi published his historic white paper on the cryptography mailing list at metzdowd.com that was titled "Bitcoin: A Peer-to-Peer Electronic Cash System."

You can read Satoshi's white paper here:

bitcoin.org/bitcoin.pdf

It's just eight pages long and easy for a layperson to understand.

On January 9, 2009, Satoshi released version 0.1 of the open-source Bitcoin software on SourceForge. He launched the network by defining the "Genesis block" (block number 0). The mining of this first block produced a reward for the miner of 50 bitcoins.

At that point, Bitcoin had achieved no established value because no transaction had yet occurred.

Embedded in the Genesis Block is the following text: "The Times 03/Jan/2009 Chancellor on brink of second bailout for banks."

This message clearly suggests that Satoshi was motivated to create an honest alternative to central bank-issued fiat currency. The fact that his message referenced news in the United Kingdom and used the British format for writing a date suggests Satoshi was probably British.

On January 11, Satoshi Nakamoto wrote the following on the Bitcointalk forum:

> Announcing the first release of Bitcoin, a new electronic cash system that uses a peer-to-peer network to prevent double-spending. It's completely decentralized with no server or central authority. [5]

Finney answered:

> Congratulations to Satoshi on this first alpha release. I am looking forward to trying it out. Total circulation will be 21,000,000 coins. It'll be distributed to network nodes when they make blocks, with the amount cut in half every 4 years.
>
> > First 4 years: 10,500,000 coins
> > Next 4 years: 5,250,000 coins
> > Next 4 years: 2,625,000 coins
> > Next 4 years: 1,312,500 coins, etc...

Finney then offered this speculation:

> It's interesting that the system can be configured to only allow a certain maximum number of coins ever to be generated. I guess the idea is that the amount of work needed to generate a new coin will become more difficult as time goes on.
>
> One immediate problem with any new currency is how to value it. Even ignoring the practical problem that virtually no one will accept it at first, there is still a difficulty in coming up with a reasonable argument in favor of a particular non-zero value for the coins.
>
> As an amusing thought experiment, imagine that Bitcoin is successful and becomes the dominant payment system in use throughout the world. Then the total value of the currency should be equal to the total value of all the wealth in the world.

---

[5] nakamotoinstitute.org

Current estimates of total worldwide household wealth that I have found range from $100 trillion to $300 trillion. With 20 million coins, that gives each coin a value of about $10 million.

So, the possibility of generating coins today with few cents of compute time may be quite a good bet, with a payoff of something like 100 million to 1! Even if the odds of Bitcoin succeeding to this degree are slim, are they really 100 million to one against? Something to think about . . .

Hal

You can find the Bitcoin mailing list threads I quote here compiled by the Satoshi Nakamoto Institute. [6]

On January 16, 2009, Satoshi provided this insight in answer to a question posted on the forum about whether Bitcoin could be said to have any real monetary value.

Satoshi posited that Bitcoin already has monetary value through its proof-of-work mechanism, even though Bitcoin had not yet been used commercially. Here's what Satoshi wrote:

It can already be used for pay-to-send e-mail. The send dialog is resizable and you can enter as long of a message as you like.

It's sent directly when it connects. The recipient double-clicks on the transaction to see the full message. If someone famous is getting more e-mail than they can read, but would still like to have a way for fans to contact them, they could set up Bitcoin and give out the IP address on their website. "Send X bitcoins to my priority hotline at this IP and I'll read the message personally."

Subscription sites that need some extra proof-of-work for their free trial so it doesn't cannibalize subscriptions could charge bitcoins for the trial. It might make sense just to get some in case it catches on. If enough people think the same way, that becomes a self-fulfilling prophecy. Once it gets bootstrapped, there are so many applications if you could effortlessly pay a few cents to a website as easily as dropping coins in a vending machine. (nakamotoinstitute.org)

One reason I think Adam Back might be Satoshi is that Back uses the colloquial word "bootstrapped" a lot in interviews I've seen with him. Here, with Satoshi, we see the phrase "bootstrapped."

---

[6] satoshi.nakamotoinstitute.org/emails/threads/

In America, we hear "Pull yourself up by your bootstraps." But I don't hear Americans use the phrase "bootstrapped." Satoshi appears to be British. Back is British. Both use the phrase "bootstrapped" to describe Bitcoin's increased adoption.

Back is also low-key and understated in the way he talks – much like Satoshi's communications on the Bitcoin forum.

Of course, this is just speculation on my part. Back says he's not Satoshi. In this same discussion thread on Bitcointalk, Satoshi offered this prediction:

> The real trick will be to get people to actually value the bitcoins so that they become currency. I would be surprised if 10 years from now we're not using electronic currency in some way, now that we know a way to do it that won't inevitably get dumbed down when the trusted third party gets cold feet.
>
> It could get started in a narrow niche like reward points, donation tokens, currency for a game or micropayments for adult sites. Initially it can be used in proof-of-work applications for services that could almost be free but not quite. [7]

Satoshi also talked about decentralization being Bitcoin's key feature:

> You know, I think there were a lot more people interested in the 90's, but after more than a decade of failed Trusted Third Party based systems (Digicash, etc.), they see it as a lost cause. I hope they can make the distinction that this is the first time I know of that we're trying a non-trust-based system.

You can find more of these fascinating posts here:
satoshi.nakamotoinstitute.org/emails/cryptography

What also makes Bitcoin very different from all, or almost all, other cryptocurrencies that came later is these early cryptographers had no expectation that they would become rich from the project. They were scientists, not venture capitalists.

They were driven by their libertarian ideology – their commitment to freedom. They wanted to find a way to create a monetary system that could just run on its own, that is incorruptible, and would be governed by math, not people.

---

[7] satoshi.nakamotoinstitute.org/emails/cryptography/17/

They wanted to create an escape hatch from corrupt money, corrupt political systems, and the coming digital prison that was being built by Google and Big Tech. There were no stakeholders or shareholders in Bitcoin. No one would own or control Bitcoin. It would just exist on its own in cyberspace.

While some imagined that Bitcoin might snowball on its own if its adoption were to grow, they thought it just as likely (more likely) that the project might not go anywhere. It might just end up like all the other failed attempts over the decades that tried to create a secure, decentralized digital money.

In none of their conversations on the Bitcoin talk forum did any of them express expectation of making a lot of money. No one said anything like "I think we're going to get rich off this idea."

In a very real sense, I consider these computer engineers as similar to America's founders.

George Washington, Thomas Jefferson, James Madison, Benjamin Franklin, and the 56 signers of America's Declaration of Independence were not trying to get rich by going to war against the British Empire, the largest empire in world history.

They were already wealthy. George Washington was a revered general in the British Army. They had everything to lose by going to war with the British Empire.

They had nothing to gain personally by launching America's War for Independence. It was almost all downside risk with almost no upside potential for America's founders.

There was a much better chance that they would end up at the end of a hangman's noose than succeed in building a new nation – the first nation in history conceived in liberty.

They were driven to go to war with the British Empire by principle, as set forth in America's founding document, the Declaration of Independence. Penned by Thomas Jefferson, the second paragraph states:

> *We hold these truths to be self-evident, that all men are created equal, that they are endowed by their Creator with certain unalienable Rights, that among these are Life, Liberty and the pursuit of Happiness.*

This was the driving idea that created the United States of

America – the first nation in history to be "conceived in liberty."

Similar to America's founders, the creators of Bitcoin were not motivated by wealth.

They could have made plenty of money, all the money they could ever want, with their expertise in software coding and computer engineering.

These computer scientists were motivated by their opposition to a creeping totalitarianism and a rising new oligarchy.

They saw the corruption of money by government as the primary threat to liberty and road to enslavement by government and/or Big Tech monopolies. The debasement of currency leads to oligarchy and the gradual transfer of wealth from the middle class and working class to the wealthy.

That's exactly what we've seen take place since America went off the gold standard in 1971 . . . because inflation is a hidden tax on those who rely on fiat money to survive – those on fixed incomes and those who live paycheck-to-paycheck.

The wealthy can afford to unload their fiat money and buy assets that appreciate relative to the dollar – such as beachfront property, stocks, rare art, gold, or bitcoin.

So, in an inflationary environment, wealth always flows in the direction of those who can afford these kinds of assets.

Not everyone is poor in Venezuela, Cuba, or in Third World countries. There's always a small group at the top who are fabulously wealthy, those who have the political power.

Political power equals wealth.

Fiat money can also be called political money. Political money flows to those in power.

America's banks and largest corporations are partners with and agents of the government. They benefit from political money.

Debasement of money is theft, especially from those who live paycheck-to-paycheck. A 7 percent inflation rate is a 7 percent added tax on these people.

At the same time, real estate and hard assets are typically appreciating at about this same 7 percent per year inflation rate when measured against the dollar.

So a 7 percent inflation tax on the working class flows directly to those holding real assets.

That's how the rich get richer, and those on wages and fixed incomes get poorer.

This was the problem these computer engineers tried to address. They saw corruption of money as a major leak in the ship of liberty. If the leak is not fixed, this ship called *Liberty* will sink.

They wanted to find a way to fix the money system. This was a project they had been working on for decades. This was their obsession.

The first successful Bitcoin transaction occurred on January 12, 2009 (Block 170), when Satoshi sent Hal Finney 10 bitcoins as a gift. On the Bitcointalk forum, Finney describes his excitement:

> When Satoshi announced the first release of the software, I grabbed it right away. I think I was the first person besides Satoshi to run bitcoin. I mined block 70-something, and I was the recipient of the first bitcoin transaction, when Satoshi sent ten coins to me as a test. I carried on an email conversation with Satoshi over the next few days, mostly me reporting bugs and him fixing them. [8]

The first successful commercial use of Bitcoin occurred on May 22, 2010, when Laszlo Hanyecz bought those two Papa John's pizzas for 10,000 bitcoins.

Satoshi Nakamoto continued to collaborate with other developers on the Bitcoin software until mid-2010.

He performed all the coding himself and then turned control of the source coding over to Gavin Andresen. On August 22, 2011, Satoshi sent his final message to the Bitcoin community:

> There's more work to do on DoS, but I'm doing a quick build of what I have so far in case it's needed, before venturing into more complex ideas. [9]

This style of writing leads me to think Satoshi might be David Chaum – who is very philosophical and who has gone on to work on other projects. Does he use the word "bootstrapped" too?

I'm not sure.

Satoshi then logged off and disappeared forever.

Some theorize that Hal Finney is Satoshi because Finney was the recipient of the first Bitcoin transaction from Satoshi – 10 bitcoins on January 12, 2009. Finney died from ALS (Lou Gehrig's disease)

---

[8] Finney, Hal Finney, "Bitcoin and Me." March 19, 2013
[9] satoshi.nakamotoinstitute.org/posts/bitcointalk/543/

in August of 2014.

Another reason some think Finney was Satoshi is Satoshi's 1,000,000 bitcoins are still sitting at Satoshi's Bitcoin address. Not a single coin has ever moved.

My bet is Satoshi refers to this group of cryptographers who worked on Bitcoin for many years, to include Hal Finney, Adam Back, Nick Szabo, David Chaum, and others.

Perhaps they have a pact to keep Satoshi's identity secret – and for good reason . . . because the entire point of Bitcoin is that no one owns Bitcoin, no one controls Bitcoin, no one runs Bitcoin.

Bitcoin is a decentralized monetary network governed by math and protocols, not people. Bitcoin is incorruptible money with a fixed set of rules, the most important rule being: There will never be more than 21 million bitcoins.

CHAPTER 4

What is Money?

One of the great gifts Bitcoin is delivering to the world is a course in economics. Bitcoin is teaching the world Economics 101.

Most people have no idea what money is or how it derives its value. People pull cash out of their wallet, which seems to work for buying things. But that's about all most people know about money.

But people are sensing more and more that something has gone seriously wrong with the money. They notice their money is buying less and less. They notice it's costing more and more to live.

Bitcoin's rising price is also causing people to wonder what Bitcoin is all about. This realization is prompting hundreds of millions of people to want to learn the basic laws of sound economics.

The mission of Bitcoin is to be incorruptible money. Through Bitcoin, the world is learning that sound money must have four key properties:

1) Sound money must have a finite supply – scarcity.

If money can just be printed at will, it's no longer finite. If it's no longer finite and scarce, then it's no longer valuable.

Gold is difficult to find and mine, so it's scarce.

Miners are able to increase the world's gold supply by about 1.5 percent each year. So gold is not quite finite. It's close to finite, and scarce. Gold is difficult to accumulate. According to the billionaire investor Warren Buffett, all the gold in the world would fit into a 67-square-foot cube. Scarcity plus demand makes gold valuable.

2) To be useful, money must be divisible into smaller amounts.

In primitive economies, transactions were (and still are) conducted via barter. "I'll dig that ditch if you pay me with corn" is a transaction using barter.

As civilizations became more advanced, people searched for and tried to develop units of exchange.

Some exchanged pretty rocks and metals. Some also maintained ledgers and agreements on what people owed each other.

The first gold coins were minted in about 550 BC under King Croesus of Lydia – a province in what today is Turkey. Gold coins became the accepted payment for goods and services.

In our U.S. economy today, we have $1, $2, $5, $10, $20, $50, and $100 bills, plus coins – although we are quickly moving toward a cashless society. Money is mostly digital today. There's only about $1.2 trillion in physical U.S. currency in circulation in a $21 trillion annual GDP economy.

So a useful currency must be easily divisible. Your house is valuable. But it's not easily divisible, so it's not useful as currency.

Gold is divisible, but not easily. If you had a few gold coins in 500 BC Lydia, you might have had trouble getting change for your purchase. To use a portion of your gold bar, you'd have to melt it down, pour a bit of it into a container, let it cool into a solid, and then weigh it to see how much it's worth.

That's not easy or convenient.

3) A good currency must be easy to carry and transport.

Paper money solved this problem. Paper gold certificates were much easier to carry and transport than gold. That's what U.S. paper currency was until 1933 – gold certificates that could be redeemed for gold at banks.

But government could not resist going off the gold standard.

The problem with paper money is there is always the temptation for governments to print more of it. That temptation is irresistible. Money printing is like crack cocaine addiction. Once you're on crack, you need more and more of it to achieve the same high.

Imagine your behavior if you had a money printer in your basement, and you could always print more money without legal consequence. Just print as much as you want when you want.

What would you do?

You would probably do exactly what governments and politicians are doing – print more and more money

The more money politicians print, the more their voters cheer.

The money printing provides a sugar-high for the economy – until it doesn't. At some point, we crash from that sugar high. At some point, we become Venezuela or the German Weimar Republic, which gave us Hitler.

4) A good money must be durable.

Food is valuable. It's necessary for survival. It's also divisible. But food is not durable. Food spoils, rots, goes bad.

Rare art can be valuable, but it's also not very durable. It can easily be destroyed. Rare art is also not divisible. Paying someone a piece of a Picasso wouldn't work well. So rare art can work as a good store of value if you keep it in a vault under perfect climate control, perhaps under vacuum seal. But it doesn't work well as a currency.

Paper money is easy to carry and transport. It's divisible into smaller amounts. But it's also easy to corrupt simply by printing more of it, which is what always happens – has never not happened. Paper money has not preserved value over time, so is not durable.

In fact, if you look at the history of fiat currency, all have dropped to zero over time.

The U.S. dollar is among the strongest of the fiat currencies. Most of the developed world pegs the value of their currency to the dollar. The dollar's value has fallen 98 percent when measured against gold since we went off the gold standard completely in 1971.

Gold is indestructible. You can melt it. You can form it into coins, bars, jewelry, or ornaments.

So gold is divisible and durable.

Gold's durability makes it a good store of value. It allows you to transmit value over time.

One problem with gold is that if it's stolen, it can't easily be identified – unlike rare art.

It's difficult for thieves to traffic in stolen rare art because art is so easy to identify.

Yet with gold, the thief can just melt it and turn it into something else. All identifying markings then disappear.

Now we have Bitcoin – which possesses all four essential properties of sound money (finite, divisible, transportable, durable) and does it better than any currency that's ever been created before.

It's a finite currency. There will never be more than 21 million bitcoins.

It's also divisible into fractions of a bitcoin – satoshis or "sats." 100,000,000 satoshis equal one bitcoin.

Bitcoin is easy to carry and transport.

You can carry your entire Bitcoin vault on your phone, on a piece of paper, or even in your head if you can remember a 12-word private key recovery phrase.

You also cannot melt a bitcoin and turn it into something else, like you can with gold.

Each bitcoin, each fraction of a bitcoin is unique and one-of-a-kind.

Bitcoin is also durable. It maintains and generally increases in value over time, at least when measured against fiat currency.

But Bitcoin has additional properties that no currency and no other asset class has ever had.

Bitcoin can be sent instantly anywhere in the world for a very low cost. Currently, fees are averaging about $2 per transaction.

Bitcoin fees are based on the amount of data being sent. You can actually send Bitcoin for free if you don't mind waiting some time for your transaction to clear.

If you use the Lightning Network, which is built on top of the Bitcoin base layer, you can send small amounts for almost free.

With the Lightning Network, I can envision a time when you might pay 10 cents to read one article in a publication without having to buy a monthly subscription.

You can't do any of this when using gold. And it's not easy to do this even with fiat money.

For merchants, credit card fees are in the 2-3 percent range, plus a flat 30-cent fee per transaction.

Fees for wiring money overseas can be enormous and can take days to finalize.

A quarter of the world's people have no access to banking. They are "unbanked." Until Bitcoin, the unbanked had to use a service like Western Union to send money.

My quick scan of Western Union's site turns up fees of $12 to $35 per transaction. There are also exchange rate fees when converting one currency to another.

Banks charge wiring fees of $25 to $35 typically. Money wires take hours to clear. If you are wiring money out of the country, it can take days for a transaction to clear.

These fees and delays are almost eliminated with Bitcoin, especially with the Lightning Network.

Your transaction is usually finalized within 10 or 20 minutes, or instantly if you use Lightning. There's no need to covert bitcoin into another currency, although you can if you want.

In a few years, transacting business using fiat currencies issued by bureaucratic central banks will look like caveman-style barter economics. We'll wonder then why anyone put up with doing business this way.

CHAPTER 5

The Mechanics of Bitcoin

This section is for those who want to know a bit more about how the Bitcoin system works under the hood – the mechanics.

Many people don't feel they need to know the precise mechanics of how things work.

Most people get in their car and drive. They don't know how the car works under the hood. It just works. Most people buy a ticket and get on a plane. They don't know the mechanics of how the jet works. The plane just gets them to where they want to go.

The phone just works. We don't need to know much more than that.

That's fine for technologies that have been around for decades and that we use every day.

But when investing in an emerging technology, I want to know more about it. I want to know at least the basics of how it works and why a competing technology is unlikely to surpass it any time soon.

Digital money created out of thin air by an anonymous inventor that runs on a computer network that basically just runs itself with no central governing authority sounds pretty sketchy to most people when they first hear about Bitcoin.

It sounds sketchier still when one learns that the value of one bitcoin was one-third of one penny in 2010 and has since risen to $[check today's price] per coin.

So, what does Bitcoin look like under the hood? How does this system actually work? And is it hackable?

Is our bitcoin safe from thieves? Can the Bitcoin network ever be destroyed by a powerful malicious actor, such as Vladimir Putin or Communist China? We want to know these things about Bitcoin

So, let's dive a bit deeper into the weeds.

The Bitcoin network is a public ledger of transactions that is updated with blocks of transactions every 10 minutes on average. This complete updated ledger is then distributed publicly to miners and nodes (computers) around the world – to anyone who has installed the Bitcoin software.

The Bitcoin network is protected by military-grade cryptography, complex math and algorithms, plus a worldwide network of nodes and "miners."

There are more than 1,000,000 Bitcoin miners and full nodes now distributed around the world. This number is increasing all the time.

This global network is what makes the Bitcoin network decentralized, which means there is no central governing authority or administrator.

Transactions are not cleared by a central authority, such as a bank or a credit card. Instead, transactions are confirmed by a consensus of nodes and miners, plus cryptographic algorithms.

Bitcoin is not hosted on Amazon AWS, Google, or the Microsoft Assure cloud. It's distributed across a network of 1,000,000 miners and nodes.

Anyone can be a miner. Just buy the right computer – an ASIC mining computer. Then download the Bitcoin software and start mining.

ASIC stands for "Application Specific Integrated Circuit." These are specialized bitcoin mining computers that cannot be used for any other purpose. A top-level bitcoin mining computer will cost in the range of $15,000 to $17,000 – such as Bitmain's Ant miner S19 Pro.

Yet you can also be a non-mining node with a $400 laptop computer if all you want to do is to monitor the network, play a role in verifying transactions, and oversee the work of the miners.

Non-mining nodes maintain a live copy of the Bitcoin ledger on their computers, monitor the network, and verify transactions, but they are not eligible for mining rewards.

Miners serve several key functions. The most important functions are to verify transactions, make sure there is no double-spending of bitcoins, and to secure the network.

Miners do the real work. They are compensated for their work with transaction fees and newly mined bitcoins.

The key point to understand is that every transaction is publicly broadcast to this network of nodes and miners. A consensus of miners and nodes is required to approve transactions.

To use the Bitcoin network, go to bitcoin.org to download your wallet.

Your wallet has a private key and a public key. Your private key is also your digital signature. More accurately, your private key generates unique, one-of-a-kind signatures for each transaction you initiate.

Your private key is what allows you to send money if you have the money in your wallet.

Your public key enables you to receive bitcoins from anyone on the network. You can publish your public key on your website or anywhere, so people can send you bitcoins or satoshis.

Your public key is like a mail slot in your vault that can only go in one direction. Anyone can drop money in your vault. Only you can take money out.

Your public key is cryptographically linked to your private key, but in such a way that no one can see your private key.

Every transaction also has a unique code that is the link between your public key and your private key. This unique transaction link between your private key and public key is what enables the person you are sending money to, as well as the Bitcoin network, to verify that the transaction is legitimate.

A transaction code is generated by the system and can never be used again. This transaction code (the link between your public and private key) is your digital signature for that particular transaction.

Without getting too far into the technicalities, the truth is there's no such thing as a bitcoin or a satoshi.

The currency is actually just the history of transactions. There are no accounts, at least not in the sense that you have an account with your bank.

Instead, ownership of funds is verified through links to previous transactions.

This is why when you first download Bitcoin's wallet software, every transaction that has ever been made on the Bitcoin network, going back to the first transaction, is also downloaded.

When you first install Bitcoin software, this process can take more than a day. But it only has to be done once.

You will then be able to see all transactions that occur live. You can also see every transaction that has ever occurred on the network. The Bitcoin network is completely transparent. Everyone can see every transaction.

To spend Bitcoin, the system must see that enough bitcoin has entered your address (vault) in the past to cover what you are trying to spend.

Once a transaction has been spent, it's considered spent, and it cannot be used again. Remember also that each transaction has a unique code that can never be reused.

The math and algorithms are complex.

If you want to do a deeper dive into how the Bitcoin network works and is secured, Google search terms like "elliptic curve digital signature algorithm," "mathematical trap door" and SHA-256.

All transactions go through several layers of verification.

Here's a most basic summary of what happens:

STEP ONE: Sender initiates transaction. Information includes the amount being sent and the address (public key) of the receiver.

STEP TWO: The system generates a SHA-256 hash. This is a 256-bit encrypted container that includes all the information (data) needed for the transaction. SHA stands for "Secure Hash Algorithm" and was developed by the U.S. military to encrypt messages. Modern SHA cryptography is considered unbreakable code. A hash in blockchain is data that flows in one direction and cannot be undone. Cryptographic hash functions are a basic tool of cryptography.

STEP THREE: The system generates an encrypted version of the sender's private key for the transaction, which is the sender's digital signature.

STEP FOUR: The receiver receives the data, the sender's public key, and sender's digital signature for the transaction.

STEP FIVE: The receiver's public key is applied to the sender's encrypted digital signature.

STEP SIX: This automatically generates a hash (code) that must equal the hash produced by the sender. If there's no match, the transaction is rejected by the system.

STEP SEVEN: If there is a match between the sender's hash and receiver's hash, the transaction is provisionally validated and moves to a mempool of pending transactions awaiting a miner to include this transaction in a block with other transactions.

As part of the SHA-256 hash function, every transaction contains the link (output/input script) to the previous transaction so the network can quickly trace the history of every transaction that has ever occurred. Cryptographic shortcuts (code reading) allow this to be completed quickly.

Every transaction is cryptographically linked back to the first bitcoin transaction. The ledger history can never be changed.

Flow Chart of How Bitcoin Works

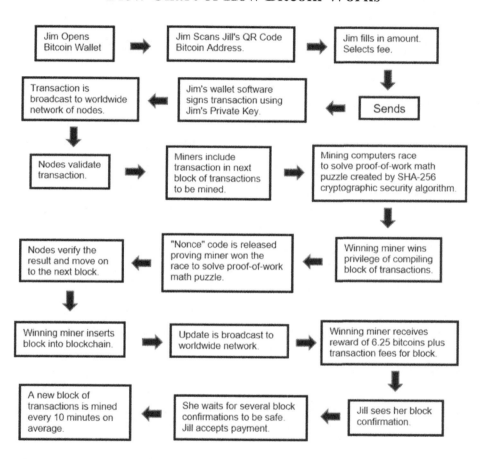

In summary then, a transaction is provisionally approved algorithmically when all keys match (private key of the sender, public key of the receiver, signatures for the transaction); is then added to the mempool of pending transactions; is then approved by the miner who won the privilege to assemble the next block of transactions; is then broadcast with other transactions in this block to the worldwide network of miners and nodes for validation; and is then accepted by the receiver.

New blocks of transactions are formed every ten minutes on average. The maximum block size on the Bitcoin network is four megabytes, which can contain about 3,000 transactions.

Remember why miners do all this work. They are competing to assemble each block of transactions for insertion into the immutable blockchain using a "proof-of-work" protocol.

This involves a race by mining computers to solve a complex math puzzle. The miner who wins the race to mine the next block receives a prize of 6.25 bitcoins.

This is the "Reusable Proof of Work" algorithm that Hal Finney outlined – a process that creates one-of-a-kind coins that are actually unique transactions, not really coins.

The miner who solves the puzzle for the privilege of mining the block first shares the result across the entire network of miners.

Solving this puzzle generates a nonce (a unique key code) that unlocks the block, so all nodes and miners can verify the transactions again and approve the block. "Nonce" means "number that can only be used once."

So this is a many-layered verification system.

The winning miner has no financial incentive to mess with the block because this miner is being awarded 6.25 bitcoins for winning the race to solve the puzzle and mine the block, to include validating transactions in the block. The miner's incentive is to protect the integrity of the network, which also protects the value of the miner's bitcoins.

In theory, a miner could include an illegitimate transaction in a block, or several illegitimate transactions. But the block would then be rejected by the network and the miner would lose his 6.25 bitcoin reward for solving the puzzle and assembling the block.

That was Satoshi's brilliant design. Everyone on the Bitcoin network is incentivized to protect the network. All transactions are public. There are 1,000,000 nodes and miners watching the work of the winning miner who has won the contest to assemble the block.

If any bitcoin miner attempts any monkey business that might jeopardize the integrity of the network and undermine people's confidence in the network, this behavior would just hurt the miner.

The only reason miners invest in expensive computers to mine for bitcoins is so they can accumulate more bitcoins, which they then hope increase in value.

If the network were ever compromised, their bitcoins would plummet in value – might become worthless.

After transactions are verified by cryptographic keys and algorithms prior to entering the mempool of pending transactions, then approved by the winning miner who is assembling the block, the worldwide network of nodes and miners then start granting their approval of transactions in the block.

Once a consensus of nodes and miners is achieved on the validity of transactions in the block, the block is inserted into the blockchain. The receivers of transactions in that block can then accept their payments.

As you can see, this is a rather slow and clunky process.

This is the nature of a decentralized monetary network that has no central administration. Transactions are approved by a consensus of a worldwide network of more than 1,000,000 nodes and miners – though in practice most transactions are accepted by the recipient after a few verifications.

Still, the Bitcoin network can only process about 3,000 transactions every ten minutes. By contrast, Visa processes about 30,000,000 transactions every ten minutes.

So Bitcoin is not a good vehicle for day-to-day transactions. Bitcoin is built for security, not speed.

For speed, you want centralized authority that can move quickly. For security, you want decentralization with many layers of protection.

Bitcoin is where you store your wealth and how you move large sums of money. For shopping at the grocery store and conducting day-to-day transactions, fiat money and Visa are superior.

Bitcoin is like an armored truck or a convoy of tanks protecting your assets. Even more than this, Bitcoin is your army of 1,000,000 soldiers (miners and nodes) singularly focused on protecting your life savings.

So let's now recap the transaction verification process by quoting directly from Satoshi's white paper:

1) New transactions are broadcast to all nodes.

2) Each node collects new transactions into a block.

3) Each node works on finding a difficult proof-of-work for its block.

4) When a node finds a proof-of-work, it broadcasts the block to all nodes.

5) Nodes accept the block only if all transactions in it are valid and not already spent.

6) Nodes express their acceptance of the block by working on creating the next block in the chain, using the hash of the accepted block as the previous hash. [10]

The money is then available to the payee.

When Satoshi wrote this, there was not yet any distinction between nodes and miners.

As the computing power needed to mine for bitcoins grew more intense, some nodes invested in powerful ASIC computers to mine, while other nodes only participated in the validation of transactions, which could be done with a $400 laptop computer.

For miners, solving the math puzzle for each block is really not so much a race as it is a lottery. Your probability of solving the puzzle is in direct proportion to the computing power of your mining computer.

This reward system is how new bitcoins enter into circulation and compensates miners for verifying transactions, maintaining the public ledger, and protecting the system.

Miners also receive transaction fees that are paid by the payer. These transaction fees vary depending on how busy the network is and how much computational energy is required to process a transaction.

The larger the amount of your transaction, the smaller the fee is as a percentage of the transaction. For large transactions, the fee is very low as a percentage of the transaction. Bitcoin fees are typically about $2 per transaction.

Once a block of transactions is approved and inserted into the blockchain ledger, it can never be undone.

The links connecting blocks are called hashes – which is cryptographic coding and information that can flow in only one direction. You can add to the blockchain, but you can never remove blocks from the chain once they are inserted.

That is how the system tracks how much bitcoin is in each wallet and tracks how much you have to spend. It tracks how much is

---

[10] bitcoin.org/bitcoin.pdf

leaving each wallet, entering each wallet, and who is paying who and when. In summary then:

1) Digital signatures safeguard money.

2) Transaction chains store the history of ownership.

3) Blockchains hold the order of transactions.

The big point here is Bitcoin is decentralized because transactions are validated and the system is protected by a vast network of Bitcoin nodes and miners who are dispersed all around the world.

The miners are rewarded for their work on Bitcoin. This reward incentivizes them to protect the network because they want to protect the value of their own bitcoin.

The math puzzle-solving function that miners compete in for the 6.25 bitcoin reward and to be able to insert the next block into the blockchain acts as a kind of subsidy until the network grows big enough for transaction fees alone to be enough to compensate the miners. Once the final 21 millionth bitcoin is mined in the spring of 2140, this subsidy will cease.

By that time, one bitcoin might be worth $1 trillion or more, if fiat currency even still exists by then. By then, everyone will likely just be using Bitcoin. The world will be on the Bitcoin standard.

Changes to the Bitcoin protocol must be approved by 95 percent of nodes and miners, who also approve changes and upgrades to the Bitcoin software whenever the benefit to the network is obvious.

Miners have approved several upgrades to the Bitcoin software and protocol during its history. More on this later.

Is Bitcoin Vulnerable to a "51 Percent Attack"?

Some observers have pointed to the fact that only a consensus of 51 percent of miners is required to verify transactions. This, they say, might be a vulnerability for Bitcoin.

But this is really not a vulnerability. It's brilliant design by Satoshi.

The reason only a 51 percent consensus is required to approve a transaction rather than 100 percent (or a supermajority) is to protect the network from a saboteur or a small group of saboteurs who might attack Bitcoin by maliciously blocking transactions and then holding the system hostage.

In reality, legit transactions will be approved by 100 percent of the miners because the cryptography underlying transactions is ironclad and military-grade.

However, some have suggested that the 51 percent rule (consensus) required to approve transactions leaves Bitcoin vulnerable to a "51 Percent Attack."

This kind of attack could happen theoretically if 51 percent of miners (more precisely, 51 percent of the computing hash power) were to team up to maliciously attack the Bitcoin network by blocking legitimate transactions, bogging down the network, and potentially creating a "double-spend."

Satoshi describes the system's defense against a potential 51 percent attack this way:

> Proof-of-work is essentially one-CPU-one-vote. The majority decision is represented by the longest chain, which has the greatest proof-of-work effort invested in it. If a majority of CPU power is controlled by honest nodes, the honest chain will grow the fastest and outpace any competing chains. To modify a past block, an attacker would have to redo the proof-of-work of the block and all blocks after it. [11]

This possibility was far more likely during the early days of Bitcoin when the network of miners was small, and the value of the coins was low. It would be very difficult today with more than 1,000,000 nodes and miners spread out across the world to protect their coins that now cost $[check today's price] to buy.

A race to mine the next block is occurring every ten minutes on average, with 1,000,000 mining computers racing to solve a proof-of-work math puzzle for each block. To revise the ledger history, the attacker would need to win every race to solve the math puzzle for many blocks in succession while simultaneously redoing the proof-of-work math puzzles for previous blocks in the blockchain.

For this reason, it appears impossible for any attackers to change the immutable blockchain history. All that might happen is for the current block of transactions to be disrupted by a "51 Percent" attack.

Furthermore, if 51 percent of miners (CPUs) were ever to collude

---

[11] bitcoin.org/bitcoin.pdf

to launch a successful "51 Percent" attack on the system, they would also risk destroying the value of their own bitcoin.

Some have theorized that if 51-percent attackers were able to sustain a successful attack over a substantial period of time, they might be able to create a new chain in secret, a "hard fork." This competing chain might then be able to overtake the competing chain, thereby becoming the official ledger.

Then, when published and distributed, the network could be thrown into disarray. The attackers might then be in position to refuse to accept blocks that were mined by legitimate miners.

This type of "51 Percent" attack can be countered by creating a "hard fork" for honest miners to follow. The market then would determine the legitimate chain.

"Hard Forks"

Creating "hard forks" in the blockchain can be used both to protect the blockchain from attackers; and can be created by malicious actors to attack the blockchain.

Miners can create a "hard fork" in the blockchain by refusing to accept an older version of the blockchain and creating a new branch of the blockchain.

The market then decides which fork to follow.

This actually happened in 2017 when a group of early Bitcoin miners and developers broke off from Bitcoin's main chain to create Bitcoin Cash.

This group, led by Roger Ver, argued that Bitcoin transactions were too slow and too expensive. They wanted to create a version that allowed faster, cheaper transactions.

They wanted larger block sizes so more transactions could be bundled together.

They claimed to be the true followers of the Satoshi vision. Ver called himself "Bitcoin Jesus." They managed to create a hard fork in the blockchain to create Bitcoin Cash.

Bitcoin Cash still exists. It's less than one percent of the size of the Bitcoin network. Satoshi explained how disputes in the blockchain are resolved:

> The majority decision is represented by the longest chain,
> which has the greatest proof-of-work effort invested in it. [12]

The market (the consensus of miners and nodes) tells us which fork is the main chain. Of course, you are also free to follow the renegade chain if you wish.

In addition to Bitcoin Cash, other hard forks created by breakaway miners include Bitcoin XT in 2014, Bitcoin Classic and Bitcoin Unlimited in 2016.

None of these chains amounted to much and were rejected by the wider Bitcoin community.

To counter a successful 51 Percent attack (or other attack), a hard fork can also be created to strand the attackers on a dead-end fork and reverse illegitimate transactions that might have already occurred.

Then the free market decides which fork to follow.

So far, a 51 Percent attack has never occurred on Bitcoin, although it has succeeded on smaller blockchains. Because of the size of the Bitcoin network, hundreds of billions of dollars of computing power and specialized ASIC hardware would now be needed to carry out a successful 51 Percent attack.

China could probably do it.

But if such an attack should occur and temporarily succeeds, it can be remedied by creating a hard fork. The community will then just follow the honest chain – which everyone can see because the Bitcoin ledger is 100 percent auditable.

So Bitcoin has many layers of defense.

Speed vs Security

Bitcoin emphasizes security over cheap, speedy transactions. Security for their bitcoin is what the market has told us people value most. Speed is important for daily transactions. But you want maximum security to protect your wealth. Bitcoin is designed to secure wealth.

People don't mind waiting a few more minutes and paying a bit more for security, especially when sending substantial sums.

---

[12] bitcoin.org/bitcoin.pdf

But new layers that allow cheaper, speedy transactions are being built on top of Bitcoin to allow instant and almost free transactions. One "Layer 2" solution is called the Lightning Network.

You can load a small amount of your bitcoin into Lightning to buy cups of coffee, groceries, and conduct routine daily transactions while using the Bitcoin base layer to protect your wealth.

Gold used to be the base layer for the dollar. Bitcoin is the base layer for the much faster Lightning Network, as well as other applications that are now being built on Bitcoin.

It's worth noting that credit card transactions are not really speedy either. Even though your credit card purchase is usually honored immediately, it can often take days for credit card transactions to settle.

That is the main advantage of centralized systems. A centralized system, like Visa, can provisionally approve transactions quickly and then wait for final settlement.

Credit card transactions are often not considered final for 30 days, 60 days, or longer. Chargebacks can happen at any time. So credit card transactions are not speedy at all for the merchant.

A Visa credit card transaction is never final for the merchant. Visa can always go into the merchant's bank account and retrieve the money. Visa is the referee and can intervene at any time, take your money, freeze your account, and effectively shut down your business.

Once a Bitcoin transaction is verified by the network of miners and accepted by the payee, there are no chargebacks, no reversing of transactions unless both agree to reverse a payment. The one who is paid on the Bitcoin system can always return the money. But that decision is between the two parties. With Bitcoin, your account can't be frozen or canceled. Your payments cannot be intercepted or stopped.

Organizations, such as the NRA, are having trouble getting banks and payment processors to work with them. Woke people in these centralized legacy financial institutions are refusing service to the NRA.

Other pro-freedom organizations are receiving the same treatment from legacy banks, credit card companies, and payment processors.

Bitcoin fixes this issue. Bitcoin does not target or discriminate against people based on political, religious or any beliefs. Bitcoin is uncensorable money. Bitcoin targets and deplatforms no one.

But why is "uncensorable" money important?

We often say bitcoin is "uncensorable" because money is a form of communication.

Distributed code is also communication.

Freedom of speech, freedom of expression, and freedom of the press are protected by the First Amendment to the Constitution of the United States. This is the first freedom protected by our Bill of Rights.

America's founders considered freedom of speech and freedom of the press as crucial to a free society. In the United States, the government is not permitted under our Constitution to censor expression, so long as there is no incitement or conspiracy to commit violence.

The freedom to transact is a version of freedom of speech.

What is paper money?

It's a note on a piece of paper. It's a communication. It's a type of contract or claim. That's what Bitcoin is.

But instead of metal coins or paper notes, Bitcoin uses encrypted code to enable the secure transmission (communication) of value.

What makes Bitcoin different from fiat currency, what makes Bitcoin different from a centrally administered banking system, is Bitcoin is unconfiscatable, uncensorable, uninterceptable money.

CHAPTER 6

How Bitcoin Fixes Corrupt Fiat Money Printing

Prior to 1933, U.S. paper money were certificates that were convertible to gold. You could actually show up at a bank and get gold in return for your paper money.

Here's what the U.S. Constitution says about money:

Article I, Section 10, Clause 1:

No State shall enter into any Treaty, Alliance, or Confederation; grant Letters of Marque and Reprisal; coin Money; emit Bills of Credit; make any Thing but gold and silver Coin a Tender in Payment of Debts; pass any Bill of Attainder, ex post facto Law, or Law impairing the Obligation of Contracts, or grant any Title of Nobility.

Relying on this clause, the U.S. Supreme Court held in 1844 (*Gwin v Breedlove*) that creditors are entitled to demand payment in gold or silver. Until 1933, U.S. paper currency was as good as gold.

This clause in the U.S. Constitution has never been amended. The U.S. Constitution is supposed to be the supreme law of our nation.

But we went off the gold standard anyway.

The big advantage of paper currency is that it makes it easy for people to conduct daily transactions. You could carry paper IOUs redeemable for gold in your wallet. Very convenient and efficient.

In 1913, under the direction of President Woodrow Wilson, Congress created the United States Federal Reserve – often called "The Fed."

Its job was to issue new currency at calibrated levels to keep the price of gold at $20.67 per ounce as measured by the dollar.

On April 5, 1933, President Franklin Roosevelt issued Executive Order 6102 that ordered all gold coins, gold bullion, and gold certificates be brought to a Federal Reserve bank branch and exchanged for paper money. People would be paid $20.67 per ounce of gold per Roosevelt's Executive Order.

This Executive Order was made under the authority of a law enacted in 1917 during World War I called the "Trading with the Enemy Act." This law is still on the books today.

On January 30, 1934, Congress passed and Roosevelt signed the Gold Reserve Act, which formally outlawed the ownership of gold. This law raised the price of gold from $20.67 to $35 per ounce, thus devaluing the dollar by 41 percent overnight.

This means 41 percent of the American people's wealth was effectively stolen by the U.S. government, a theft that intensified and prolonged the Great Depression.

But at least the price of gold remained at $35 per ounce until President Richard Nixon took the United States off the gold standard completely in 1971.

By the end of World War II, the United States was the most powerful country in the world by far. Europe, Japan, and most of the world were decimated by the war. The U.S. also held most of the world's gold supply.

In July of 1944, the United States and 44 other countries met in Bretton Woods, New Hampshire. The United States agreed to keep gold as the basis for the value of the dollar. Other counties did not have much gold, so agreed to use the dollar as the basis to value their own currencies.

The Bretton Woods Agreement also created two powerful new organizations – the International Monetary Fund (IMF) and the World Bank.

The famous British economist John Maynard Keynes and the U.S. Treasury economist Harry Dexter White were the primary architects of the Bretton Woods system.

Then on August 15, 1971, Richard Nixon announced that the U.S. dollar would no longer be pegged to the price of gold at all.

Why did that happen?

Because the U.S. government wanted to be free to print as much money as needed to fund the Vietnam War and Lyndon Johnson's Great Society welfare programs.

Increasing taxes is always politically unpopular. Printing money is easier and doesn't require the approval of Congress.

Rampant money printing would produce a hidden tax called inflation. That's how an ounce of gold went from $35 in 1971 to

$1,800 today. This is how and why the dollar has lost 98 percent of its value since 1971.

But you might counter that America appears to be much wealthier today and living better overall than it did in 1971. So perhaps it's good we went off the gold standard.

It's true that Americans today are living better overall than they did in 1971. But that's not because we went off the gold standard. It's because of advances in technology, science, and overall human progress.

When the U.S. Bureau of Labor Statistics releases its inflation data each month, what it calls its Consumer Price Index (CPI), it often sounds like the inflation number is pretty low and reasonable.

For the past decade, we've seen annual inflation rates, as measured by the Consumer Price Index, in the 2-3 percent range.

But since the start of the Covid pandemic in March of 2020 and all the extra money printing that took place during the pandemic to prop up the economy, we've seen the inflation rate as measured by CPI rise to 7 percent-plus.

But remember what the Consumer Price Index actually measures. CPI measures price fluctuations in relation to the goods and services consumers buy regularly – designated by the U.S. Government as the cost of living.

Constant technological advances and more efficient mass-production are deflationary forces that push costs and prices down steadily. We've found more efficient ways to mass-produce food, cars, furniture, build homes, drill for petroleum and natural gas, and produce what we need to live than was possible in 1971.

The U.S. Federal Reserve also calibrates its money printing to keep the prices of things you buy and need to live relatively stable. Prices go up, but not so much each year that it causes a revolution.

People believe that 3 percent or even 5 percent inflation each year is bad, but most think we can live with that level of inflation. It doesn't seem like much in the overall scheme of things.

However, the inflation rate is really much higher if you factor in technological innovation that would actually be pushing prices down dramatically if we had honest money. Most of the things we buy should be getting cheaper and cheaper every year, not more expensive.

Instead of paying an average of $40,000 for a car, you should be paying more like $1,000 for a nice car, perhaps less – if we were still on the gold standard.

As I write this book, the Covid global pandemic has been going on for more than two years. The U.S. has increased the money supply by 60 percent during this period. However, the official CPI inflation number we get from the government is showing inflation running at 7 percent (which is still very high).

That's because the official CPI inflation numbers we get from the government are manipulated to make inflation appear lower than it actually is. The government has a major self-interest in doing this, in order to:

1) Keep Cost of Living Increases (COLAs) on Social Security benefits lower than true inflation.

2) Keep interest payments on our $30 trillion national debt as low as possible.

3) Enable much more government spending without appearing to increase taxes much.

4) Con voters into believing inflation is not really as high as it is, so politicians can win reelection and so there isn't a revolution.

When the government increases the money supply by 60 percent in 24 months, this is actually a massive tax on your money, a massive tax on your life savings.

Inflation does not appear all that dramatic to most because technological improvements (such as robotics and more efficient manufacturing) apply relentless downward pressure on prices.

Still, just keep in mind that you would be paying $1,000 or less for your new car instead of $40,000 if the U.S. had not gone off the gold standard in 1971.

Let that sink in.

Before 1971, the stock market was not of much interest to the general public. Stocks were considered risky and speculative. People generally bought bonds – often a mix of government bonds (such as from the U.S. Treasury) and high-grade AAA corporate bonds. People could retire and live on 4 percent annual interest they received from their savings.

That's no longer the case.

Today, investors are mostly interested in super-fast-growing stocks, which are much riskier. Investors today feel they need the growth, despite the greatly added risk, to stay ahead of inflation. If true inflation is more like 15 percent (not the official 7 percent CPI number), this means you need 20 percent annual stock market returns just to stay slightly ahead of inflation.

So full retirement is just about impossible today for most people. Retirement used to be considered normal before 1971. Retirement is what most people expected and did at age 65. That's almost impossible today for 95 percent of Americans because of the skyrocketing cost-of-living and the steady decline in value of fiat currencies.

The U.S. Government's massive money-printing operation is how it finances America's $30 trillion national debt (rapidly heading to $100 trillion).

By printing trillions and trillions of new dollars every year, the Fed brings the value of the national debt down in real terms because the national debt is in nominal dollars – dollars that are devalued daily by the Fed's money-printing operation

The government would like to pay ten cents on each dollar of debt, or one cent on each dollar of debt owed, if possible.

The U.S. Federal Reserve also sets interest rates.

Right now, the interest rate is around 2 percent on the U.S. national debt. That's also money the U.S. Government essentially owes itself.

The government just prints more money to pay the IOUs (Treasury bonds) it's also printed.

"Printing money" is not quite what happens. There's only about $1.2 trillion of physical currency in circulation in our current $21 trillion annual GDP U.S. economy.

Most of the money the Fed creates is digital notations on a ledger. It's digital money.

The way the Fed creates money is by printing up bonds (IOUs) and selling them on the open market.

But there's not much of a market for Treasury bonds these days because the interest rate being paid to buyers of these bonds is only 2 percent on 10-year Treasury notes, as of this writing.

So the Fed buys a lot of its own bonds with the new money it creates and then calls these bonds "assets."

But it's really just money the Fed owes itself.

The Fed also buys bonds from banks. That's how the Fed injects more money into the economy.

Right now, the Fed charges banks a near-zero interest rate for this money.

So it's effectively free money for the banks. The banks then lend this money out at 3-4 percent to people who have good credit, and at higher interest rates to people who are less creditworthy.

Those without resources and who have shaky credit have no access to this low-interest-rate money. This is another way the rich get richer and the poor get poorer in fiat money systems.

The bonds the Fed buys from banks with the new money the Fed has just created are also called assets. So both the bonds the Fed prints and the bonds the Fed buys from banks it calls "assets."

Few would consider IOUs you issue to yourself as "assets." If you tried to claim the IOUs you write to yourself as assets on a mortgage application, you would be committing a federal crime – mortgage application fraud, which is a form of bank fraud.

But that's what the Fed does when it publishes its balance sheet each month. Its balance sheet shows the Fed's assets rising, almost straight up on the Fed's graph. That really means the Fed is printing an insane amount of money.

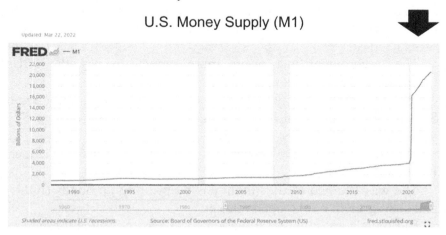

The system for creating new money is set up this way to confuse the public. The Fed's Board of Governors (economists) uses terms that few Americans understand.

The Fed doesn't say it's "printing money." The Fed calls what it's doing "quantitative easing."

When the Fed decides to print slightly less money, they call that "tapering." They are still printing a lot more money all the time, just not quite as much as they were. That's "tapering."

When the Fed announces its "tapering," this usually sends the stock market into a nosedive.

So even though most of the money the Fed creates is just digital notations on a ledger, most people call it money printing for simplicity's sake. It's a convenient term for creating money out of thin air.

If interest rates were set by the market instead of by fiat central bankers, the interest rate would be more like 12-15 percent instead of 2 percent due to all the money printing.

So we're living in an "Alice in Wonderland" Ponzi scheme.

If you and I ran our finances the same way, we'd go to jail. But this is how our fiat money system has been working since 1971 – and really since FDR outlawed the ownership of gold by citizens and unilaterally changed the price of gold from $20.67 to $35 per ounce, thus devaluing the dollar by 41 percent overnight – which is really the same as seizing 41 percent of everyone's cash.

If you or I tried to print dollars, we would also go to prison for a long time for counterfeiting.

Counterfeiting U.S. money is considered one of the worst crimes possible under U.S. law, at least in terms of punishments handed out for counterfeiting.

Counterfeiting is considered much worse than theft. It's considered an attack on the state, an attack on civilization itself. Counterfeiting is considered similar to committing treason under U.S. law.

Yet the U.S. Federal Reserve prints trillions and trillions of new dollars every year, devaluing the dollars you have earned with your time, labor, and ingenuity.

Once the dollar was untethered from gold and became a fiat money printing scheme, it became 100 percent certain that the dollar would melt to zero in value over time.

The dollar has already lost 98 percent of its value since 1971. So it's almost gone to zero within half a century.

This is what happens in all fiat money systems. In all fiat money systems, the currency eventually falls to zero.

The average lifespan of a fiat currency is about 35 years. The fact that U.S. fiat currency has lasted 50 years and lost only 98 percent of its value makes the dollar one of the better fiat currencies in the world. The situation in other countries is far more dire.

In Venezuela, the annual inflation rate is 2,255 percent, in Zimbabwe 557 percent, in Sudan 163 percent, and in Argentina 52 percent, as of this writing.

In a number of European countries, we now see negative interest rates. That means you don't pay interest to borrow money. The government pays you to borrow money. We see this now in Switzerland, which was once a model of sound money. Japan also has negative interest rates.

I had never heard of such a thing before the Covid pandemic. Now governments are actually paying people to borrow money. This continues to be the practice even though the pandemic is over.

The U.S. and European central banks are charging banks near zero percent interest rates to borrow money.

This means U.S. and European currencies have no value, according to interest rates set by the U.S. and the European Union central banks.

This fact alone should tell you how fraudulent our system of money actually is.

The average person doesn't pay near-zero percent for loans. Rich people and big corporations pay near-zero percent for loans. Banks actually pay near-zero percent interest to central banks for all the new money the central banks print at a manic pace all day every day.

That's how these governments keep their economies propped up. That's how they hope to keep this fiat money Ponzi Scheme going for as long as possible.

But at some point, the house of cards collapses, like what happened in the German Weimar Republic, which gave the world Hitler.

To understand why politicians are so addicted to printing money, think about how politicians are incentivized. Politicians are incentivized by winning reelection. If they can keep the Ponzi scheme going for just one more election cycle, that's all they care about.

That's why they don't care about running up a $100 trillion national debt and increasing the money supply by 60 percent in just 20 months. They just want to make it through the next election.

If they can juice the economy with a free-money sugar high for another two years of rampant spending and money printing, that's all these politicians need to make it through another election cycle.

So they print more money and give a few crumbs to people at the bottom of the economic ladder.

Lower-income people will be placated with crumbs from the table because at least it's something. It looks like free money – for a little while. But all this money printing hurts low-income folks most.

What wealthy people do is get rid of their fiat money as fast as possible. Wealthy people use their fiat money to buy other assets that tend to appreciate in value when measured against fiat money.

Wealthy people buy real estate, tech stocks, and gold. Now they also buy bitcoin. They are able to buy these assets on leverage for a near-zero percent interest rate.

Low-income folks have no excess cash to buy appreciating assets. So their purchasing power always goes down. Fiat money printing is actually a massive wealth transfer program from the poor and middle class to the rich.

CHAPTER 7

Is Bitcoin a Good Investment?

Y ou need to make your own investment decisions. All I can do is tell you what I do and why.

I can describe my own thought process. You then can take this information to make your own decisions. You also need to do your own studying and due diligence.

I don't invest in anything until I've put at least 100 hours of study into it.

Once I'm convinced investing in a particular asset is probably a good bet, I start buying a little. I buy a little to start because owning a little motivates me to study that asset further and follow it closely.

On May 22, 2010, when Laszlo Hanyecz bought two pizzas for 10,000 bitcoins, one bitcoin cost about 1/3rd of one penny.

As of this writing in July of 2022, it will cost your more than $20,000 to buy one bitcoin.

Is Bitcoin Similar to the Dutch Tulip Mania of 1636?

Some have compared this stunning rise in the value of a single bitcoin to something like the Dutch tulip mania of 1636. The Dutch tulip mania often serves as a parable for how people can get badly hurt by speculative asset bubbles.

What happened was tulip bulbs arrived in the Dutch Republic from Turkey. People loved the beauty of the flower. So the price of tulip bulbs was bid up higher, up to six times the average person's annual salary. At the peak of this mania, you could buy a mansion in exchange for one tulip bulb.

The price then crashed to near zero when it was discovered that tulip bulbs were really not rare at all, and could easily be imported from Turkey and elsewhere.

But there are some key differences between the tulip mania of 1636 and Bitcoin.

The tulip mania lasted just three months. There's no fixed supply of tulips. Also, tulips are perishable, so tulips would not be a good store of value even if there was a fixed supply of tulips.

The Bitcoin monetary network has been building and getting stronger since 2009.

I watched Amazon closely for 15 years before investing any money in Amazon.

My first investment in Amazon was in 2012. By that time, it was clear to me that Amazon had a business model that was working. The Amazon stock price then went up 1,600 percent over the next nine years.

Many now ask: Is it too late to start buying bitcoin?

My answer: Was 2012 too late to start buying Amazon, Google, Microsoft, Apple, or Facebook?

I still think all the Big Tech stocks are good investments and will continue to rise in value – just not as explosively as over the past decade because they are now more mature companies and industries.

My own belief is Bitcoin is still in its infancy, just getting started. Bitcoin is still very much an emerging technology.

My view is that Bitcoin is bigger than Amazon, Google, Microsoft, Apple or any one company because Bitcoin is potentially the new money of the world. It's potentially the new money because it's superior money.

For any new technology to be widely adopted, it must be clearly superior to what we are using now – exponentially superior. Otherwise, people will just stick with the old and familiar.

It's my view and the view of approximately 150,000,000 Bitcoin users that Bitcoin is orders of magnitude superior to fiat money. It's also superior to gold as way to store value. In addition, Bitcoin acts as insurance against economic and societal collapse.

Bitcoin has become legal tender in El Salvador. Bitcoin is becoming the primary unit of exchange for people in countries like Nigeria, Venezuela, Sudan, much of Africa, Latin America, and other countries with collapsed economic and political systems.

Within the next decade, it's likely bitcoin will be broadly accepted as the preferred money of the world. It's already the preferred money in much of the Third World.

Still, whenever you are making investment decisions, you must really study and understand what you are investing in.

The current Chairman of the U.S. Securities and Exchange

Commission (SEC) is Gary Gensler. He taught a course at MIT on Bitcoin. I'm no fan of President Joe Biden, who I view as completely incompetent. But Gary Gensler knows a lot about Bitcoin.

When I became interested in Bitcoin, I took Gensler's MIT course on Bitcoin and cryptocurrencies online.

Anyone else can just go online and take this course for free. Just Google "Gary Gensler MIT Bitcoin course." It's easy to find.

I listened carefully to all 24 of Gensler's lectures. I did all the reading. I've read and reread Satoshi Nakamoto's eight-page white paper on Bitcoin many times. Every time I read Satoshi's white paper, I learn something new. I find a new gem.

It takes at least 100 hours of study to really understand how Bitcoin works. But you could spend thousands of hours on it if you really wanted to get into the weeds of cryptography and blockchain technology.

I now feel like I understand Bitcoin conceptually. No, I don't know cryptography. I know very little software coding. But I feel I understand conceptually how Bitcoin works.

The structure of Bitcoin is what's so brilliant. The technological building blocks for Bitcoin all existed in the 1990s (or earlier) long before Satoshi's white paper. The challenge was to use these technology building blocks to create the perfect indestructible digital money.

The tools needed to paint a picture existed for thousands of years: paint and brushes. But we needed Leonardo da Vinci to create the Mona Lisa.

What Satoshi created with Bitcoin, in my view, is the Mona Lisa of decentralized, indestructible, unconfiscatable, uncensorable digital money.

Thousands of other cryptocurrencies have attempted to emulate Bitcoin's success.

They either tried essentially to copy Bitcoin – usually to make transactions speedier. Or they tried to create crypto assets with more features. None of the other cryptos are any good, at least so far. The other cryptocurrencies and projects are like my paintings when compared to the Mona Lisa. There is no comparison.

More on this point later in my chapter on why I don't invest in Ethereum or any other cryptocurrency or asset. This doesn't mean I won't in the future. Something great might come along. But Bitcoin is the only crypto asset I invest in at this point.

Anyone who follows the news has seen the enormous price swings in Bitcoin. Price swings of 50 percent and more are not uncommon for Bitcoin.

This is always the case for an emerging technology.

In any emerging technology, there will be wild price swings as investors try to assess the value of an asset. A thorough understanding of what you are investing in allows you to emotionally withstand and survive the volatility.

Your thorough knowledge about what you are investing in provides you confidence. Lack of understanding creates fear, triggers panic, produces poor decisions. A thorough knowledge of what you are investing in prevents you from selling during inevitable price drops, allows you to weather storms.

I feel good about Bitcoin. I'm confident in the asset over the long-term because of the time I've spent studying it

Could I be wrong?

Absolutely.

There's no such thing as certainty in life.

Black Swan events do occur.

A Black Swan event is an event that is difficult, if not impossible, to foresee or anticipate. As the late Secretary of Defense Don Rumsfeld famously said:

> There are known knowns. There are things we know we know. We also know there are known unknowns; that is to say, we know there are some things we do not know. But there are also unknown unknowns — the ones we don't know we don't know. [13]

So I agree with Rumsfeld. There's no way to see or predict every hazard out there. All we can do is make intelligent bets where the odds appear to favor success.

I started watching Bitcoin closely in 2017 when the Bitcoin price rose from about $1,000 a coin to $20,000 per coin. Then I watched it crash 83 percent by December of 2018 to about $3,100 per coin.

My conclusion in December of 2018 was that Bitcoin was basically a fascinating lab experiment, brilliantly conceived in many

---

[13] U.S. Department of Defense transcript. Secretary of Defense Donald H. Rumsfeld February 12, 2002.

ways. I thought it should work, or something like it should work at some point. But by the end of 2018, Bitcoin did not look stable enough for me to invest in.

I was concerned someone might be able to hack the technology and destroy the system. I was most concerned about an attack by the governments if Bitcoin ever really gained traction against fiat currencies issued by the central banks.

Then when Bitcoin crashed 83 percent in 2018 from its December 2017 peak, it looked to me like Bitcoin might be finished.

But I kept watching – not as intently as I had watched Bitcoin during the spectacular 2,000 percent runup in 2017. But I kept an eye on Bitcoin because it clearly wasn't yet dead.

I started paying close attention again as Bitcoin started to come back in 2019, rising from $3,400 per coin in February of 2019 to $11,800 per coin in June of that year, a 200 percent increase in just five months.

For me, this was validation of Bitcoin and its underlying technology.

Amazon followed a similar track. Amazon went on the public stock market in 1997. Its stock then collapsed 93 percent during the tech stock bubble and crash in 2000.

This is what happens in all emerging technologies, as investors try to figure out the value of what they are buying. We saw similar patterns in stock prices for Apple, Google, Microsoft and other tech companies.

The stock prices of these companies experienced many crashes of 50 percent or more.

That's just the nature of investing in emerging technologies. You must be prepared for wild price swings on these assets. This is why I urge against investing more than 10 percent of one's assets in any one stock. The same rule applies to Bitcoin.

Diversification is a key pillar of intelligent investing.

I also encourage dollar-cost-averaging in – meaning don't buy all at once. Invest in increments over time. This way, if you buy at a peak and the price crashes, you won't feel devastated. You will have money left (dry powder) to buy more at a good price after a price crash.

Bitcoin is very volatile. There are parabolic price increases followed by blow-off tops all the time. You want some dry powder for the inevitable price drops.

Once I saw that Bitcoin was coming back and coming back strong from its 83 percent price collapse in 2018, I started buying Bitcoin in July of 2019 when the price was about $11,000 per coin.

Unfortunately, this was a short-term peak for Bitcoin. Right after I bought, the price started dropping. Then the Covid pandemic hit in March of 2020. The price of Bitcoin dropped to about $6,000 a coin, approximately a 45 percent drop from where I bought it.

But then the price started rising again. I became even more focused on Bitcoin when the Federal Reserve started its massive money-printing program (far more even than usual) and Congress launched a manic spending spree.

Between the new money printing from the Fed and trillions of dollars in new spending by Congress, upwards of $11 trillion dollars in new money was dumped into the U.S. economy in 2020. The national debt jumped from about $16 trillion at the end of 2019 to $27 trillion one year later by the end of 2020.

When I saw this happening, I started buying more bitcoin in April of 2020 for $7,000 a coin.

I saw Bitcoin as having been designed for this exact situation. The overall value of the Bitcoin (market cap) rose to $200 million and then $400 million.

Right now, Bitcoin represents about 10 percent of my investment portfolio, outside of real estate.

I have made a commitment never to sell any of my bitcoin – the primary reason being my belief that the money printing will continue.

Once money printing starts, it becomes politically impossible to stop – which is why political currencies always go to zero eventually.

Sure, the Fed might slow the money printing some and do what it calls "tapering."

But it's politically impossible for government to stop money printing completely and increase interest rates to what they should be if we actually still had a free-market system.

The stock market would collapse. The value of people's homes would crash. Wall Street financial institutions, which are heavily leveraged, would implode.

Imagine if the U.S. government were suddenly required to pay a

12 percent interest rate on America's $30 trillion national debt – which is about what the interest rate would be if the free market were actually allowed to operate. The interest rate would probably be even higher in today's environment and be more like 18 percent if we had a true free market system instead of a fiat money system.

The U.S. government can't afford to pay market-based interest rates on the national debt because the entire federal budget would become only interest payments. There would be no room in the federal budget for national defense, Social Security, Medicare, welfare programs, roads, or anything else.

That's why the Fed won't increase interest rates in any meaningful way; and why the Fed can't afford to taper much on its money printing. What's far more likely is for the money printing to accelerate.

If the money printing press were to stop, and if we were suddenly to return to the gold standard, we would have an instant depression because the economy has been built on debt and cheap (almost free) money.

Going back to the gold standard would be like forcing a heroin addict to suddenly go cold turkey.

The heroin addict would likely die. Getting off heroin must be done slowly. Most heroin addicts also relapse. The success rate for getting off heroin is less than 30 percent for those who actually try.

The fiat money standard is every bit as addictive. The odds that the U.S. government, or any government, will go back to the gold standard or any kind of honest money is just about zero.

It would be just too painful to do it. If you're stuck on top of a mountain with gangrene making its way up your leg, and if you know the only way you can stay alive is to hack your leg off with a saw without anesthesia, what are you going to do?

Most of us would rather die than do what's needed to stop the gangrene.

So that's pretty close to the situation with our economy and fiat money printing system. Politicians and most Americans won't tolerate the pain required to put our system back on honest money.

So expect the money printing to continue and even accelerate in the years ahead.

The only answer is self-defense on the part of individuals.

It's the responsibility of each of us as individuals to protect ourselves and our loved ones from the political money printing press by adopting the Bitcoin standard.

By the way, *The Bitcoin Standard* is also the title of a superb book by economist Saifedean Ammous who, like me, sees Bitcoin as our best protection from this corruption of the money by manic fiat money printing.

That doesn't mean I've completely left the fiat money system. I keep enough fiat money to pay my family's monthly bills. I invest in real estate and tech stocks. Bitcoin represents about 10 percent of of my investment portfolio outside real estate.

For me and my family, Bitcoin is insurance against economic collapse and the steady ongoing erosion of the dollar by all this money printing. It's also diversification of assets in the event of a stock market collapse.

In the event of a total economic and political system collapse, such as has happened in Venezuela and other countries, Bitcoin will allow me, my wife Wanda, and any family members who want to come along, to escape to wherever civilization might still exist in some form.

Perhaps we'll move to El Salvador, which has adopted Bitcoin as its legal tender. Other countries, mostly in the Third World, are also moving toward adopting the Bitcoin standard.

CHAPTER 8

Is Bitcoin Secure?

This is the big question people have when thinking about buying a significant amount of bitcoin. Is Bitcoin secure?

The Bitcoin network has now been in place since 2009. It's now nearly a $400 billion network.

If it wasn't secure, surely very smart hackers, China or Russia, would have figured out a way to hack Bitcoin by now.

It's also passed the "Lindy Test" – which says the longer something's been around, the longer it's likely to last. Take the internet as an example. The internet is a decentralized communications network that was developed by the U.S. Department of Defense. It was designed to survive a nuclear attack.

No one's been able to destroy the internet.

People have been able to hack and destroy applications built on the internet, but not the internet itself. Bitcoin is like the internet. It's a decentralized protocol, designed for security – designed to survive thermonuclear war.

This is not an original insight by me. I learned this history by following the work of a brilliant aeronautics and computer science engineer from MIT named Jason Lowery, who is a director of space launch operations for the U.S. Space Force.

Lowery notes in his Ph.D. dissertation that the three key building blocks of Bitcoin were developed for U.S. national security purposes. These include:

1) SHA-256 Cryptography

SHA stands for "secure hash algorithms" and was first developed by the U.S. National Security Agency (NSA) in 1993 to secure applications and protocols. Bitcoin uses SHA-256 to verify transactions and calculate proof-of-work math puzzles.

The rise of ASIC SHA-2 accelerator chips in the early 2000s led to the use of script-based proof-of-work systems.

The National Security Agency's SHA algorithms were first published in 2001.

2) The Internet

The internet was first developed for military purposes to ensure a decentralized communications system that would be difficult to destroy. The Defense Advanced Research Projects Agency (DARPA) launched the project in 1968.

The project was called ARPANET (Advanced Research Projects Agency Network). The ARPANET incorporated distributed computation and frequent re-computation of routing tables. This increased the survivability of the network in the event of a nuclear war.

The protocol was permitted to be used for civilian and commercial purposes in 1983 under the TCP/IP protocol, which stands for Transmission Control Protocol/Internet Protocol, better known as the internet.

Notice that, in the view of the U.S. military, a key pillar of security is decentralization. The more decentralized a communications system is, the more difficult it is to attack and destroy.

That was the concept behind the military's creation of the internet.

3) GPS – Global Positioning System

The Global Positioning System (GPS) project was started by the U.S. Department of Defense in 1973. Its primary purpose was to allow submarines to launch intercontinental ballistic nuclear missiles accurately at the Soviet Union if the Soviet Union were to launch a first strike nuclear missile attack against us.

This was a key pillar of the Mutual Assured Destruction (MAD) doctrine that kept the Cold War from becoming a nuclear war. The U.S. nuclear response involved a triad: Land-based intercontinental ballistic missiles (ICBMs), Airstrikes, and submarine-launched missiles.

Missiles fired from land can be aimed. Missiles fired from submarines are not accurate unless guided by satellite-based GPS.

When a missile is fired from a submarine, it's first ejected by high-pressure gas. After the missile breaks the surface of the water, the rocket stage fires. The missile then must be guided to its target. This requires GPS – which requires satellites.

Satellites also became an important pillar of our internet and communications systems – communications systems that are difficult to attack.

It's difficult to attack a network of satellites.

These three building blocks were all developed during the Cold War by the U.S. Department of Defense to protect our civilization from thermonuclear war.

Satoshi Nakamoto (or a group of cryptographers) took these national security building blocks developed by the U.S. military to create encrypted digitalized communication built on a decentralized protocol to create indestructible money. Bitcoin is the internet of money.

In a very real sense, Bitcoin is one of the most powerful defensive weapons on the planet.

Think how difficult it is to defeat a guerilla army – whether in the jungles of Vietnam or the mountains of Afghanistan.

The British Empire and the Soviet Union could not conquer Afghanistan. The United States did not fare well in Afghanistan either.

The U.S. military had immensely more firepower than the Communist guerillas in Vietnam in the 1960s and '70s. But the Viet Kong's guerilla-style of warfare made it very difficult for the U.S. military to successfully fight them.

It's difficult to fight and defeat an enemy you can't find.

That is why it would be so difficult for any government to take down the Bitcoin network, with its more than 1,000,000 miners and nodes spread out across the globe connected by a decentralized internet, including via satellite.

China found out how difficult it is to take out Bitcoin.

China banned bitcoin mining and transactions in the summer of 2021.

This temporarily caused the price of Bitcoin to drop because half the world's bitcoin miners were located in China.

Mining hash power was cut in half as mining computers in China shut down.

Chinese miners left China for more hospitable countries. Within a few months, mining computing hash power was back to where it was before China's crackdown on bitcoin miners.

Throughout China's crackdown on bitcoin miners in the summer of 2021, the Bitcoin network never missed a beat. Transactions were processed with minimal delay. Satoshi's "Difficulty Adjustment" temporarily eased automatically and kept block mining on schedule, one block mined every ten minutes on average.

I'll explain Satoshi's "difficulty adjustment" algorithm later in this book – because it's ingenious.

Bitcoin withstood a state attack by the world's largest country without much trouble.

In summary, as Jason Lowery points out, Bitcoin is a military-grade defensive weapon engineered to protect your wealth from government or other attack.

Bitcoin uses advanced military technology to put a digital iron dome over your wealth.

Your wealth is then protected by a worldwide guerrilla army of more than 1,000,000 miners and nodes. The bigger the Bitcoin network becomes, the more difficult it will be to attack.

There has only been one breach of Bitcoin's security in its entire history. It occurred in the very early days of Bitcoin, before Satoshi disappeared.

On August 6, 2010, a serious flaw in Bitcoin's protocol was discovered.

Transactions weren't being properly verified before they were included in the transaction blockchain.

This issue allowed users to create an unlimited number of bitcoins. On August 15, 2010, more than 184 billion bitcoins were generated in a transaction and sent to two addresses on the network.

That transaction was quickly spotted and erased from the transaction log after the bug was fixed. The network was then forked to an updated version of the Bitcoin protocol.

This was the only security breach in Bitcoin's history – occurring before Satoshi left the scene, when Bitcoin was still basically a lab experiment.

Since then, no one has been able to counterfeit bitcoins, double-spend bitcoins, or create additional bitcoins outside the protocol.

The cryptography behind Bitcoin is based on the SHA-256 algorithm designed by the U.S. National Security Agency. Cracking it appears to be impossible as there are more possible private keys than there are atoms in the universe.

And this is just one layer of security built on many other layers of security.

Elon Musk believes Bitcoin is secure.

Tesla bought 42,902 bitcoins in January of 2021. Just about everyone would say Elon is very smart.

Not only is he an expert software engineer himself, but Tesla has some of the best software engineers in the world.

If Elon and Tesla's top software engineers believe Bitcoin is secure and unhackable, that's pretty strong evidence in my mind.

MicroStrategy, run by tech entrepreneur Michael Saylor, bought 129,218 bitcoins starting in 2020. MicroStrategy and Michael Saylor continue to accumulate bitcoin.

Square, run by the tech titan Jack Dorsey who also founded Twitter, owns 8,027 bitcoins. Dorsey recently changed the name of Square to Block (as in blockchain).

Jack Dorsey is a Bitcoin maximalist – meaning he's not impressed with any of the other crypto projects out there.

Dorsey calls Bitcoin "the native currency of the internet."

Dorsey believes so strongly in Bitcoin that he quit as CEO of Twitter (which he founded) to dedicate his life to making Bitcoin easily accessible to the impoverished and unbanked of the world.

These are some of the world's best-known tech entrepreneurs. They all believe Bitcoin is secure.

Some have theorized that the development of quantum computers in the future might be able to crack Bitcoin's cryptography. The math puzzle "difficulty adjustment" Satoshi built into the system, however, should be able to account for increasingly powerful computers, including quantum computers.

We'll get into Bitcoin's "difficulty adjustment" algorithm in a moment. But yes, anything is possible. The sudden emergence of a quantum computer might destroy Bitcoin. The planet might also get hit by a meteor. A solar flare might wipe out all life on earth.

Black Swan events do occur and certainly will occur. But if you are looking 10-20 years out, the odds look good for Bitcoin.

The odds of Bitcoin going to $500,000 a coin over the next ten years appear to be much better than Bitcoin going to $0. That's how I look at investments. What is the upside potential? Does the potential upside exponentially exceed the downside risk?

You should never invest more in any one asset or asset class than you can afford to lose in the event of some unforeseen catastrophe – because unforeseen catastrophes happen all the time.

What I also like about Bitcoin is it's a new asset class, different from the stock market, different from real estate. So if the stock market crashes, if real estate values collapse, there's a high probability, in my view, that Bitcoin will rise in that environment.

Or . . . maybe it won't if no one has any money because the economy has collapsed and we're living in another Dark Ages.

So yes, that might happen. But short of some huge catastrophe, I believe Bitcoin is a good bet for some portion of one's assets.

My view is also that if Bitcoin had been hackable, it would have been hacked by now.

China or Russia would have hacked it – or some other bad actor by now. Yet Bitcoin just keeps building, exactly as Satoshi predicted.

Could something happen to Bitcoin?

Sure. The future is unknown. If I were 100 percent certain about Bitcoin and its future, I would put all my assets into Bitcoin. But I'm not 100 percent certain about anything. This is why I diversify into a number of assets that I consider to be good bets.

One-third of my net worth is in real estate and rental properties.

Approximately 55 percent of my assets are in stocks – tech stocks. My two largest holdings are Bitcoin and Tesla. You can't know anything with certainty – which is why you want to intelligently diversify.

The Mt. Gox Exchange Hack

Some point to the hack of the Mt. Gox Bitcoin exchange in 2011 to argue that Bitcoin is hackable.

In 2010, a video game programmer and early Bitcoiner named Jeb McCaleb launched the first Bitcoin exchange.

His goal was to make it easier for the general public to buy bitcoin. He called his exchange Mt. Gox.

McCaleb originally set up his exchange as a way for fans of the game "Magic: The Gathering" to trade cards online. The name "Mt. Gox" was the acronym for "Magic: The Gathering Online Exchange."

McCaleb became an avid believer in Bitcoin. So he repurposed his Mt. Gox site in late 2010 as a Bitcoin exchange.

Mt. Gox then exploded in popularity.

McCaleb sold his exchange website in 2011 to a French developer named Mark Karpelès, who was living in Japan at the time. McCaleb thought Karpelès was better equipped to take his exchange to the next level.

Unfortunately, Karpelès was not good at securing the site. The Mt. Gox site was hacked. Private Bitcoin keys were stolen, along with approximately 650,000 bitcoins valued at about $365 million at the time.

Karpelès was convicted of some minor offenses (basically not following correct custodial procedures), but not theft. He served no time in prison.

Important to note is that no one hacked Bitcoin's underlying technology. If a thief can get your private key, he can steal your Bitcoin.

The problem here was the lack of security for this low-grade primitive exchange. Hackers were able to get the keys on the exchange.

If anything, the hack of the Mt. Gox exchange points to the danger of having your bitcoin held on centrally administered exchanges, which can be hacked.

After selling the Mt. Gox exchange to Karpelès, McCaleb went on to develop another cryptocurrency in 2011 called Ripple. In 2014 he co-founded another crypto asset called Stellar. In 2018, *Forbes* reported McCaleb's Ripple holdings had a value then of $20 billion.

McCaleb appears to be involved in cryptocurrency more for the money than to advance the cause of liberty. This appears to be the driving force behind all the other crypto assets I've looked at, except for Bitcoin.

More on this later, in my chapter on Ethereum and other crypto assets. All the other crypto assets are venture capital projects, that fit the legal definition of securities under regulation and oversight of the Securities Exchange Commission (SEC).

Among all the crypto assets, only Bitcoin fits the description of property or a commodity – like gold – because no one owns or controls Bitcoin.

How to Secure Your Bitcoin

If you store your private keys in the cloud, on your laptop, or anything connected to the internet, you risk having your keys stolen.

Anyone who has your private key code has your bitcoin.

You want to store your private keys in an offline hardware wallet.

Modern exchanges, such as Coinbase.com, are far more secure today than the early Mt. Gox Bitcoin exchange in 2011. Mt. Gox was an amateur shoestring operation. But the reality remains: If you store your private keys on a centrally administered exchange or anywhere in the cloud, you are trusting the exchange to keep your private keys safe from hackers and thieves.

You are also trusting this third-party custodian with your wealth.

We know humans are fallible and corrupt.

If your bitcoin is on a custodial exchange, it can be seized by the government or frozen in a civil action at any time.

The exchange might go bankrupt.

If you are not in sole possession of your private keys, you really don't own your bitcoin. The third-party custodian has your keys, so effectively owns your bitcoin.

What many investors do is purchase their bitcoin through an exchange, such as Coinbase.com, and then move their bitcoin off the exchange to "cold storage" hardware wallets.

"Hot Wallets" refer to any cryptocurrency wallet that is connected to the internet.

"Cold Storage" is a hardware wallet that is not connected to the internet, is usually a USB flash drive device that is password protected.

Offline hardware USB drive cold storage wallets (such as Ledger, Trezor, and KeepKey) are protected by the PIN number you choose; and are compatible with two-factor identity authentication, specifically with Fido UF2, which was developed by Google and is the standard.

So offline hardware wallets are quite secure. They are equipped with narrow-purpose interface apps for your devices that allow you to buy, spend and move your bitcoin and other crypto assets you might own, plus store your passwords.

I use Ledger hardware wallets. No external software (bots, malware, cookies) can enter a Ledger hardware wallet. I assume the same is true for Trezor and KeepKey, but I've never used them.

These are the three most popular.

There's also the military-grade IronKey.

Now, the truth is, your hardware wallet is touching the internet when it's plugged into your laptop, and you're buying, or selling, or moving your bitcoin.

You can't completely avoid the internet. Bitcoin is the native currency of the internet.

Security breaches are always possible when you are touching the internet. Though your risk is greatly reduced if you've advanced this far – that is, if you've moved your bitcoin off the exchange (such as Coinbase); moved it to a self-custody hot wallet (such as Electrum or BlueWallet); then moved it to a new address you've created for your offline cold storage USB drive hardware wallet (such as Ledger).

Only move small amounts from one wallet address to another until you become very comfortable with the process.

It sounds complicated when you first hear about it. But the process becomes second nature. Learning to drive a car was probably scary at first, but then became second nature.

This is important . . .

I use a Linux-based Purism Librem laptop to conduct all my financial transactions. There's no Microsoft Office, no Google Chrome installed. The operating system is PureOS, designed for privacy. No tracking. This laptop is only connected to the internet when I need to conduct financial activity. I have another laptop for surfing the Web, watching YouTube, and general use.

Next Level Security

If you want to take security to the next level, do this.

First, learn how to generate your own wallet addresses without relying on a commercial product to do this for you.

Head on over to bitaddress.org to create yet another wallet by using the tool you'll see on the page.

Download this page onto your computer – preferably a new virgin laptop computer that's unlikely to be polluted with malware.

Once you've downloaded the bitaddress.org page and tool, disconnect from the Internet. Then start moving your mouse around your screen randomly for 20 seconds or so until the tool tells you it has enough information to generate your new wallet (private and public key).

The tool will give you a 52-digit alphanumeric code, upper and lower case – plus a corresponding QR code. That's your private key.

The tool will also provide your public key and QR code.

Alternatively, you could flip a coin 256 times, write down the result of each flip, and generate your 256 bit code that way – hence the name SHA-256.

But that's overkill. Just use the tool at bitaddress.org.

Print the page with your wallet info and QR code. Store it somewhere safe temporarily, until you've carried out this next step.

Buy a Military Dog Tag Metal Stamping Kit

Stamp your 52-digit private key code on stainless steel tags. Stamping the code into the steel is better than engraving it.

For more detailed information on this, go on YouTube and type "store bitcoins on steel military dog tags" or "stamp military dog tags" or "emboss military dog tags." Lots of videos will come up.

Stamping numbers and letters (upper and lower case) into stainless steel is heavy-duty. Engraving can wear off over time.

Buy some stainless steel credit card holders or wallets.

Place your stamped dog tag in a stainless steel credit card holder case, and bury it somewhere on your property. Just remember where you buried it. Do this several times, burying your tags in different locations.

Your buried stainless steel tags will survive corrosion, flood, fire, and thermonuclear war.

This is where you store your emergency fund, for when all Hell breaks loose and socio-economic collapse ensues.

Yes, this is ultra-hardcore. But this is what you do if security is your #1 concern. But begin first with baby steps.

It's fine to start buying bitcoin on a custodial exchange to start, such as Coinbase.com. Then you will want to get off the training wheels and graduate to self-custody . . . because exchanges really are not safe. Even Coinbase (probably the best exchange) recommends this.

China, Russia, Iran, North Korea, and bad actors are working 24-7-365 to hack America's financial institutions. The U.S. government, including the IRS, can grab your money at any time.

A civil litigant can freeze your account with a court order, which is not difficult to get.

So self-custody should be the goal for all Bitcoiners.

Let's recap:

1) Buy some bitcoin (satsoshis) on Coinbase.com.
2) Go to bitcoin.org and download one of their recommended self-custody hot wallets, such as Electrum or BlueWallet, which will provide you a new address, different from your Coinbase address.
3) Move small amounts of your bitcoin from Coinbase to your self-custody hot wallet. Get used to the process.
4) Order a hardware cold-storage wallet, with USB flash drive, such as Ledger, which will generate new private and public keys for you. You can store a near infinite number of keys on this drive. Order directly from manufacturer, not from Amazon or third-party seller.
5) Practice moving some bitcoin from your hot wallet to your cold storage wallet.
6) Buy stainless steel military ID dog tags for about $1 each, along with metal stamping kit for about $35.
7) Learn to generate your own bitcoin wallets, without using a commercial product, by going to bitaddress.org. Download page. Disconnect from internet. Follow instructions. Use tool. Print page.
8) Stamp 52-digit private key code on stainless steel dog tags.
9) Practice moving small amounts of bitcoin to this new address.
10) Check your balance by going to blockchain.info or blockexplorer.com and enter your public Bitcoin address. Don't enter your private key. Yikes! Enter only your public key. Follow instructions carefully.
11) Purchase stainless steel credit card case or wallet for $7-15, or about $60 if you want titanium. Put dog tag in case. Bury on your property where only you know about it, plus perhaps one other loved one who can be trusted. Repeat process two more times. Bury in different locations.
12) Rehearse your knowledge of your buried treasure locations in your mind at least once a month.

Most people won't get past STEP ONE on this list.

They'll buy some bitcoin on Coinbase.com and leave it there.

That's fine.

Coinbase.com is probably secure, so long as it stays in business and so long as the government (IRS) doesn't want your money or your account isn't frozen or seized in a civil lawsuit.

It took me one year of owning some bitcoin before I ventured beyond STEP ONE and took my coins off the exchange.

If you make it through STEP 5 on this list, you're a true Bitcoiner.

If you make it through STEP 12 on this list, you're a bona fide survivalist, prepared for societal and economic collapse, and ready to make a quick escape to wherever civilization might still exist in some form.

Seed Word Wallet Recovery Phrases

Hot wallets (like Electrum or BlueWallet) and offline cold storage wallets (like Ledger, Trezor, and KeepKey) have tools to help you create random 12-24 word recovery phrases in case you lose your private key code.

These hardware wallets use these 12-24 word seed phrases to create your wallet keys. If you use these hardware wallet tools to generate your random words off line, that's secure.

You then write down the words the tool gives you in the proper order. You then enter the phrases back into the tool by hand. And out come your wallet addresses. Cool.

Some worry that these hardware devices contain software that might hijack your codes. This is possible, but if you use one of these reputable ones (Ledger, Trezor, KeepKey, or the military-grade IronKey), security is their entire business.

These devices have millions of customers. If shown to be not secure, they go out of business. The one I use, Ledger, has 3,000,000 customers in 190 countries. If had a bug, a hole, a backdoor, we would have heard about it by now.

So it appears to be good. I've had no security issues with Ledger.

But there are further precautions you can take.

Another way to generate seed words for your phrase is to use the tool at bitaps.com/mnemonic

Download this page on your laptop. Then disconnect from the

internet. Then pull up this page from your laptop.

Hit whether you want a 12, 15, 18, 21, or 24 seed-word phrase.

When the random words appear, hit load.

Your new keys will appear along with your seed words.

Print page. Hide the page in some secure location until you're ready to secure your keys, such as with the above described metal dog tag stamping method.

You can also generate random seed word phrases in ways that don't involve touching the internet or using a commercial hardware wallet product.

One involves using two 20-sided die plus two 10-sided die, along with something called a BIP39 word list. You select one of among 2,048 available BIP39 word indexes.

You'll also want to conduct what's called a "saltwater balance check" to make sure the die you are properly balanced. Sometimes slight manufacturing issues can create tiny flaws in the die that can throw off randomness.

The "saltwater balance" test will ensure the die are properly balanced, to therefore produce a truly random result. Google "saltwater balance test for dice" if you want more info.

The details of this method of random seed word selection are way beyond the scope of this book. And, honestly, it's just part of my bizarre brand of humor to even be touching on some of these topics in a "beginner's guide."

But if this has grabbed your attention and you want more detail on all this, just type "bitcoin seed word generation with dice" into Google.

Seed words can also be generated with a scientific calculator set to random mode. For more info on this method, type "generate bitcoin seed phrase with a calculator" into Google.

Mathematicians say that blindfolding yourself and pointing to random words in a dictionary doesn't actually produce a random selection of words. I don't know why. But I take their word for it. Probably has to do with how the human body instinctively moves, following predictable patterns.

My guess is because the natural human tendency is to pick from the center of the book rather than the edges, similar to cutting a deck of cards. People tend to cut the card deck near the middle.

It's important to note that seed-word recovery phrases are used to recover lost private key codes, but your private key code cannot be used to generate seed word recovery phrases.

That's because, in cryptography, information flows in one direction. It cannot be reversed. It's like putting a cow into a meat grinder. The cow comes out the other end as hamburger meat. It's the exact same material from an atomic and molecular perspective. But you can't push the hamburger meat back through the machine and reassemble the cow.

This is what make cryptographic coding secure.

SHA-256 is considered by experts to an unbreakable coding algorithm. How did they come up with all this?

Mindbending.

These nuggets of detail are just intended to give you a taste of some of the more arcane aspects of Bitcoin World. And the arcanery goes way beyond this.

This rabbit hole called Bitcoin is deep . . . infinite.

You can go as deep into this rabbit hole as you want. But this book is just an introduction to the topic.

Let's now go back to the world in which most people live – Beginner Land.

For offline cold storage wallets (such as Ledger, Trezor, and KeepKey), make sure you have multiple back-up copies, hidden in multiple secure locations (not all in your house). USB drives can fail. Fires, floods, and robberies happen. And make sure your hardware wallets are all protected by strong passcodes.

In the event one of your USB hard wallet drives is stolen or lost, make sure you have another Bitcoin hardware wallet that has a different private key and move your bitcoin to that wallet.

Assuming your stolen USB drive wallet is protected by a good passcode, it will take the thief some time to break into your USB drive hardware wallet.

Some people also write their private key code on a piece of paper, laminate the paper, and store it in a safe in their home or safe deposit box at a bank. No good. Paper, even laminated paper, is easily destroyed. Paper can accidentally be thrown in the trash, swept away, lost. Everyone knows that a safe in your home is where your valuables are. So that's no good.

And a safe deposit box in a bank means you are trusting the bank to keep your private key safe. You are then trusting a custodian with your wealth, which largely defeats the point of Bitcoin.

The Pros and Cons of Being Your Own Bank

The big advantage of Bitcoin is that it's a decentralized system. No central authority can block your transactions or seize your bitcoin. But this is also a double-edged sword.

The downside is you are responsible for keeping your private keys secure because if you ever lose your private key, your bitcoin associated with that key is gone forever.

In Bitcoin World, you are sovereign over yourself. You are your own bank. There's no authority you can appeal to if you lose your private key. You can't call the bank and say: "I lost my passcode. Can we reset it?"

But also, no one can freeze your account. No one can seize your funds, unless they have your private key.

Remember, the SHA-256 cryptographic algorithm can generate more possibilities for wallets than there are atoms in the universe, say some. So if you lose your bitcoin, the problem isn't SHA-256.

The problem is you.

Many people believe the bank won't freeze their account, believe the government won't seize their money. But this happens all the time.

You also should not let people know how much bitcoin you own. Otherwise, kidnappers might get hold of you and start tearing off your fingers one by one until you give them your private keys.

So there's that risk. You can't completely eliminate risk. Kidnappers can also take your child hostage.

Freedom Requires Taking Responsibility

Bitcoin liberates you from central authority and central control.

Bitcoin separates your money from the government, also separates your money from banking. Bitcoin is your off-ramp from the corrupt fiat money printing system.

Not everyone is comfortable with freedom. With freedom comes responsibility. Responsibility is hard to handle.

The sad truth is, most people (80-90 percent) prefer to be told what to do. Most people want to be taken care of. Most people want to believe the government is looking out for them. Most people want to believe our leaders in government know what they're doing.

This belief is how Hitler happens.

Bitcoin is your escape route.

On the flip side, an estimated 3.7 million bitcoins have been lost over the years – not stolen, just lost. These lost bitcoins will never find their way back into circulation.

This means Bitcoin is even more scarce than you might think. 19 million bitcoins have been mined and put into circulation, but 3.7 million bitcoins have been lost and are out of circulation forever.

This means there are really only 15.3 million bitcoins in circulation, not 19 million. It also means that instead of a 21 million cap on bitcoin supply, the maximum number of bitcoins that will ever be in circulation is more like 17.3 million.

Most of the 3.7 million lost bitcoins were lost in the early years when people had no idea about the future value of their bitcoin.

They lost their bitcoin when it was worth $1 or $10 per coin. They stored their private keys on a laptop that they then threw away without thinking.

This happened to the political commentator Alex Jones.

One of the early Bitcoiners Max Keiser reportedly gave Alex Jones 10,000 bitcoins in 2010 when the price was about $1 per coin. When Jones' laptop got outdated, he bought a new laptop and threw the old one away, forgetting his old laptop contained his private key.

He just wasn't thinking about Bitcoin, not until years later. He thought Bitcoin sounded like a joke, or that it just wasn't worth wasting any brainpower on the topic. His 10,000 bitcoins are gone.

Multiply 10,000 bitcoin by today's price to check Jones' loss.

Another famous case involves a software engineer named Stephan Thomas. He was paid 7,002 bitcoins in 2011 for some software work he did back when bitcoin was super cheap, just a few dollars a coin. He lost his key code.

Thomas was actually pretty careful. He kept his key code in three places. He then lost two of them.

He also stored his key on an IronKey encrypted flash drive. No one can break into an IronKey because it's indestructible encrypted military-grade hardware. Not even the company that makes the device, Kingston Technology, can get into an IronKey without the passcode.

You're only allowed ten attempts to guess the passcode of an IronKey. Thomas has reportedly tried eight times. He has two guesses left.

After that, all the data stored on his IronKey drive, including his Bitcoin key, will be erased automatically and forever lost.

Today, people tend to be extra careful with their bitcoin. Still, accidents, mistakes, and computer hacks can happen.

Take precautions. There's a right way (and many wrong ways) to secure your bitcoin. This is something you must get used to if you want to be a true Bitcoiner.

Taking custody and securing your bitcoin is a skill you must learn. It's a survival skill. You learn by doing.

Start slow. Do a little at a time. Start by moving a few satoshis from address to address that are under your control. Take baby steps.

Learning how to take custody and control of your bitcoin is a big part of how you graduate from being a mouse in someone else's maze . . . to become a free, independent, and sovereign individual who has options.

CHAPTER 9

Does Bitcoin Make Criminal Activity Easier?

Senator Elizabeth Warren and other critics of Bitcoin claim Bitcoin is a vehicle for drug cartels, money laundering, black marketeers, and criminal activity. These critics point to the so-called "Silk Road" black market website that was founded in 2011 by Ross Ulbricht (then age 27) and that operated until 2013.

This, of course, was in the very early days of Bitcoin, when few had heard of the network.

Ulbricht went under the pseudonym "Dread Pirate Roberts," the character in the movie *Princess Bride*, evidently because he liked the libertarian themes in the movie.

"Silk Road" was one of the first incarnations of the "dark web," which operated as an underground marketplace mostly for illegal drugs, opioids, erotica, and fake driver's licenses. Other items sold on the site included cigarettes, art, books, clothing, jewelry, rooms for rent, even freelance writing and art services.

So it also operated as a kind of flea market or Craig's List.

Terms of service included a ban on selling anything that intended to "harm or defraud," including child pornography, stolen credit cards, weapons, murder-for-hire, arson, or any kind of paid violence.

Silk Road hid the identities of users by hosting the marketplace as a Tor site, which conceals IP addresses.

Buyers on the site rated and reviewed merchants. This was a big part of the site's success.

Though all Bitcoin transactions are broadcast publicly on the open-source ledger, the identities of Bitcoin users are concealed by cryptography.

The site's "Silk Road" name was taken from the name of an ancient trade route between the Roman Empire and China, later between Medieval Europe and China.

The FBI shut down Silk Road and arrested Ulbricht in October of 2013. He was arrested while using a computer to conduct his business at a public library in San Francisco. [14]

The FBI can track you down pretty easily if you are using a public computer in a public library to conduct your illegal business activities. The FBI found 44,342 bitcoins on Ulbricht's computer.

The criminal complaint against Ulbricht in the Southern District of New York United States District Court stated as follows:

> From February 6, 2011 to July 23, 2013 there were approximately 1,229,465 transactions completed on the site. The total revenue generated from these sales was 9,519,664 bitcoins, and the total commissions collected by Silk Road from the sales amounted to 614,305 bitcoins. [15]

Prosecutors also initially claimed that Ulbricht tried to have five people killed, though could find no example of a murder that had occurred in connection with Silk Road.

Nor was Ulbricht ever prosecuted for solicitation of murder, which would be a serious crime. There is no evidence in Ulbricht's history to suggest he was ever prone to any kind of violence.

An ideological libertarian, his posts consistently denounced violence – including the monopoly on legal violence that the state can use against you.

In February of 2015, Ulbricht was convicted of running an ongoing criminal enterprise, trafficking in illegal narcotics, money laundering, and computer hacking.

U.S. District Court Judge Katherine Forest sentenced Ulbricht to two life sentences without the possibility of parole and ordered Ulbricht to pay $183 million. [16]

Later in 2015, two federal law enforcement agents were convicted of keeping the bitcoin Ulbricht had paid them to keep Ulbricht informed about the investigation. DEA agent Carl Mark Force IV and Secret Service agent Shaun Bridges were each

---

[14] Donna Leinwand Leger. "How the FBI Brought Down Cyber-Underworld Site Silk Road." *USA Today*, October 21, 2013.
[15] "Silk Road – Tale of First Darknet Market," first published on darkweb.wiki - Anthony Frank
[16] Roberts, Jeff John. "Why a Judge Threw the Book at Silk Road's Founder." Fortune magazine, June 1, 2015.

sentenced to six years in prison – which sure is light compared to two life sentences for Ulbricht.

Isn't corruption by federal law enforcement, including profiting from Silk Road, actually worse than Ulbricht's non-violent crimes?

There's not even any evidence Ulbricht ever stole any money.

While Ulbricht was certainly engaging in criminal activity by facilitating commerce in illegal drugs (along with legal products), there's no evidence he killed or even tried to kill anyone or hurt anyone.

He certainly deserved some jail time, but not more than those corrupt federal agents. Not two life sentences!

There needs to be a sense of proportion.

Ulbricht claims he was acting out of libertarian ideals.

There are many in libertarian circles who believe drugs should be legalized, arguing that buying drugs peacefully from the safety of home is preferable to the violence of the global drug war and interacting with gangs in the street drug trade.

I don't agree with the legalization of powerful narcotics. Some substances – such as heroin, crack cocaine, and meth –are so addictive that they are almost impossible to break free from. Fentanyl is 50 times more powerful than heroin.

Opioids, including Fentanyl, are killing more than 100,000 Americans per year.

So count me as a "no" on legalizing these kinds of drugs, though there's a case for legalizing cannabis and milder drugs.

I also don't view Ulbricht as anything close to the level of a dangerous violent killer, many of whom serve a few years and then are back out on the street committing more crimes. The Silk Road site did have a policy prohibiting the sale of child pornography, weapons of any kind, or any kind of violence for hire.

Here are some quotes from Ulbricht's writings as "Dread Pirate Roberts" on the Silk Road forum prior to his arrest. These quotes were assembled by Andy Greenberg for *Forbes* in 2013. [17]

Ulbricht on why he started Silk Road:

> Silk Road was founded on libertarian principles and
> continues to be operated on them. It is a great idea and a

---

[17] Andy Greenberg. "Collected Quotations of the Dread Pirate Roberts, Founder of Underground Drug Site Silk Road." *Forbes*, April 29, 2013.

great practical system...It is not a utopia. It is regulated by market forces, not a central power (even I am subject to market forces by my competition. No one is forced to be here). The same principles that have allowed Silk Road to flourish can and do work anywhere human beings come together. The only difference is that the State is unable to get its thieving murderous mitts on it. [10/1/2012]

Ulbricht on Silk Road being a vehicle for drug cartels:

Cartels are nearly impossible to maintain without the use of violence, especially in an environment as competitive as Silk Road. There is also nothing morally wrong with them. If a cartel were to form, I would not attempt to break it up unless its members were breaking other rules. If you want an explanation for why cartels are nearly impossible to maintain in a free market environment, please read "Man, Economy and State" chapter 10, part 2, section D. [3/21/2013]

Agree with Ulbricht or not, he wrote thoughtful things under the "Dread Pirate Roberts" name as a young man on the Silk Road forum. He appears to have been motivated as much by his libertarian ideology as by profit. He's no John Gacy, Jeffrey Dahmer, or even Al Capone who only got seven years.

Capone was one of the most famous and dangerous gangsters in U.S. history. Only seven years for him, but two life sentences for Ulbricht. There is no evidence Ulbricht tried to hire someone to have anyone hurt or killed.

Violence is antithetical to his libertarian beliefs.

He certainly broke the law.

But two life sentences with no possibility of parole for running an underground online marketplace is excessive.

This Silk Road example cited by critics of Bitcoin is not a persuasive argument against Bitcoin.

The fact that every transaction is public and broadcast live to the world as it occurs makes Bitcoin a poor vehicle for a criminal enterprise.

For criminal activity, it's far more effective to use cash than to conduct transactions on the internet and on a public blockchain ledger. Internet transactions can be tracked.

While Bitcoin addresses cannot be accessed without the private key to the wallet, we can track the balances of every Bitcoin address.

We know, for example, that Satoshi's address contains 1,000,000 bitcoins, which have never moved.

If the government puts enough effort and resources into it, they can track your bitcoin transactions. They'll just follow your transactions from address to address until they find you – most likely when you try to convert your bitcoin to fiat money through a crypto exchange or centrally-controlled digital wallet.

Physical fiat cash is much more difficult for the government to trace, which is one big reason government wants to eliminate the cash economy.

There have been several attempts to restart Silk Road.

In November of 2014, the FBI announced the arrest of Blake Benthall and others who had tried to reboot Silk Road as Silk Road 2.0. In January 2015, the FBI shut down Silk Road 3 and arrested more people.

In November of 2020, the U.S. Justice Department announced it found and seized 69,370 bitcoins from "Individual X" who stole the coins from Ulbricht by hacking Silk Road.

As of this writing in 2022, these coins are worth about $2 billion.

The IRS Criminal Investigation unit used computer forensics specialists to track down the coins and "Individual X."

In a deal with prosecutors, Individual X agreed to hand over the loot in exchange for no jail time and keeping his identity concealed.

SIDEBAR: A Las Vegas businessman named Jay Bloom claims in a civil court filing that Individual X is a man called Raymond Ngan. Bloom won a $2.2 billion default judgment against Ngan who failed to show up in court.

Ngan says in a federal bankruptcy court filing that he only has $500 in a checking account.

Bloom's suit claims Ngan failed to provide him $160 million in financing Ngan allegedly promised. Not much is known about Ngan, who appears to be a refugee from Cambodia.

END SIDEBAR.

One of the great side aspects of Bitcoin World are the stories and colorful characters associated with the network.

But the lesson of Silk Road is not that Bitcoin makes crime easier. The lesson is that if the FBI and the IRS put the effort in, these government agencies can probably track you down if they want to.

Yes, your bitcoins are secured by your private keys. But if the government gets hold of you, it can probably get your bitcoins.

The government will just hold you in prison until you give up your private keys.

The IRS asks about your crypto holdings on tax forms.

Your best approach is to be honest with the IRS about your crypto holdings, pay your taxes, and not engage in illegal activity – unless you plan to flee the country to some remote location that has no extradition treaty with the United States.

But that's a tough way to live. Our government can be annoying. Taxes are too high and there's too much nonsensical government regulation. But the United States is still the best place on the planet to live.

Bitcoin is a hedge against dishonest money. It's not a license to break the law – at least not until we descend into some form of totalitarianism.

If this happens, it will be good to have some bitcoin.

CHAPTER 10

What Makes Bitcoin Valuable?

One argument you often hear against Bitcoin is that its value is based on nothing. Of course, the value of the dollar and fiat currency is also based on nothing. U.S. paper money used to be gold certificates redeemable for actual gold.

There's not much inherent value in gold either. You can use it for jewelry and decoration. It has utility in electronics. But other than these uses, gold doesn't have much use and not much inherent value.

Gold is considered valuable because it's scarce and because it's "perceived" to have value. Its value is in the perception. This perception of value was achieved because gold had the properties people were looking for in a unit of exchange. These include:

1) Gold is finite and scarce.
2) Gold is divisible.
3) Gold is portable.
4) Gold is durable.

Because gold possesses this combination of properties, gold has been used as a unit of exchange for 6,000 years.

What makes a Picasso painting valuable?

A Picasso painting is valuable because many people agree it has value.

If you found a paper napkin with a doodle on it, you'd probably think this napkin with a doodle on it doesn't have much value. You would probably toss it in the trash. But what if you learned the doodle on this napkin was created by Picasso?

Then this doodle would have enormous value.

The value is in the perception. Something becomes valuable because people agree it's valuable. This is a basic principle of 19th Century Austrian economics, which we'll get into later in this book.

So scarcity alone does not create value. Lots of things are unique and one-of-a-kind. A pile of mud is unique. "There will never be another pile of mud exactly like that particular pile of mud right there."

That uniqueness doesn't make a pile of mud valuable.

Value is created once a lot of people agree something is valuable – whether it's a rare baseball card, a comic book, a stamp, or a piece of art. A pile of mud could conceivably become valuable if enough people agree it has value.

Bitcoin might never have gained value in people's minds – might just as easily have remained an interesting lab experiment. Just because the supply of bitcoins is limited doesn't mean many people would care.

It's difficult to say why Bitcoin got traction in the minds of people so quickly. I believe it first gained traction in the minds of people because it was an inherently interesting project.

When I first read Satoshi's white paper on Bitcoin, I was blown away by it. That white paper is only eight pages long. I'm no tech expert at all. Other than the math equations and coding, Satoshi's white paper was easy for me to understand.

You can Google it, pull it up, and read it. You should read it before you buy any bitcoin.

When you read Satoshi's white paper, you will find it difficult to avoid being sucked into this rabbit hole called Bitcoin. The design of Bitcoin's structure is both brilliant and surprisingly simple – so simple that even I, an English Literature major, can understand it.

It's simple in design like an hourglass. It's perfectly designed for what it's trying to achieve.

And that makes sense. The more complex the coding (or anything for that matter), the easier it is to attack it

An underground bunker encased in steel and concrete is more secure than a moving tank.

Less than one page of Satoshi's paper consists of code and math equations. I skipped these parts and just followed his layman's description of Bitcoin's structure, which includes a number of helpful diagrams.

So Bitcoin gained traction in the minds of people – first among a small circle of cryptographers and the tech-savvy, then among a wider circle of libertarian types and the intellectually curious; then gained wider attention as the price of one bitcoin rose from a few pennies to a few dollars, to hundreds of dollars, to thousands of dollars and higher.

But it's also not true to say that the value of Bitcoin is based on nothing.

People buy bitcoin with their hard-earned money.

Money represents people's labor, time, and ingenuity. Money is a way we store the value of our work, creativity, and inventions in a way that we can easily and efficiently send some of this value to others, or save this value for later use.

When someone gets cheated out of their "life savings," most of us recoil in horror. To be cheated out of one's life savings in effect means that someone has stolen your life.

The entire mission of Bitcoin was to create an honest money system that does not allow government or any central authority to steal your labor, your time, your ingenuity, and your life savings by simply printing more fake confetti money.

What is your work?

Your work is your energy. Bitcoin is an impenetrable dome of encrypted energy that protects your life's work.

"Network Effect" Creates Value

Bitcoin gains more value as more and more people buy it and use it. This creates a "Network Effect" – also called "Metcalf's Law."

Metcalf's law states that the value of a telecommunications network is proportional to the square of the number of connected users to the system.

If there were only one phone in the world, it would not be very valuable because there would be no way to use it. Phones gain value as more people get phones.

The same is true with the internet. The internet was not very valuable when only a few people knew what it was and could access it. At that point, the internet was just an interesting lab experiment.

Facebook gained value because of its Network Effect.

Facebook started as essentially a bulletin board at Harvard where guys could rate the "hotness" of female students. Pretty tasteless and juvenile. But Facebook quickly became something bigger, spread to other campuses, and then to wider society.

People join Facebook to stay connected or to reconnect with family and friends, and to find new friends. Facebook has three billion users. This makes Facebook an enormously powerful advertising platform.

Facebook has a stock market value (market cap) of $500 billion.

More than one billion people own an Apple iPhone. This allows Apple to launch a new product to one billion people in minutes.

That's powerful.

Apple has leveraged this Network Effect to become the world's most profitable company, now with a $3 trillion market cap.

The value of almost all internet businesses comes from this Network Effect – variations of Metcalf's Law.

Microsoft is valuable because so many businesses and people use Microsoft software products.

Microsoft software has become standard. There have been better word processing programs than Microsoft Word, in my view. I preferred Word Perfect back in the 1980s and early '90s. Microsoft Word gained traction with the public and became the standard.

I used to use Lotus for my spreadsheets. But Microsoft Excel gained dominance in the market, so became the standard. Maybe something else is better. But it doesn't really matter because everyone uses Excel.

Gold also became valuable because of this Network Effect.

There are other metals that are scarcer than gold – platinum, palladium, osmium, rhenium, rhodium, tantalum, and I'm sure others.

But gold gained traction in people's minds, so became the standard, perhaps because gold is prettier or perhaps because a metal that is too rare would not serve the purpose of currency as well.

If you can't find enough of a metal, that metal doesn't work well as a unit of exchange. If you can't instantly tell the difference between platinum, titanium and silver, that doesn't work so well. And if the metal is too plentiful, that won't work either.

Silver works as a currency. About 20 times more silver has been mined than gold. Currently, about nine ounces of silver are mined per year to one ounce of gold.

Silver has also worked fine as a currency for thousands of years – good for smaller daily transactions, but not as good as gold as a long-term store of value.

So gold gained critical mass in people's minds, primarily as a long-term store of value that is also portable.

Still, gold is really too valuable to be used as a daily currency. You might get robbed. So people are more likely to store and hide their gold than actually use it in daily life.

Bitcoin is something like gold – digital gold.

It has similar properties to gold. It's scarce, has a limited supply. But it's more portable. You can carry it on your phone or in your head if you can remember a 12-word seed phrase. Bitcoin has also gained wide recognition as valuable – up from 3/10ths of one penny 12 years ago to . . . well, just check price today.

And you can send your Bitcoin, or a fraction of it (satoshis), anywhere on the planet instantly and at very low cost.

You can't do that with gold.

Let's say you own a 24-karat gold bar. That gold bar is worth about $625,000.

Let's say you want to send your $625,000 gold bar from New York to London.

How would you do it? What would it cost? How would you secure your gold bar?

You would need to buy insurance. That would be costly. You would need to hire a bonded transport and delivery service. That would be costly.

You could carry it yourself. But it would be heavy. You would have trouble getting it through airport security and through customs. You might also get robbed if someone finds out you're carrying a gold bar.

It's complicated to transport gold – usually requires armored trucks. Even then, it's no sure bet your gold bullion reaches its destination.

This task becomes exponentially more complex if you want to transport your gold bar to a Third World country, say Nigeria. How would you do that?

With Bitcoin, you can transmit unlimited value in minutes securely with just a few keystrokes on your computer or phone.

In March of 2020, Tesla announced it had purchased 49,902 bitcoins for an average price of about $32,000 a coin – a total value of $1.6 billion at the time.

A couple of months later, Elon Musk announced that Tesla had sold about $300 million in bitcoin, not because he had soured on Bitcoin. He was just testing it to find out how liquid bitcoin was. He wanted to see if it was possible to sell $300 million in bitcoin quickly. Elon said he had no problem with the transaction.

One year later, Tesla sold 75 percent of its bitcoin holdings ($936 million) in June of 2022 – again, not because Elon had soured on bitcoin, but because Tesla needed the cash for its business. Tesla had no trouble quickly selling nearly $1 billion in bitcoin, had no trouble finding buyers.

You can't do that with gold, not this easily. You can't even transact this much money this easily and quickly using fiat currency.

Senior bank officials would need to get involved. There would be meetings. Multiple-signature authorizations would have to be signed. The IRS would be alerted.

None of this happens with Bitcoin – though you can set up private keys so that more than one signature is required to spend bitcoin. But that's up to you – not a bank.

So how much more useful and efficient is Bitcoin than your gold bar or fiat currency?

Then there's the problem of storing your gold bar.

You wouldn't want to keep it in your house. Someone might learn about it and steal it.

You could bury your gold bar in the ground. But someone might find it, might see you burying it, wonder what it is, and then go get it. You could ask your bank to store it. But then you're trusting someone else to protect your gold bar.

Let's say someone sues you and subpoenas all your bank records. Then let's say that litigant (whether the government or private party) gets a court order to freeze all your assets.

Your gold bar is then no longer yours. It's in the custody of the bank, which is really an arm of government. The government now has your gold bar.

Your bitcoin is under no one's custody but yours – IF you take custody of your bitcoin and don't keep your bitcoin on a centrally-managed exchange.

With Bitcoin, you are your own bank. No one, not even the government, can get your bitcoin unless you give them your private key. Your bitcoin is in a digital vault protected by impenetrable military-grade cryptography.

How much better is that than gold?

How much better is this than fiat currency?

That's the appeal of Bitcoin.

It should be noted that news of Tesla's selling of nearly $1 billion of its bitcoin holdings had almost no impact on bitcoin's price. Tesla had no trouble finding buyers. Bitcoin's price actually started heading up soon after the public learned about Tesla's sale, as investors saw bitcoin's resilience.

I believe one reason gold has not been rising much in price over the past couple of years, despite all the manic money-printing by the Fed, is because many people are looking at Bitcoin as being superior to gold. Bitcoin is a better store of value than gold. Bitcoin is also portable and easy to use.

Gold right now is about a $10 trillion asset.

Bitcoin is an $400 billion asset. If people start migrating in a major way from gold to Bitcoin because Bitcoin is a superior asset, it's not unreasonable to think that Bitcoin could rise to $100,000 a coin within the next few years.

The world bond market is worth $120 trillion. What if a portion of this money, even just one or two percent, started flowing into Bitcoin as a hedge or as diversification?

The worldwide stock market is $100 trillion. What if just five percent of this money started flowing into Bitcoin as a hedge against stock market crashes?

It's not outlandish to envision a $500,000 bitcoin price within ten years as adoption grows.

Bitcoin's price movements often appear to track closely with the stock market, especially with emerging tech growth stocks. That's because Bitcoin is seen by many as an emerging technology.

But as Bitcoin matures as an asset class, it should decouple from the stock market and follow its own path (if my thesis is correct).

Bitcoin's long-term non-correlation to the stock market will be appealing to investors looking to hedge against a crashing stock market and a crashing dollar.

If the fiat economy starts collapsing, Bitcoin should rise, at least over the long term.

Perhaps it crashes at first with the stock market, but then it should start heading upward as people look for an escape hatch from the collapsing fiat money system.

Bitcoin right now has 150 million users. Bitcoin is where the internet was in 1997 in terms of number of users.

Bitcoin

The internet started being used in the 1960s as a way for government researchers to share information. It took 30 years for the internet to reach 150 million users. Bitcoin achieved this level in just 11 years, an observation made by Bitcoin analyst Willy Woo.

At its current rate of growth, Bitcoin will have one billion users within about five years (from 2022), notes Woo – which would be the same number of internet users in 2005. But if we need to wait until 2030 or 2035 for Bitcoin to hit the one billion user level, that's fine with me. We can't predict Bitcoin's timetable. Bitcoin will take its own path in its own time.

Rate of Adoption

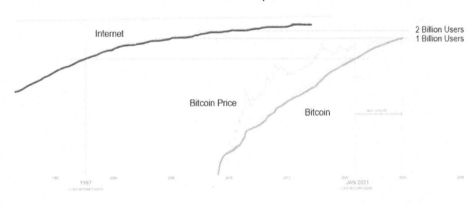

Source: Willy Woo. Woobull.com

This chart is on a log scale.

So if Bitcoin goes from 150 million users to one billion users over the next five or ten years, as Willy Woo projects, that would obviously be very good for the price. Willy's one of the most widely followed Bitcoin analysts.

Now let's get back under the hood and look at some more intriguing details of Bitcoin.

CHAPTER 11

Why Does Bitcoin Have to Be Mined?

Gold is valuable because it's scarce. Gold is also valuable because it's difficult to find and mine.

Winning a gold medal in the Olympics is valuable because it's so difficult to do. It requires a lot of work and a major commitment.

Satoshi sought to approximate gold mining in his design of the Bitcoin system.

He also built a competition element into bitcoin mining with the math puzzle-solving contest system I described earlier called "Proof of Work."

If new bitcoins were produced automatically – with no effort, no investment, no commitment by people – the coins created would not be perceived as valuable.

If you give your child a bicycle, she won't value it as much as she would if she had to work and save her money to buy the bicycle. You value what you work for. The work itself has value.

Money is a storage system for all the hard work you've done to earn that money – a store of value that you can use to purchase things of value you will want later or to transmit value to your children later when you depart this world.

The proof-of-work system Satoshi used is the only known way to produce a truly decentralized money system that is more secure than Fort Knox.

A decentralized network of miners is required to maintain the network, protect the network, and verify transactions.

The miners must be paid for their work. They are paid with transaction fees. They also earn rewards by solving complex proof-of-work math puzzles by using powerful computers.

Every 10 minutes on average, a new math puzzle must be solved, and a new block of transactions inserted into the blockchain to keep to Satoshi's timetable.

As pending transactions enter the mempool for verification, a race ensues among the miners (ASIC computers) to solve this math puzzle. Once the puzzle is solved and the winning miner has verified transactions in the block, the block is unlocked by a "nonce" for verification by the worldwide network of nodes and miners. If the block of transactions is approved by a consensus of the network, the winning miner inserts the block into the blockchain.

The winning miner is then rewarded with 6.25 bitcoins.

This race to solve the math puzzle does not occur among humans, but among powerful specialized ASIC bitcoin mining computers. Of course, humans own these computers. These computers can only be used to mine bitcoin, no other purpose.

This is really more like a lottery than a race. Your probability of winning the 6.25 bitcoin reward is directly proportional to the amount of computing power your machine is expending.

Often miners join pools of miners to ensure they win at least some bitcoin regularly and to keep cash flow steady. We now have a number of publicly-traded bitcoin mining companies – such as Riot Blockchain, Marathon, Bit Farms, Hut 8, Canaan, and many others.

Bitcoin mining is now a multibillion-dollar industry.

In contrast to gold mining companies, bitcoin miners are not looking to sell their bitcoin. The only reason they sell bitcoins is to fund their mining operations or to live. They mine for bitcoin for one reason: to accumulate more bitcoin. Gold mining companies sell the gold they mine as quickly as they acquire it. Gold mining companies hold very little gold. This difference in behavior is a strong indicator of the direction bitcoin miners believe the price of bitcoin is heading.

As the price of bitcoin increases in value, the competition for bitcoin becomes more and more intense.

This means that the math puzzles ("Proof of Work") that must be solved must become increasingly difficult for the network to stay on Satoshi's timetable of one new block of transactions mined and produced every ten minutes on average.

When one bitcoin cost just $1 and there weren't many miners, all you needed was a low-grade laptop computer to mine Bitcoin.

Today, you need a powerful specialized ASIC computer designed specifically for mining Bitcoin.

ASIC stands for Application-Specific Integrated Circuit.

It's hard to imagine how much computing power will eventually be required when the price of one coin hits $500,000 and then $1,000,000.

This is why bitcoin mining operations have mostly moved off the grid where power is plentiful and free or almost free. Increasingly, bitcoin mining operations are powered by solar, water (hydro) and wind.

Some have criticized the enormous amount of energy that bitcoin mining consumes. Bitcoin mining consumes more power than some small countries do.

Tech titan Jack Dorsey has a different view. He believes Bitcoin can actually accelerate the transition to cheap renewable clean energy – the reason being that bitcoin mining is most profitable if it's done off the grid and uses free or nearly free solar power, wind power, and hydropower to power mining rigs.

These forms of power are renewable and infinite.

The sun is a giant nuclear reactor in the sky. Power produced by the sun is infinite. Wind is free. Hydropower just requires placing turbines in the path of flowing water, such as at the base of a glacier.

Bitcoin miners go to where the power is free or almost free, which is off the grid – nowhere near population centers. So Bitcoin miners are taking energy from no one. They are incentivized not to use fossil fuels, which are expensive.

Bitcoin mining operations will create new power grids built on infinite renewable solar, wind, and hydropower. This will incentivize the distribution (rather than concentration) of populations – which is good for the environment.

Note that the theme and impact of Bitcoin is always to incentivize decentralization. It's also well worth underscoring that sustaining and propping up the dollar consumes enormous energy.

Think of the enormous amount of energy our military consumes to defend and prop up the dollar. How much energy is consumed by banks, the Fed's money printing press, and all our financial institutions?

Remember, the U.S. dollar is no longer convertible to gold, no longer backed by gold. The U.S. dollar, we're always told, is backed by the "full faith and credit of the United States government."

In other words, the value of the dollar is decreed by the U.S. government. This means the value of the dollar is really backed by the military, law enforcement, and the threat of prison. The value of the dollar is in effect backed by the U.S. government's threats of violence against you.

The rest of the developed world has agreed to peg the value of their currencies to the dollar.

So the value of the dollar and fiat currencies of the developed world are all backed by the NATO alliance and the combined militaries, banking systems, and law enforcement agencies of the developed world.

How much energy is all this consuming to protect the dollar as the world reserve currency?

Bitcoin's energy consumption is minuscule in comparison. It's also been noted that more energy is consumed by video gamers than by the Bitcoin network. More energy is consumed by Christmas lights than by bitcoin miners.

So it becomes a matter of priorities. What's it worth to have an honest money system that is accessible by everyone, including the unbanked poor in the Third World?

So yes, the Bitcoin network requires a lot of power. But it's this expenditure of energy that protects the network. How much is it worth to protect a $400 billion monetary system that's on its way to becoming a trillion-dollar money network, a $10 trillion network, and possibly even the standard money for the world?

A quarter of the world's people have no access to banking. Many in the undeveloped world live under annual inflation rates of 100 percent, 1,000 percent, and more. These people effectively have no access to money.

How much is it worth to give these people in impoverished countries and collapsed economies access to honest money so they can build a better life for themselves?

Jack Dorsey built Twitter and Square (now renamed Block). He is liberal-left politically.

He's very concerned about the environment. He wants clean air, clean water. We all want this.

Jack Dorsey believes the benefits Bitcoin provides to the unbanked and impoverished people of the world are well worth Bitcoin's energy use. Dorsey believes Bitcoin is the world's greatest engine for freedom and human progress.

Dorsey quit his position as CEO of Twitter so he could dedicate his life to building the Bitcoin network and make it easily accessible to everyone on earth.

Is there an alternative to proof-of-work mining, an alternative that does not consume so much energy?

Yes. It's called "Proof of Stake."

Is a proof-of-stake system any good?

ANSWER: No. Not if you value security; and not if you value decentralization – which is essential to security.

The purpose of Bitcoin's proof-of-work mining system is to make the cost of attacking the system prohibitively expensive, because to take over the system, an attacker would need to use more computing power than the entire combined computing power of the network, and then sustain that attack for days.

This means the attacker would actually need exponentially more computing power than the combined computing power of the entire Bitcoin network.

Proof-of-work is akin to national defense, but in the digital world.

This is the point developed by MIT aeronautics and computer engineer Jason Lowery in his Ph.D. dissertation. Again, Lowery is a director of space launch operations for the U.S. Space Force, so knows what he's talking about.

Our military is expensive. We spend $1.2 trillion per year on our military to protect the country. Many think we spend too much on the military.

But, as we discovered with the attack on Pearl Harbor, it's better to be too strong than too weak. Better to be overprepared than underprepared.

Proof-of-work is the strongest fortress we know how to build in the digital world, says Lowery. Building and maintaining this digital fortress requires energy, requires power.

Proof-of-work is just one pillar in Bitcoin's security triad – the other two pillars being decentralization and military-grade cryptographic algorithms. All three security pillars work together and are interlocking pieces of Bitcoin's protective digital dome of encrypted energy.

Once the 21 millionth bitcoin is mined in the spring of 2140, the contest to mine for new bitcoin will stop. Transaction fees alone will be enough to sustain and protect the network.

A key component that protects the network is that the miners have a big incentive to protect its integrity. The miners own a lot of bitcoin. Plus, bitcoin miners have invested a lot of money in their expensive ASIC computer mining rigs.

If there were ever a "double-spend" or if ever the integrity of the network was compromised, the value of their bitcoin would crash, perhaps to zero. The miners, plus military-grade cryptography, will keep Bitcoin secure.

Billionaire tech entrepreneur, Michael Saylor, has likened Bitcoin's miners to a swarm of cyberhornets protecting their growing nest. The Bitcoin nest keeps getting bigger, as both the price of bitcoin increases and the network of users grows.

The incentives of every bitcoin owner, miner, and node are perfectly aligned to secure the network. As the network grows, it becomes more secure, more impenetrable.

This was Satoshi's brilliant design.

The Difficulty Adjustment

One of the most intriguing features of Satoshi's system is what is called the "difficulty adjustment."

The difficulty of the math puzzles that miners must solve (proof-of-work) adjusts, depending on the average time it takes to mine a block.

This difficulty adjustment occurs about every two days – every 2,016 blocks. This is so Bitcoin sticks to Satoshi's timetable of one block mined every 10 minutes on average until the final 21 millionth bitcoin is mined in 2140.

Generally, the difficulty adjusts upward as Bitcoin increases in value and the number of miners and users grows. So the trend for the difficulty of the math puzzle that mining computers must solve is to become more intense over time.

The difficulty adjustment doesn't actually track with price, but with "hash rate" (computing power) used by the network to solve the math puzzle. If the "difficulty adjustment" must be increased to keep to Satoshi's timetable of a new block mined every 10 minutes, this increases the "hash rate" (computing power) of the network.

However, it's often the case that an increase in "hash power" correlates with an increase in the price of one bitcoin over time.

But the "difficulty adjustment" does not always increase.

Sometimes the difficulty of the math puzzle adjusts downward –

becomes easier. For example, when China banned bitcoin mining and transactions in the summer of 2021, miners were forced to shut down their operations in China. Time was needed for Chinese miners to move their mining operations out of China.

Because of this temporary reduction in mining operations, the difficulty of the math puzzle had to be lowered. Satoshi's algorithm performs this "difficulty adjustment" automatically every 2,016 blocks, like clockwork.

What Happens in the Event of a Tie Between Miners?

There are times when miners solve the puzzle for the blocks they are working on at the same time, or almost the same time.

This situation is unusual because of the ten-minute time gap between blocks.

But this ten-minute timeframe is just an average over two days. Sometimes blocks arrive within seconds of each other. At other times, blocks are 20 minutes or more apart. The amount of time between blocks goes up and down throughout the day and night depending on how busy the network is.

The math puzzle difficulty is adjusted every 2016 blocks (about every two days) to keep the average at ten minutes between blocks.

But ties can still occur when blocks arrive in the blockchain at exactly or almost exactly the same time.

This doesn't happen often. But when it does, it can create an "accidental fork." In this case, the miners wait for the addition of the next block. Whichever branch of the blockchain is longest then becomes the official blockchain.

The transactions in the "orphaned" block are then dumped back into the mempool of pending transactions to be collected in a new block to be mined again.

This circumstance could delay your transaction. It's also why you should wait for several block confirmations to come through before you accept your payment.

But what happens if a payee in a confirmed block never accepts the transaction?

If the payee never accepts the transaction for whatever reason, then that transaction is treated as never having occurred. The other completed transactions in the block still remain valid.

The purpose of blocks is simply to group and order transactions in a manageable format for a miner to handle. The block itself has nothing to do with the validity of individual transactions. Blocks are containers for transactions. Blocks link to blocks and represent a timeframe.

Transactions link to transactions. Blocks link to blocks.

Timestamps

Important to the Bitcoin system is the "Timestamp" embedded in each block.

This is not a time designation like we're used to – such as Eastern Standard Time or Greenwich Mean Time, now called Universal Time. Satoshi deployed the Unix time system, which is a running total of seconds. This count started at the Unix Epoch at 00:00:00 on January 1, 1970.

This was computer time set by early Unix engineers because they needed a uniform date for the start of computer time.

The timestamp tells us the exact moment a block was validated by the Bitcoin network and inserted into the blockchain.

This helps ensure that this block can never be duplicated and is a further safeguard against the dreaded "double-spend."

Following this principle, traditional banks use timestamps for tracking deposits and withdrawals. This enables banks to track how much you have to spend, how and when money flows in and out of your account, and prevents you from spending more than you have in your account.

Ledgers must be recorded in linear order – even though the actual transaction might not have occurred at the exact time recorded in the ledger.

Banks don't keep perfect time. A bank might not know your account is overdrawn until the next morning, after it's completed its reconciliation for the previous day – at which point you might get hit with an overdraft fee if you spent more than you had in your account.

Banks also batch checks together in what would be an approximate order they arrived, but not in perfect order. This was especially true before the internet age.

Bitcoin does not keep perfect time either. But a blockchain ledger must be in linear order.

This is the only way to keep track of money, how much is going in and out.

Transactions in a block are treated as if they all occurred at about the same time – within that ten-minute timeframe between blocks.

The timestamp of a Bitcoin block shows everyone exactly when the block was approved by the network of nodes and inserted into the blockchain. The timestamp shows that the network has agreed on the history of transactions.

Timestamps are also important to Bitcoin's system because the system operates on a clock. Each block must be mined every ten minutes on average. The difficulty adjustment keeps Bitcoin on schedule.

The Halving Cycle

Every 210,000 blocks (roughly every four years), the block reward for the miners is cut in half.

This is called the "Halving Cycle."

This means the supply of new bitcoins entering the system is cut in half as well.?

When Bitcoin first launched in 2009, the reward for mining a block was 50 bitcoins.

There were no transactions in the early blocks, so the blocks were just empty containers.

The ten-minute average timeframe between blocks continues regardless of the number of transactions available for being grouped into a block.

The first transaction occurred in Block 170, when Satoshi sent ten bitcoins to Hal Finney.

In 2012, the reward was cut in half to 25 bitcoins for the miner who solved the math puzzle for a block. In 2016, the reward for the miner and supply of new bitcoins was cut to 12.5 every 10 minutes. In May of 2020, the reward was cut to 6.25 bitcoins for each new block mined.

Right now, about 900 new bitcoins are entering the system each day. The next halving will occur in the spring of 2024 when the supply of new bitcoins will be cut to 3.125 every ten minutes on average, so 450 new bitcoins will enter circulation each day.

The final bitcoin will be mined in the spring of 2140. To be precise, the final number will be 20,999,999,976 bitcoins.

After this, there will never be another bitcoin or satsohi added into circulation.

I don't know why Satoshi picked this number and not an even 21 million.

Satoshi must have had a reason. He (or they) had a good reason for every element of their design of the Bitcoin protocol.

So far, 19 million bitcoins have been mined, which means we have just 2 million bitcoins still to be mined. It sounds like we're almost there – except more than 100 years will pass before the final coin is mined.

But why is the total bitcoin supply being released so slowly. Why not just create all 21 million bitcoins all at once or at least more rapidly?

Because Satoshi knew that time would be needed for the adoption of Bitcoin to gain traction, if it gained traction at all.

Remember that the first successful commercial transaction was the purchase of two Papa John's pizzas in 2010 for 10,000 bitcoins.

If 21 million bitcoins had been dumped on the market then, there would not have been enough users.

There would have been too much supply.

If there were only a few thousand users then for 21 million bitcoins, there would have been no scarcity. Therefore, no value. Value is created by scarcity plus demand.

There was still very low demand for Bitcoin in 2010. Few people knew about Bitcoin.

Satoshi calibrated and predicted rising adoption, which produces rising demand. Then you can roll out more supply, carefully calibrated so as not to create too much supply too quickly.

A satoshi is the smallest unit of a Bitcoin. 100,000,000 satoshis equal one bitcoin.

This gives you an idea how big Satoshi thought Bitcoin might grow. He must have thought it was possible for the price of one bitcoin to reach $100 million, or perhaps more. The vision was that, at a certain point, fiat currency might be replaced entirely by bitcoin, that everyone will want to be paid in bitcoin.

Of course, there was no guarantee this would happen. There was no guarantee Bitcoin would capture the public's attention and imagination the way it has. But it did. Satoshi's protocol is working exactly as it was designed and is succeeding on a grander scale than perhaps even Satoshi imagined.

Unlike ordinary products that increase supply to meet rising demand, Satoshi's Bitcoin protocol does the opposite. Bitcoin's rate of new supply decreases over time as demand increases, ultimately caps out at 21 million in 2140.

So one bitcoin has gone from being worth $1/3^{rd}$ of one penny in 2010 to what it is now.

Satoshi designed Bitcoin to be like a growing rolling snowball, which once it reaches a certain critical mass, probably can't be stopped. Once it reaches critical mass, Bitcoin becomes an unstoppable Death Star aimed at corrupt central banks and fiat currency.

I believe Bitcoin has now reached critical mass, much like the internet did in the mid-1990s.

We're coming to a point in the not-too-distant future when the average person will become comfortable transacting in bitcoin and bitcoin-based derivatives. Bitcoin will just become a regular and natural part of everyday life for most people. Everyone will then be on the Bitcoin standard.

CHAPTER 12

Is Bitcoin Too Difficult to Change?

One critique we often hear about Bitcoin is that it's "too difficult to change." I believe this is one of Bitcoin's strengths. Bitcoin is stable, like gold. It's digital gold.

There's a finite supply. There will never be more than 21 million bitcoins.

If this were ever to change, that would be the end of Bitcoin.

Bitcoin is a protocol, similar to railroad tracks.

Railroad tracks would not work well if the width between the tracks were constantly changing. Bitcoin's main selling proposition is that it's stable, like the Rock of Gibraltar – like the sun in the sky. We know exactly when the sun will rise and set each day. That's Bitcoin.

Bitcoin is not in the applications business. In the applications business, applications are constantly changing, constantly adding new features. Microsoft Office today is very different from what it was in 2004.

Microsoft Office is always changing. Microsoft Office must keep changing to remain competitive.

Bitcoin is not trying to compete in the applications world. Bitcoin is trying to be just one thing – perfect digital money. Perfect money must be stable.

However, there have been upgrades to the Bitcoin software over the years. For an upgrade to be adopted, 95 percent of miners and nodes must approve of the upgrade.

Segregated Witness

The first Bitcoin upgrade was called "Segregated Witness" (SegWit). It aimed to make Bitcoin more scalable by:

1) Making Bitcoin transactions smaller in terms of taking up less space in the block.

2) Increasing the maximum block size from one
megabyte to four megabytes. Increasing the size of
the block allows for more transactions per block.

As the Bitcoin network grew, the massive increase in number of transactions bogged down the network. It was sometimes taking hours for the network to process transactions. Without the SegWit upgrade, Bitcoin transaction validation by the network would slow to crawl. This would make the network almost unusable.

Segregated Witness refers to removing "witness" information from the input field of the block to free up space. The SegWit protocol splits a transaction into two parts.

The unlocking signature (called the "witness" data) is removed from the input field, but is still included as part of the blockchain in a separate structure. So one portion holds the transaction data, which includes the public address of the sender and receiver, the amount of bitcoin being sent, and a transaction fee for the miners.

The separate "witness" structure contains the scripts and digital signatures.

By segregating the data, more space is freed up in the block, making room for more transactions, and thereby speeding up the network.

To be more precise, the increase in maximum block size was actually an increase in weight more than size, or weight units (WUs). So, under SegWit, the maximum Bitcoin block size increased from 1,000,000 WUs to 4,000,000 WUs. Most people say megabytes, though Bitcoin actually uses weight units.

Under the old protocol, it was possible to have blocks bigger than 1 MB if 1,000,000 or less WUs. Under SegWit, it's possible to have blocks bigger than 4 MBs if 4,000,000 or less WUs. Most laypeople have never heard of WUs, but understand MBs. So it's easier just to say megabytes.

Changing the block size or weight was contentious because a small block size allowed nodes to maintain a complete blockchain ledger history on a cheap $400 laptop computer.

The larger the blocks, the more computer power and memory would be needed to operate as a full node. This would lead to fewer people operating as nodes and to more centralization, as fewer nodes would be able to afford more expensive computers.

Larger block sizes allow for more and faster transactions, but require more computing power by nodes, so would lead to more centralization.

But the thinking was that, by 2015, computers had become much more powerful than they were in 2008 when Satoshi published his white paper. A $400 laptop in 2015 would be capable of maintaining the full Bitcoin blockchain ledger even with a maximum 4 MB block size. So the SegWit upgrade would be in keeping with the goals of Satoshi to maximize decentralization of the network.

The argument over block size triggered a kind of civil war in the Bitcoin community. As mentioned earlier, a faction of miners and developers wanted blocks to be as big as 32 MB to enable much faster transactions. They managed to create a hard fork in the blockchain, which became Bitcoin Cash.

Bitcoin Cash did not gain much traction. It still exists, but is less than one percent of the size of Bitcoin in terms of market cap.

It turns out people are more interested in security and maximizing decentralization than transaction speed, at least when it comes to Bitcoin.

Larger blocks are less secure than small blocks because large blocks potentially allow malicious actors to bombard a block with fake transactions, clogging up the network. This is called a denial-of-service (DoS) attack. In a denial-of-service attack, money is not stolen, but a sustained DoS attack can paralyze a network.

A DoS attack is analogous to a large crowd standing at the entrance of a store preventing real customers from entering the store.

A DoS attack has never succeeded against Bitcoin because of small blocks and the size of the network. DoS attacks are too costly and difficult to sustain against Bitcoin for reasons I outline later in this book.

The SegWit upgrade was proposed in 2015 and approved by the Bitcoin community in August of 2017.

The SegWit upgrade also paved the way for implementation of the Lightning Network, a "Layer 2" solution that utilizes "smart contracts" to enable instant microtransactions for free, or almost free.

Lightning enables fast transactions by allowing users to agree to a transaction on a separate channel outside the blockchain. The blockchain then updates accounts accordingly.

This can be done without centrally administered third-party wallets, intermediaries, and without miners.

Lightning is what Bitcoiners will use to buy their coffee at Starbucks and point-of-sale terminals. It's less secure than the main blockchain. But it's instant, almost free, and is good for small transactions.

Lightning will ultimately enable a near-infinite number of transactions per second worldwide. It addresses the "Bitcoin is too slow for daily use" objection.

I was never concerned about Bitcoin's speed. I use fiat currency and credit cards for my daily transactions. Bitcoin, to me, is digital gold – a store of value. Bitcoin purists will use Lightning.

I'll probably continue to use fiat currency for my daily transactions, at least for the time being. But this is likely to change as merchants transition to accepting bitcoin.

And if you're living in a Third World country where there's hyperinflation and your local currency is worthless, Lighting becomes the practical solution. SegWit plus Lightning solve Bitcoin's scalability and speed issue.

Taproot

Taproot is the second major upgrade in Bitcoin's history. It achieved the 95 percent approval threshold from the Bitcoin network in June of 2021. Taproot further addresses Bitcoin scalability. Taproot enables the batching of multiple signatures together and streamlines the process of transaction verification.

Before Taproot, each digital signature had to be validated against a public key. This made the verification process cumbersome. Taproot allows for the aggregation of signatures.

Specifically, Bitcoin uses an Elliptic Curve Digital Signature Algorithm (ECDSA) to generate keys and verify transactions. The Taproot upgrade incorporates what are called Schnorr signatures. Those in the know, say these signatures are simple to implement, while still just as secure.

Schnorr signatures streamline verification by using a sum of public keys to match a sum of signatures to verify a sum of transactions, instead of each transaction having to be verified separately.

The Taproot upgrade combines single-signature and multi-signature transactions into one verification process. By decreasing the size of transactions (in terms of weight, or WUs), Taproot increases the number of transactions that can be included in a block, lowers the cost of transactions, and increases transaction speeds.

This upgrade isn't essential to me because all this could be accomplished with Layer 2 solutions, such as Lightning. But the Taproot upgrade was not contentious with the Bitcoin community.

All this shows that upgrades and improvements to Bitcoin are possible and do happen when 95 percent of the network of Bitcoin nodes and miners approve. And they will approve upgrades if it's in the interest of the community to do so. In the Bitcoin network, incentives for everyone in the network are aligned – the prime directive being to protect the value of everyone's bitcoin.

Speed of transactions, "smart contracts," and enabling more functionality and innovation are secondary issues that can best be addressed on Layer 2, Layer 3, Layer 4, and so on. Bitcoin is the base layer, the vault full of gold. Bitcoin is the rock on which all else sits. Bitcoin is the foundation that must be stable and permanent. Bitcoin is not a product, like Microsoft Office.

Bitcoin is a protocol, like the internet is a protocol. Applications are built on top of the internet protocol, often referred to as *TCP/IP* – which stands for Transmission Control Protocol (TCP) and the Internet Protocol (IP).

Upgrades and improvements to the base protocol can be made as warranted. Railroad tracks were improved with track switches, intersections, lights, electrification, stronger steel, etc. But the basic railroad tracks always stay the same, follow a standard.

Skyscrapers, Ferris wheels, and roller coasters must be built on solid rock, not shifting sand.

Bitcoin must remain solid rock. Almost everyone in the Bitcoin community agrees with this principle. So if 95 percent of the Bitcoin community approves a software upgrade, I'll assume it was needed.

CHAPTER 13

What About Ethereum and Other Crypto Assets?

C NBC reports that there are more 19,000 cryptocurrencies and assets out there. Only a handful have a following of any size.

Ethereum is the #2 asset in the world of crypto.

It's about half the size of Bitcoin in terms of market value.

All other crypto assets are tiny in comparison.

I'm an investor in emerging technologies.

My usual approach when investing in emerging technologies is to invest in the two or perhaps three leaders in a space, based on the thesis that, in the world of technology, the winner takes most.

However, we often don't know who the winner will be.

So, using this guideline, I should be an investor in Ethereum – since it's the #2 crypto asset in terms of market cap. But I'm not an investor in Ethereum.

Why not?

Primarily because Ethereum is not yet a functioning product. It's promising to be a product. But it's not a functioning product yet. I'm not sure it ever will be a functioning product.

So what is Ethereum?

First, Ethereum is not a cryptocurrency. It does have a native currency as part of its ecosystem called ether or ETH. To use the Ethereum platform, you burn ether – called "gas fees."

Ethereum is trying to create a decentralized platform built on blockchain technology that allows developers to build decentralized applications (DAPPs).

It's trying to be a decentralized internet.

Ethereum is not competing with Bitcoin. It's not purporting to be sound money. Ethereum is in the applications business. It's trying to build a decentralized internet for decentralized applications.

So it's a completely different animal from Bitcoin.

Ethereum's founder, Vitalik Buterin, jokingly says he was inspired to launch Ethereum when he was about age 19 because the digital video gaming company Blizzard spoiled his game of World of Warcraft by eliminating one of his weapons. Here's how Vitalik describes what happened in his "About Me" bio:

> I happily played World of Warcraft during 2007-2010, but one day Blizzard removed the damage component from my beloved warlock's Siphon Life spell. I cried myself to sleep, and on that day, I realized what horrors centralized services can bring. [18]

Vitalik was also involved in cryptography and was a co-founder of *Bitcoin* magazine in 2011.

Apparently, Vitalik grew frustrated with the Bitcoin community's resistance to adding functionality and features to Bitcoin. He had a vision for building a decentralized internet.

This sounds like a great thought – especially given the increasingly totalitarian nature of YouTube, Facebook, Twitter, social media, Google, and Big Tech.

The internet has become more and more centralized over time. It's been taken over by a few big tech companies.

Amazon controls 33 percent of the traffic on the internet because so many big websites are hosted on Amazon's AWS cloud.

So if Amazon just pushes a button, Amazon can take down one-third of the internet. Another 18 percent of internet traffic runs through Microsoft Assure, while 9 percent is hosted on Google cloud.

That's a total of 60 percent of the internet running through three big tech companies.

These three companies have the power to instantly collapse the world economy, potentially even kill hundreds of millions of people simply by pushing a few buttons. If 60 percent of the internet went down, food and medicine deliveries would stop, supply chains would be disrupted, and power grids would go down. There would be chaos on the streets.

Civilization would collapse. Society would quickly look like the movie *The Road*.

Short of this, these tech companies have the power to shut down your business if they don't like you.

---

[18] Owen Good. Polygon, October 24, 2021.

Twitter deplatformed the President of the United States.

President Trump then went over to a more freedom-oriented social media site called Parler and started posting there.

So then Amazon pushed a button and shut down Parler because Parler was hosted on Amazon's AWS cloud. Google and Apple also deleted the Parler App from its stores. This made it impossible for Parler to function. Parler went dark.

Parler was able to get back online a few months later. But its user base was decimated; so Parler was essentially dead as an ongoing enterprise.

Whether you like or dislike President Trump is not the point.

This should never happen in a free society.

Young Vitalik Buterin wanted to create an internet for decentralized applications where people could not be deplatformed for their political views or censored in other ways.

So that's what Ethereum set out to achieve. It's a noble vision – a goal I fully support.

Here's how Vitalik describes what he had in mind in his 2013 white paper that launched Ethereum, titled "A Next-Generation Smart Contract and Decentralized Application Platform":

> Satoshi Nakamoto's development of Bitcoin in 2009 has often been hailed as a radical development in money and currency, being the first example of a digital asset, which simultaneously has no backing or "intrinsic value" and no centralized issuer or controller. However, another, arguably more important, part of the Bitcoin experiment is the underlying blockchain technology as a tool of distributed consensus, and attention is rapidly starting to shift to this other aspect of Bitcoin . . .

> What Ethereum intends to provide is a blockchain with a built-in fully fledged Turing-complete programming language that can be used to create "contracts" that can be used to encode arbitrary state transition functions. [19]

Vitalik goes on to say that blockchain technology can be used to create "Decentralized Autonomous Organizations" (DAOs).

His White Paper states: "The general concept of a 'decentralized autonomous organization' is that of a virtual entity that has a certain set of members or shareholders which, perhaps with a 67 percent

---

[19] ethereum.org/en/whitepaper

majority, have the right to spend the entity's funds and modify its code."

Vitalik posits: "Not only would there be clauses, there would also be an open record of all open storage changes. Eventually, there could be a more sophisticated system.

There would be a built-in voting system that would approve transactions, along with adding or removing members. This could even pave the way for a Liquid Democracy. In this, anyone could assign an individual to vote in their place."

At various times, Vitalik has said Ethereum aims to be a new kind of decentralized internet with decentralized applications (DAPPs), a decentralized "world computer," and a platform for decentralized finance (DeFi). So for an investor, the question then becomes: How is it going so far?

Well, it's achieved the #2 position in Crypto World behind Bitcoin. Everything below Ethereum is a flea by comparison. And it's about half the size of Bitcoin in terms of market cap.

So it's certainly succeeding by this metric.

But is this decentralized internet running on blockchain technology really working?

Is it delivering the goods? Is it providing a good user experience?

Or if not, will it work at some point?

For me, the answer is a big unknown because Ethereum is not a finished product. It's also encountering a lot of operational problems, some of which appear to me to be fatal.

The problem with building a decentralized internet on blockchain technology is that operations on blockchain are slow.

Bitcoin transactions are slow too. But that isn't a big problem for what Bitcoin is trying to achieve.

If we're trying to move a bar of gold from one location to another, we expect this to be slow. We're going to be careful. We're going to insure it, hire an armored truck, and take steps to secure the gold.

We don't expect moving gold bars to be quick.

A similar thought process is at work for moving and sending Bitcoin.

If you are sending someone overseas $1,000 in Bitcoin, you're not going to be too upset if the transaction takes 10 minutes or it takes 20 minutes. You can also send $1,000,000 in Bitcoin and it will take the same amount of time.

Speed is not the issue when you are sending substantial sums of money. Security is the issue people are concerned about because people who send Bitcoin tend to send sizeable amounts.

But you don't want to wait ten minutes for your email or your Microsoft Word document to open. Video games need to be fast, hyper-speed, and realistic. Virtual reality is the goal.

Speed requires centralization. Decentralization is good for security, but bad for speed.

That's the big problem Ethereum has run up against.

My Test of The Top Applications on Ethereum

Before investing in something, I want to know: Is the product they are putting out any good?

So I decided to try out some of Ethereum's decentralized applications (DAPPs) for myself.

The first challenge I encountered was: How do I do this?

I conduct research. I learn I need to go to ethereum.org.

When I do that, I'm given instructions.

I'm told I need to download a crypto wallet. They give me a number of choices, but steer me to one called Metamask, which seems to be the most popular choice for active Ethereum users.

I use this wallet to buy $500 worth of ETH. The transaction (gas) fee for this transaction was $37.45.

So that's a 7.5 percent transaction fee, pretty high.

As with Bitcoin, transaction fees on Ethereum vary depending on how congested the network is. The average transaction fee on the Bitcoin network is about $2.

$2 is a lot if you're sending $10. It's not much if you're sending $1,000 or $10,000.

Bitcoin is good for sending sizeable amounts, not so good for $5 transactions.

To send $10 on Ethereum is likely to cost you $50 – the approximately $40 transaction fee plus the $10 you're sending. So Ethereum is no good as any kind of currency unless you are sending a hefty amount – $10,000 or more.

What governs transaction fees is not the amount of money you are sending, but the amount of computing power (hash rate) needed by miners to process the transaction.

Transaction fees on the Bitcoin network are typically about 1/20th what they are on Ethereum.

Why is this?

Well, because Ethereum is trying to be a decentralized internet for all kinds of applications, including streaming video and video games.

Bitcoin is just a money ledger, so doesn't require much computing power to operate compared to Ethereum.

I proceed with my mission to try one or two of the more popular applications built on Ethereum. I decided on the category of gaming, which also combines NFTs that I had been hearing so much about.

What is an NFT?

It's described by Ethereum as a "non-fungible token" and as a "unique and non-interchangeable unit of data stored on a digital ledger."

An NFT can be any reproducible digital file, such as artwork, a photo, a video, a song.

It's supposed to be non-fungible. In theory, it might be a way a way for artists to protect their art without having to go to court and file a copyright claim. You could not reproduce it without consent from the artist.

At least, that's the promise. So far, this isn't happening. But maybe it will at some point.

As of now, all an NFT does is provide proof of ownership. It does not actually prevent anyone from reproducing it. So far, NFTs don't appear to have much practical utility. You would still need to go to court to file your claim of copyright infringement.

There would then be a question of whether a court would understand this proof of ownership.

NFTs are also characters in the most popular games on the Ethereum blockchain. I looked up the most popular game on Ethereum and discovered that it's a game called "CryptoKitties."

How do I access "CryptoKitties"?

I do some research and find cryptokitties.com

I go there. I click "I installed Metamask button."

To unlock my Metamask wallet for CryptoKitties, I accept the "Terms of Use."

I'm asked to set a password. I'm then asked to create 12 seed words and save them somewhere safe.

I go through a bunch more steps. I enter my account nickname and email address. I hit the "Save Account Info" button. The next screen is "Terms of Service." Metamask pops up a window. I press the "sign" button, so Metamask knows this is my account.

Now I'm in my CryptoKitties wallet, at which point I'm supposed to buy a cartoon cat.

But I don't have any money in my CryptoKitties wallet.

How do I put some money in?

I do this by opening my Metamask wallet. I decide to send 0.02 ETH to CryptoKitties, or about $80.

I then go back to CryptoKitties to see if any ETH has shown up in my CryptoKitties wallet.

Not yet. I wait a few minutes.

Nothing.

I go to the kitchen to make myself a sandwich.

Ten minutes later, I come back to my computer with my sandwich and some V8 juice.

The money is now in my CryptoKitties wallet.

So it's a complicated process to start this game.

I'm now ready to play.

The first step is to shop from a catalog of cartoon cats.

The cartoon cats aren't cheap. Looks like the average price is around $65. Some are very expensive – thousands of dollars.

The cats all look pretty much the same. They're just cartoon cats that don't move.

I pick a cheap one for about $9. That still seems like a lot to pay for my cartoon cat character.

Now what am I supposed to do?

Well, I'm supposed to "breed" the cat. How do I do that?

Turns out I have to buy another cat and push the "breed" button.

Then a new cat is supposed to be produced that's one-of-a-kind – a random blend of the parent cats created by an algorithm.

So I buy another kitty for around $9 – the cheapest I can find.

I hit the "breed" button. I watch for 15 minutes. Nothing happens.

I get up and take a swim in our pool. I come back. Still no third cat. I cruise over to YouTube to watch a video. I check back with CryptoKitties to see what's happening.

After 63 minutes, a new cartoon kitty is produced, which has its own traits and characteristics – a random blend of the parent cats.

So now what am I supposed to do?

Well, I can put the new kitty up for sale. I can either set a price for it or put it up for auction. If I can get someone to pay more for my cat than I paid, I theoretically make money.

But here's the catch. I'm incurring "gas" fees every step of the way. The $80 I had in my CryptoKitties wallet is now drained.

Turns out I did not put nearly enough money in to make much progress in the game.

There's also no animation in the game. The kitties don't do anything. They don't jump around, don't do anything cute. They're just inanimate cartoons, like Garfield in the newspaper comic strip.

So how does the CryptoKitties company make money?

They charge a transaction fee of 3.75 percent. Plus, when you buy a Generation Zero cat, these cats are released every 15 minutes. The CryptoKitties company then keeps the money.

This is a far cry from centralized video games that are realistic and action-packed. It sure isn't anything like "Call of Duty" – which is both much better and much cheaper to play.

I try another game – a game called "Axie Infinity," which operates in a similar way.

In this game, the characters do move around some and have certain properties. But the level of animation is primitive – about the level of Pokémon in the 1990s.

What you're supposed to do here is buy three characters (NFTs) and play against someone else who has done the same. The characters have various weapons and properties that you select.

The way players try to make money is by breeding the Axie creatures (similar to CryptoKitties), so they acquire new properties and weapons. They can then auction off these characters.

When players win a battle, they are rewarded with Small Love Potions (SLPs), one of the game's native currencies. The game's second native currency is called Axis Infinity Shard (AXS).

A combination of AXS and SLP can be used to breed new Axies – which are valuable in the context of the game.

The new baby Axie inherits the properties, features, and weapons of its parents, plus can acquire unique new weapons and properties. An especially powerful Axie can sell for thousands of dollars. In 2020, an Axie character by the name of Angel sold for $130,000.

Many suspect that the astounding selling prices we read about in the news for these characters are arranged (bid up and bought) by the owners of the game to hype enthusiasm.

Players can also earn money by fighting other players in Arena Mode and by completing all daily missions and quests assigned. Some claim they are actually earning a living by playing these games. Players need Smooth Love Potions (SLPs) to breed new Axies. So SLPs also have value and can be sold.

Keep in mind that you burn "gas" (money) every step of the way while playing this game. The average price of an Axie character is now running at about $355. You need three characters to play. So to start a game of Axie will cost you about $1,000 . . . or more.

Similar to CryptoKitties, the appeal here is online gambling.

The animation is primitive, early 1990s level (at best).

The owners of Axie Infinity make money by charging a 4.25 percent transaction fee. Okay. I'm done with gaming.

It was nothing at all like the gaming experience on a centralized platform. Plus, these games on the Ethereum platform are not decentralized. They're products created by entrepreneurs. They're businesses with marketing teams.

What other kinds of applications are there on Ethereum?

As of now, there are no applications on the Ethereum blockchain that look especially appealing or that are decentralized.

Ethereum says it's trying to be a decentralized internet for decentralized applications (DAPPs). But in the world of computer applications, people want applications that are lightning-fast.

If the applications aren't just as fast on Ethereum, people will use equivalent speedier applications on the centralized system.

This is the problem Ethereum is facing. The apps aren't working well because the network is too slow and "gas fees" are too high – 20 times higher per transaction than Bitcoin on average.

The reason gas fees on Ethereum are so high is because Ethereum is trying to do so much on blockchain technology. It's trying to be a new kind of internet.

Again, the native currency on the Ethereum platform is called ether (ETH). Applications burn ether (called gas fees) to run their applications. This is theoretically how Ethereum stakeholders and ETH coin owners make money.

Each activity burns ether, which reduces the number of coins. The price of the coins should then go up.

The problem is there is no limit to the number of ETH coins that can be issued. There is no 21 million coin cap, as there is with Bitcoin. There is no fixed monetary policy, no fixed supply of ETH.

About 18 million new ETH coins have been entering the system each year on average. But the number entering the system fluctuates wildly from year to year and from month to month.

Also, there is no final limit to the number of ETH coins that can be issued. The potential number of ETH coins that might be issued is infinite. As of now, there are about 118 million ETH coins in existence. That's compared to the 19 million bitcoins that have been issued to date – with a cap of 21 million.

Bitcoin has a finite supply. ETH's potential supply is infinite.

Ethereum's Uncertain Transition from a Proof-of-Work to a Proof-of-Stake System

Similar to Bitcoin, Ethereum has been built on a proof-of-work mining system that secures the network and adds new ETH coins to the system. However, Ethereum is now transitioning to a proof-of-stake system because proof-of-work is too slow for what Ethereum is trying to build – a decentralized internet.

Under Ethereum's current system, one block can be mined at a time, as is also the case with Bitcoin.

Decentralized blockchain technology is awesome if what you value most is secure transactions. But it's no good if you are trying to create a new kind of internet with speedy, attractive applications that the general public will want to use.

So Vitalik and a core group of Ethereum developers are in the process of transitioning Ethereum from a proof-of-work system to a proof-of-stake system.

Proof-of-work requires the expenditure of electrical power – which is why the Bitcoin network requires a lot of energy to run.

In proof-of-stake, stakeholders validate blocks of transactions according to how many coins the stakeholders hold. The more coins a stakeholder has staked, the more votes he has in the consensus needed to confirm transactions.

The problem with proof-of-stake is those stakeholders with the most coins can more easily take over the network. It operates much like a publicly-traded company. Stakeholders are effectively like shareholders. Elon Musk owns 17 percent of Tesla, so he has enormous influence over what Tesla does.

Of course, Tesla is not purporting to be a decentralized project. It's run by Elon and his hand-picked Board of Directors.

There's nothing wrong with that. That's what corporations are. But Ethereum says it's a decentralized internet for decentralized applications. According to the research firm Chainanalysis, 376 Ether holders own 33 percent of the current supply.

So Ethereum ownership is in a few hands – which has important ramifications as Ethereum transitions into a proof-of-stake system. Under proof-of-stake, the number of transaction validator votes one has is in proportion to the number of coins a validator has staked in the Ethereum network.

To be the lowest level Ethereum validator when it does transition to its proof-of-stake system, you will need to stake a minimum of 32 ETH. Multiply by today's ETH price to find amount. And that's to be the lowest level validator, the bottom of the barrel schlub.

As we'll see, Ethereum has a very hierarchical governing structure.

By contrast, you can buy a top-of-the-line ASIC bitcoin mining rig for $15,000. You can buy a good one for about $10,000.

That's if you want to be a miner. However, you can be a validating Bitcoin node on a $400 laptop computer. You just need about 2 GB of RAM, 7 GB of storage space, a read/write speed of 100 MBs, and you can run a full validating Bitcoin node, which all Bitcoiners should do.

This is why Bitcoin is so decentralized – more than 1,000,000 miners and nodes worldwide. There are only about 6,167 validating nodes on the Ethereum network, according to Ethernodes.org

Because Ethereum is trying to be a blockchain platform for decentralized applications, much more space and a much more powerful computer are needed to host the entire Ethereum blockchain ledger.

With video games running on the Ethereum blockchain, soon you'll need an entire data center to house the live blockchain of activity. This level of functionality (DAPPs) Ethereum is striving for requires centralization.

Bitcoin's blockchain doesn't require massive storage space, RAM, and processing speed because the Bitcoin blockchain is just doing one thing – tracking money transactions. This activity doesn't require anywhere near the computing power, RAM, processing speed, or data storage space that Ethereum requires.

The other uncertainty of Ethereum transitioning from a proof-of-work system to a proof-of-stake system is no one knows if proof-of-stake will actually work. This planned transition is something like trying to rebuild the foundation of a skyscraper without first tearing down the skyscraper.

Maybe they can do it, but this looks like a very difficult task.

This transition has been in the works for years, and they keep pushing the date back further.

They are making this transition because the current proof-of-work system is not working for what they are trying to build – a decentralized internet for decentralized applications.

So far, the applications aren't working well. They are too slow and too primitive. It's like dial-up-internet in the early 1990s when AOL arrived in the mail on a disk.

As an investor, I have to ask this question: Do I want to buy a skyscraper that was built on a foundation using the wrong materials, a skyscraper I might need to tear down and rebuild from scratch?

That's basically what Ethereum is doing now. I further have to ask: Why didn't someone who is as smart as Vitalik see this problem long before Ethereum reached this point?

Many Ethereum miners are angry about this transition from proof-of-work to proof-of-stake, as they watch their substantial investment in time and money for mining rigs get flushed down the toilet. Their livelihoods are being wiped out.

The outrage by Ethereum miners expressed on Twitter is extensive – much of the language used unprintable here.

Ethereum's success will hinge on whether they really can build a decentralized internet on blockchain technology that can run decentralized applications that are as good as centralized applications on the regular internet.

Currently, a beta version of Ethereum's proof-of-stake system is running parallel to Ethereum's "Main Net" proof-of-work mining system. The beta version of Ethereum's proof-of-stake system is called the "Beacon Chain."

No word on whether the Beacon Chain is working. It's a beta test and still hasn't incorporated "smart contracts," as of this writing.

Ethereum is planning another step to speed up its system.

Instead of one single blockchain, the way Bitcoin is structured and Ethereum is currently structured, Vitalik and his "Open Market Committee" are enacting a "shard system."

This new system will have 64 blockchains, like spokes on a wheel. Most nodes will only be able to monitor and validate what's happening on their spoke (or shard). Only a few "super full nodes" will be able to see what's happening on all the shards.

As of this writing, Ethereum describes the levels of nodes as follows:

> **Single-shard node**. This node will only be able to monitor and validate transactions on one of the 64 shards.
>
> **Top-level node**. This node only processes data on Beacon Chain blocks, signatures and headers of the shard blocks, but cannot download and track all transaction data on the network.
>
> **Super-full node**. This node downloads all transaction data on the network.
>
> **Light node.** This node can only download and read block headers and summaries. [20]

This is in stark contrast to Bitcoin where every node and miner on the network can verify and audit every transaction back to the first block that was ever mined. Everyone on the Bitcoin network can see every transaction live, in real-time, and inspect every transaction that has ever occurred.

Bitcoin's distributed ledger is 100 percent transparent, except for identities of the transactors – unless the transactor wants her identity known. With Ethereum, users must trust the "Super Full Nodes" to be honest. "Super Full Nodes" have also staked the most, so have the most votes, and so control the network.

Bitcoin is a "zero trust" protocol. Ethereum is a black box for everyone but "Super Full Nodes." Ethereum doesn't even qualify as a protocol at the moment. It's governed by an arbitrary set of rules that are always changing. We don't even know how many ETH coins there are in circulation. There are only estimates.

With Ethereum, the rules are always changing. The rules are whatever Vitalik says they are that day. But he might change his

---

[20] ethereum.org/en/developers/docs/nodes-and-clients

mind tomorrow. It's a day-to-day moving target.

I would rather invest in Tesla, where I can read the financials and track the money. This brings up another problem with the proof-of-stake model that is operating on multiple blockchains (shards).

Since your validation votes on the system are in proportion to the number of coins you have staked, and no work (energy) is spent on verifying transactions, there's nothing to prevent a large stakeholder from verifying all splits on chains with their coins. There's no cost to being wrong.

In contrast, on Bitcoin's system, if the mining reward winner is wrong about a transaction in his block being legitimate, he will lose his 6.25 bitcoin block mining reward, plus the cost of all the energy he used to solve the puzzle and win the reward.

Bitcoin's proof-of-work system incentivizes accuracy and security, while the proof-of-stake plus shard system (multiple chains) appears to incentivize the opposite – or, at the very least, opens the door to shenanigans.

The shard system (multiple chains) also makes a 51 Percent attack on one of the shards (chains) easier to execute. Ethereum's proof-of-stake shard system will require a tremendous amount of detailed centralized management and coordination.

A single chain proof-of-work system is easy to track. If a fork develops by error or due to attack, it's obvious what the main chain is. Blocks not on the main chain fall back into the mempool for remining. Or in the event of a hard fork, the market decides the main chain – such as what happened with Bitcoin Cash.

Ethereum's proof-of-stake shard system (64 separate block-chains) will require intense centralized human management. Ethereum is a non-auditable black box with no fixed set of rules. It's not a fixed protocol at all.

Are Complex "Decentralized Autonomous Organizations" Governed by "Smart Contracts" Even Possible?

One of the features of Ethereum we hear most about is that it offers "smart contracts" – which is important we're told for decentralized finance (DeFi). Smart contracts allow for more complex transactions where certain conditions must be fulfilled before a transaction is finalized.

A research paper by Microsoft finds that writing unhackable smart contracts for decentralized blockchains is very difficult to execute and presents vulnerabilities for attackers to exploit.

There have indeed been multiple hacks of Ethereum's "smart contract" technology. One example is the infamous "DAO hack" on Ethereum that occurred in 2016.

DAO was a venture capital firm launched on the Ethereum platform. Vitalik's vision for decentralized organizations was that it might be possible to run an enterprise without human beings by way of smart contracts and "Turing complete" AI algorithms.

In May of 2016, $150 million in Ether was raised for the DAO project. But then hackers drained a wallet of $50 million.

What was the remedy?

Well, Vitalik and his "Open Market Committee" simply reversed the hack and restored the money. This demonstrated two issues with Ethereum:

1) Vitalik can easily reverse transactions if he wants to – no different than Visa. This means Ethereum is not decentralized at all.

2) The DAO hack shows the vulnerability of "smart contracts."

As Microsoft notes in its report, "smart contracts" are difficult to pull off due to their complexity. The hacker did not actually crack Ethereum's underlying blockchain code. Instead, it exploited a loophole in the Ethereum DAO smart contract.

This event casts doubt over whether complex "smart contracts" are even possible on decentralized blockchains, much less whether Vitalik's promise of Ethereum becoming a decentralized blockchain-based "world computer" is possible.

It's difficult to write an air-tight contract, which is why paper contracts in the physical world are so long and why the court system is bogged down often for years in disputes over contracts and various interpretations of what those contracts say.

Good contracts are difficult to write, which is why a good lawyer costs $300 to $1,000 or more per hour.

Simple contracts do exist on Bitcoin's system, as Satoshi

explained in his white paper:

> Transactions that are computationally impractical to reverse would protect sellers from fraud, and routine escrow mechanisms could easily be implemented to protect buyers.

Still, any complex contract needs a human referee to resolve disputes and enforce judgements.

In August of 2021, a hacker drained more than $610 million from the Poly Network, a "smart contracts" platform built on Ethereum and other blockchains. Again, the hacker exploited a loophole in the "smart contract" to grab the money.

During the ensuing 15 days, the hacker restored all funds stolen with a note saying he was showing how easy "smart contracts" are to hack. Poly Network offered to make the hacker its security chief. There's been no response from the hacker.

In March of 2022, a gaming network on the Ethereum platform called Ronin (creator of the previously discussed Axie Infinity game) announced that hackers had managed to find a back door and stole $625 million in ether (ETH) and USDC stablecoins.

A statement by Ronin explains that "the attacker found a backdoor through our gas-free RPC node, which they abused to get the signature for the Axie DAO validator." Oh. Welp, gee wiz.

In other words, sophisticated and secure "decentralized finance" (DeFi) and "decentralized applications" (DAPPs) built on "smart contracts" appear to be a long way from reality.

The Top Example of "Decentralized Finance" on Ethereum

The biggest application on Ethereum is called MakerDao, which issues an "algorithmic" stablecoin called *Dai*.

As mentioned, a stablecoin is pegged to the U.S. dollar or other fiat currency. The largest stablecoins are USDT and USDC.

USDT has about a $50 billion market cap and is issued by Tether Holdings, headquartered in Hong Kong – Communist China.

What makes stablecoins useful is they are easy to send across borders. You don't need to wire money from a bank, use Western Union, or incur currency conversion costs.

The second biggest stablecoin in terms of market cap is USDC, issued by a company in Boston called Circle Pay and built on blockchain technology. USDC is backed by actual U.S. dollars. In July of 2021, Circle announced a plan to merge with a special-purpose acquisition company (SPAC) called Concord Acquisition Corporation and go public, a deal that values the company at $4.5 billion. The USDC stablecoin has a market cap of about $30 billion.

Stablecoins are supposed to be backed 100 percent by dollars or a dollar-equivalent asset, such as U.S. Treasury bonds. If the stablecoin is only backed by, let's say, 50 percent dollar reserves, it becomes just another money-printing operation.

Government regulators are now looking closely at stablecoins.

In 2021, Tether agreed to pay a $41 million fine to settle charges with the SEC. The SEC argued that Tether misled buyers by claiming its tokens were at all times fully backed by the U.S. dollar and other fiat currencies.

In 2019, Tether revised language on its website to say: "Every Tether is always 100 percent backed by our reserves, which include traditional currency and cash equivalents and, from time to time, may include other assets and receivables."

These two stablecoins, USDT and USDC, are not decentralized, and don't purport to be. They appear to work fine as a way to quickly transmit money across borders. These two stablecoins don't appear to be scams, but they're not places to store sizable sums of money.

To try to create a more decentralized stablecoin, a Danish Entrepreneur named Rune Christensen launched a stablecoin product called MakerDAO. Its stablecoin is called *Dai*.

He built MakerDAO (with "Dai" as the native currency) on the Ethereum blockchain using "smart contracts."

In 2018, a venture capital firm called Andreessen Horowitz invested $15 million in MakerDAO by purchasing 6 percent of all the Dai tokens. So this is not a decentralized product either.

It's using a simple "smart contracts" protocol. Instead of Dai being backed by actual dollar reserves (or dollar equivalents), what you do is deposit supported cryptocurrencies to the Maker protocol. You can withdraw its Dai token in accordance with a percentage of what you have deposited.

However, you must deposit substantially more than you are using. So MakerDAO's stablecoin works by being over-collateralized. If you want to borrow 1,000 Dai, you must deposit 1.5 times that amount in ETH, Bitcoin, or other approved crypto asset. So it's a simple and smart contract, just not decentralized.

It's also the most expensive stablecoin to use because of Ethereum's gas fees. Every action on the Ethereum blockchain incurs gas fees.

That is probably why not many are using MakerDAO's Dai, which is one-eighth the size of Tether's USDT and a quarter the size of USDC. When people use stablecoins, they are looking for cheap speedy transactions. On Bitcoin's Layer 2 Lightning Network, transactions are free, or almost free.

MakerDAO is also supposed to be an example of Decentralized Finance (DeFi) that we hear so much about because you can borrow against your Dai and get paid interest on your Dai savings.

For it to be worthwhile, you need to trust that your Dai is secure. But MakerDAO was hacked.

Because MakerDAO is a small network, criminals were able to use a denial-of-service (DoS) attack tactic in August of 2021 to steal $8.3 million of collateral on MakerDAO.

Attackers swamped Maker with fake spam transactions, which froze Maker's mempool of pending transactions. This allowed hackers to win zero-bid auctions for ETH on MakerDAO by exploiting a hole in Maker's smart-contract protocol.

So the biggest application built on Ethereum, MakerDAO, fails on every level.

In all, approximately $1 billion per year is hacked (stolen) from applications built on the Ethereum blockchain. There's nothing secure about it.

So, at least so far, I see no applications on Ethereum's platform that are attractive.

Ethereum Operates More Like a Private Company Than Anything Decentralized

Although Ethereum is organized as a non-profit foundation, it resembles a private for-profit corporation in many ways – but without the accountability of a public corporation.

Ethereum was founded in 2014 by Vitalik Buterin, Gavin Wood, Charles Hoskinson, Mihai Alisie, Amir Chetrit, Jeffrey Wilcke, Joseph Lubin, and Anthony Di Iorio.

But, apparently, Vitalik was always the decider.

The launch of Ethereum was announced at a Bitcoin conference in Miami in January of 2014.

The audience of Bitcoiners were very supportive. Sure, we need a decentralized internet with decentralized applications.

That sounds great.

The eight founders gathered a few months later in Zug, Switzerland, in July of 2014 to decide how Ethereum would be structured and plan the initial coin offering (ICO).

An ICO is like an IPO – but a coin offering instead of a public stock offering.

In a 2014 video, Vitalik says they chose Switzerland for launching the ICO because of Switzerland's more lax regulatory environment – in other words, to avoid U.S. laws governing securities.

Before coins were available to the public, Ethereum conducted a pre-mine of 72 million coins. This pre-mine represented about half of Ethereum's current supply that was mined prior to the ICO.

During this pre-mine, 12 million tokens were distributed to Ethereum's founders and early managers.

In August of 2014, Ethereum launched its initial coin offering (ICO) to the public. About 50 million ETHs were sold at a price of $0.31 per coin, which raised about $16 million for the project.

We don't know how many ETH coins were bought by Ethereum's founders for around $0.31 apiece at the launch of the ICO.

Before Ethereum's pre-mine, the pre-mine practice had been rejected by the cryptocurrency community as a red flag signaling a scam.

A pre-mine has been the hallmark of "pump and dump" schemes that we've seen in many crypto assets. But after Ethereum launched with a pre-mine for the founders, pre-mines prior to token ICO launches became common in the crypto world.

Today, the Ethereum Foundation in Switzerland holds 394,787 ETH coins. Multiply by today's ETH price to find current value.

Vitalik runs the Ethereum Foundation, which has 16 employees.

According to *Forbes*, Vitalik's wallets that we know about contain 325,104 ETH. Again, just multiply by today's ETH price to find value of Vitalik's personal trove.

He might have additional wallets that we don't know about.

Though structured as a non-profit, the project has certainly been very profitable for Vitalik.

Nothing at all wrong with making money. Nothing at all wrong with profit. But Ethereum is not a decentralized system. Nor is it a transparent system. All of this is in stark contrast to Bitcoin – which is truly decentralized, fully transparent, governed by fixed rules, and with no pre-mine for the founders.

None of the original founders remain involved with Ethereum except for Vitalik.

Charles Hoskinson quit at the 2014 Switzerland meeting prior to the ICO, apparently not on good terms with Vitalik. Hoskinson went off to start Cardano to compete with Ethereum.

Vitalik fired Amir Chetrit and Ethereum's primary early financier Anthony Di Iorio. The rest quit.

None of this means Vitalik has done anything wrong. People often have disagreements, falling outs, and differing visions.

But, as an investor, a mass exodus of all the founders except one raises a yellow flag for me, at a minimum.

Ethereum claims to be decentralized, but clearly isn't. It's under the total control of Vitalik.

Ethereum is Hosted on Centralized Servers

Much of Ethereum is hosted on Infura, which is hosted on Amazon's AWS cloud. So we have two more layers of centralization for Ethereum. Either Amazon or Infura could press a button and much of Ethereum would disappear.

On its website, here's how Infura describes its services for the Ethereum ecosystem: "Infura provides the tools and infrastructure that allow developers to easily take their blockchain application from testing to scaled deployment - with simple, reliable access to Ethereum."

Now, you might think it's unlikely that Infura or Amazon would push a button and take down Ethereum.

But Amazon pushed a button and took down the Parler social networking site after President Trump was deplatformed by Twitter. Trump set up an account on Parler. So Amazon took down Parler – to make sure President Trump could not have a voice.

If you're in the applications business, you need developers, which requires hosted services with tools for developers.

Bitcoin does not rely on any hosted service. Bitcoin is not in the applications business. Bitcoin is a synchronized ledger distributed live to more than 1,000,000 computers around the world.

If the U.S. government told Amazon to shut down Ethereum, Amazon would just push a button. Poof! Most of Ethereum would be gone. Most of its applications wouldn't work.

Amazon did this to WikiLeaks. Just shut it down. WikiLeaks had to find new servers overseas in order to operate.

WikiLeaks also used Bitcoin as the medium of exchange to fund its operations because Western countries cut off WikiLeaks from banking services.

Ethereum has another Achilles Heel. Any rogue government, terrorist organization, or criminal cartel could kidnap Vitalik and torture him until he gives them all the Ether they want.

He proved with his reversal of the DAO hack that he has the power to reverse transactions, empty wallets, and move money around the Ethereum ecosystem any time he wants.

That's why the fact that no one knows who created Bitcoin is such a strength.

Even if the identity of Bitcoin's creator were known, even if he were still alive, the Bitcoin protocol could not be changed without 95 percent approval by miners and nodes.

There would be no way for Satoshi to hack Bitcoin. There's no backdoor. Bitcoin software is open source. Anyone can propose changes, improvements, and upgrades.

But any change Satoshi tried to implement could not be achieved without 95 percent support from the worldwide network of miners and nodes. Bitcoin is truly decentralized.

Ethereum is both centralized and has many vulnerabilities to attack.

Bitcoin is not trying to be a decentralized internet or a decentralized "world computer." It's not trying to build a decentralized stock market or decentralized financial system. It's not offering decentralized video gaming or gambling. It's not trying to be an art auction.

Bitcoin has just one mission: To be honest indestructible money.

Ethereum Has Significant Competitors

Ethereum is in the applications business – says it's trying to build a decentralized internet, a decentralized world computer with decentralized applications that will be run by complex "smart contracts" without the need for human intervention.

As of now, none of this has happened. None of the applications are any good. Furthermore, Ethereum has serious competition in the applications space.

Charles Hoskinson, one of Ethereum's original founders, quit Ethereum and launched a competing blockchain called Cardano, also for applications and supposedly decentralized.

Cardano is said by those in crypto world to be better and faster than Ethereum. Cardano operates on a proof-of-stake model.

For investors, one question to ask is: Can Ethereum hold its market cap lead over Cardano and other competing crypto projects while it's trying to transition from a proof-of-work system to a proof-of-stake system?

Ethereum's transition from proof-of-work to proof-of-stake is taking many years. And there's no indication right now it will succeed.

Hoskinson claims Cardano overcomes existing problems in the crypto marketplace. He says Bitcoin is too slow and inflexible, and that Ethereum is neither safe nor scalable.

Never mind that Bitcoin is inflexible by design. It's immutable (like the sun) . . . because it's just trying to be one thing – honest indestructible money that can never be debased.

In 2019, New Balance sneakers announced a pilot program to track the authenticity of its newest basketball sneaker using the Cardano blockchain.

So that's a possible application for blockchain technology. Good for Cardano. But it has nothing to do with decentralization – which no crypto asset has as yet achieved other than Bitcoin.

There are many other competitors in the blockchain applications space.

The Solana blockchain platform was launched in 2019 by Anatoly Yakovenko. It's said to be better than Cardano – if "better" means faster.

Avalanche is another competitor.

These projects are all tiny compared to Ethereum and appear to be running into many of the same problems that Ethereum is experiencing. It's difficult, perhaps impossible, to build decentralized high-quality applications using decentralized blockchain technology.

All these other crypto projects were started by venture capital investors. Solana raised $314 million in start-up capital. Cardano raised $62 million in start-up capital from investors. It then raised $600 million with its initial coin offering (ICO).

These are all businesses – which is why the Securities Exchange Commission (SEC) is looking closely at these projects and is suing some of them. There's nothing at all decentralized about them.

This is in stark contrast to Bitcoin.

The Bitcoin protocol was simply delivered by Satoshi in the form of open-source code that everyone could see. There was no pre-mine. There were no venture capital investors. There was no initial coin offering. Anyone who had a computer could just start mining in accordance with the protocol.

169 Bitcoin blocks were also mined before the first actual transaction occurred, when Satoshi sent 10 bitcoins to Hal Finney on January 12, 2009 (Block 170).

But that transaction had no monetary value.

The first commercial transaction was the purchase of two pizzas for 10,000 bitcoins on May 22, 2010 – a year-and-a-half after the first block, the Genesis Block, was mined.

Bitcoin was no venture capital scheme. It was no effort to get rich. Bitcoin was a lab experiment that a collection of computer scientists had been working on for decades, sharing their ideas openly on the Bitcoin forum. Bitcoin is always an open book for anyone interested in getting involved and contributing to the project.

The goal of these early cryptographers was to find a way to use computer code to fix the money system – create a monetary system that could not be corrupted by humans.

Bitcoin is the only truly decentralized system. Bitcoin is not hosted anywhere. It's not run by anyone. It exists in cyberspace as an immutable protocol – a cryptographically protected uneditable ledger that's distributed on more than 1,000,000 nodes worldwide.

No one owns Bitcoin. No one controls Bitcoin. Everyone has equal access to Bitcoin. Anyone can get involved in validating transactions. Anyone can just start mining for bitcoins.

It's very clear to me what Bitcoin is trying to achieve. It's all laid out in Satoshi's eight-page white paper.

Bitcoin has a very specific mission. Vitalik's white paper is more aspirational. It's vague. There's no protocol described in his white paper.

By contrast, the key rules of the Bitcoin protocol have never changed since it was launched. Bitcoin blocks will always be mined at a rate of one every 10 minutes on average. The supply of new bitcoins to the blockchain is cut in half every 210,000 blocks until the 21 millionth bitcoin is mined in the spring of 2140.

The only significant change was to increase the maximum block size from 1 WU to 4 WUs as part of the 2017 SegWit upgrade, for reasons explained earlier – an upgrade that was approved by 95 percent of miners and nodes, and in accordance with the protocol.

All the other cryptos are still experiments or outright scams. Some good ones might emerge. But I haven't seen another one that looks investible . . . because centralization actually works much better for most applications.

But centralization doesn't work for money, as we've seen. All fiat currencies issued by central banks eventually go to zero. Bitcoin is not an application. It's an asset, now worth about $400 billion in terms of market cap.

It's a property in the same way that Miami beech front is property. Miami beech front is a desirable property in the physical world. And there's only a fixed amount of it.

We can't add to Miami beech front, which is a big reason why Miami Beach property values keep going up over time.

Bitcoin is a property in the digital world with only a fixed amount. Bitcoin has 150 million users (owners). This number goes up every day as more and more people learn about it, come to understand how it works, and see others using it.

Owning one Bitcoin is analogous to owning property in Manhattan – except Bitcoin World doesn't have politicians who can impair the value of your property with taxes or steal your property.

In Bitcoin World, the individual is sovereign, not the state.

Bitcoin separates money from state. That's what Bitcoin does.

How the U.S. Government Views Bitcoin Vs. Ethereum and Other Cryptos

The U.S. government is still trying to figure out how to treat cryptocurrencies under the law.

The U.S. Securities Exchange Commission sees Bitcoin as an asset, so has no jurisdiction over Bitcoin. But the SEC appears to see the other major cryptos as securities or as substitutes for the dollar (stablecoins), so they are subject to U.S. laws that govern securities.

Financial services are regulated by government. Securities are regulated by the SEC.

If you are offering a dollar equivalent (such as a check), it needs to be backed by dollars in a bank. Stablecoins are similar to checks and must be backed 1-to-1 by dollars or collateralized in some way.

Gold is not regulated by government because it's considered an asset, a commodity. Bitcoin is not a security or a financial service, and it's not a stablecoin. The SEC sees bitcoin as an asset, similar in character to gold, so is not subject to the jurisdiction of the SEC.

Ethereum, Cardano, Solana, Avalanche, Polygon and similar projects look and act like companies. They were launched with venture capital, had initial public offerings, and are owned or controlled by someone or some group.

So the SEC is viewing these organizations as businesses and subject to the jurisdiction of the SEC.

The SEC sees Bitcoin as property or like a commodity, so not under the jurisdiction of the SEC because Bitcoin does not operate like a corporation.

No one owns Bitcoin. No one controls it. There was no initial coin offering (ICO). There was no venture capital raised.

It just exists on its own in cyberspace, similar to air. Bitcoin is a commodity, not a security.

Because Bitcoin is truly decentralized on more than 1,000,000 computers that are guarding the integrity of a protocol, that requires a consensus of nodes and miners to approve every transaction, it's not speedy. But it's fast enough for what it's trying to be, which is honest money.

There is only one way to achieve speed – more centralization.

Dictators are able to act faster than decentralized representative democracies. Hitler was able to move at lightning speed.

If you're in the computer applications business, your product will be judged by speed and its number of features.

Bitcoin is not designed for speed. It's designed for security – to be able to transmit value over both space and time.

It doesn't have many features. It has a single purpose: To be honest immutable money. That's it.

Bitcoin is Insurance Against Economic and Political System Collapse

For me, Bitcoin is insurance. It's insurance against financial collapse and against political system collapse.

Bitcoin enables me to leave the country quickly if necessary. It can also work as an investment during the "adoption phase" of this emerging technology.

People are just learning about Bitcoin, trying to understand how it works, why it has value, and whether it's secure. So its price fluctuates wildly at times as people try to assess its value and where the price is heading. Bitcoin's price behaves as an emerging technology stock price.

We are still very early in the adoption of Bitcoin, about where the internet was in 1997 in terms of adoption.

The more people who see the manic money printing, feel and fear financial uncertainty and the potential for economic collapse, the more people will see Bitcoin as insurance, a possible escape hatch and protection for their wealth. It's far from outlandish to wonder if what happened in Venezuela or Argentina can happen here.

From the 1950s through the 1990s, Venezuela was one of the most prosperous countries in Latin America. Today Venezuela is among the poorest countries in Latin America, with an annual inflation rate exceeding 1,000 percent.

In the early 20th Century, Argentina was one of the most prosperous countries in the world. In 1913, Argentina was wealthier than Germany, France, and much of the developed world. Argentina ranked in the top ten in the world in per capita GDP.

Argentina began its decline in the late 1940s under the corrupt authoritarian rule of Juan Peron and the Peron family. When Peron died in 1974, his third wife ran the country until 1976 when she was deposed in a military coup.

Political systems and economies can collapse in even the most successful and most prosperous countries. Collapse can also happen quickly.

Look what happened in Germany. The German Weimar Republic tried to finance World War I by going off the gold standard and printing money wildly. This triggered hyperinflation, hitting 10,000 percent, which then produced Hitler.

This disaster can happen anywhere – even here in America. We have many failed states south of our border, including Mexico. These failed states can spill over to the U.S. and are doing so now.

That's what Bitcoin is for. Bitcoin is the off-ramp from political and economic corruption and collapse. Bitcoin is the escape hatch.

How is this escape hatch working?

Well, we had a test case when China tried to shut down Bitcoin in the summer of 2021 by banning mining and banning Bitcoin transactions. At that point, about half the world's bitcoin mining was located in China. Many thought this concentration of bitcoin mining in China was Bitcoin's most serious vulnerability.

When China banned bitcoin mining, the hash rate (computer mining power) was cut in half as bitcoin miners in China had to shut down their computers. China's miners then moved to Kazakhstan, the United States, and more hospitable locations around the world.

Within a few months, the bitcoin mining hash rate was back to where it was before China banned Bitcoin. The United States became the bitcoin mining capital of the world.

Bitcoin achieved exactly what it was designed to achieve. It survived a state attack by the world's biggest country – a totalitarian regime with 1.4 billion people.

Not only did Bitcoin survive. The network didn't skip a beat. Blocks were mined every ten minutes on average, transactions processed as usual – exactly as prescribed by the protocol.

Bitcoin allows you to quickly carry or transport your wealth anywhere that still has a civilized situation.

Ethereum is not solving this problem. It might be addressing some minor problems. We will see as time passes.

The problem with Ethereum, from an investor's standpoint, is there's not yet any product. There's only a promise of a product. So far, Ethereum has failed by its own measure – the goal being to create a decentralized internet for decentralized applications that are uncensorable.

None of this has happened. None of the applications on the Ethereum platform work on any acceptable level.

That's why Ethereum is changing its system from proof-of-work to proof-of-stake. But how is proof-of-stake any different from my investment in Tesla?

It's not – except that Ethereum is not auditable. So my investment in Tesla is actually far more secure. Today, Bitcoin has 150 million users. In contrast, Ethereum only has about 550,000 users.

So there are 300 Bitcoin users for every one Ethereum user.

Why?

Because there are more users of money than there are software developers. Everyone needs and uses money. Not everyone is a software developer. Ethereum appeals to a small niche of software developers who are interested in DAPPs and DeFi.

The addressable market for Bitcoin is everyone on the planet because everyone wants the best money – money that will hold its value, not have its value eroded by five percent, ten percent, or more each year.

The addressable market for Ethereum is a niche group of software developers who are interested in building decentralized applications on decentralized blockchain technology – which doesn't appear possible at this point, at least not applications that are high performance and that people will want to use.

I'm not looking for applications. We have plenty of applications. I have dozens of applications on my phone – and I only use a few.

I'm looking for bitcoin to be one thing – honest money; digital gold that I can send and transport anywhere in the world instantly.

If all Hell breaks loose here in America, if there's a socialist takeover (or worse), I want to be able to get out with some assets – with my bitcoin.

I can't carry my house with me or my rental properties. But I can carry my bitcoin, either on my phone or in my head. That's what Bitcoin is for – clean and simple.

Bitcoin is similar to gold in that it's primarily a life raft if everything else collapses and America becomes Venezuela. Bitcoin is insurance.

That's its attraction for me. But it's much better than gold because you can carry it or send it anywhere instantly.

Bitcoin doubles as an investment. It's both a life raft and an investment. It appears many others now see it the same way.

On its current trajectory of adoption, Bitcoin will have one billion users within the next five years or so.

Ethereum is not yet a product. It's promising to be a product. But isn't a product yet.

That's why I haven't invested in Ethereum.

CHAPTER 14

The Strange Case of Do Kwon

L et's review the strange case of a young South Korean crypto entrepreneur named Do Kwon, age 30.

He cost investors about $40 billion in the course of a few hours in May of 2022 when his Luna coin-backed algorithmic stablecoin UST collapsed. $40 billion gone. Poof!

Kwon co-founded Terra Labs to compete with Ethereum in the Decentralized Finance (DeFi) arena. Kwon's "stablecoin" is called UST, and was supposed to be pegged to the dollar. It relied on an automated "smart contracts" algorithm, similar to Maker DAO on Ethereum, to maintain UST's peg to the dollar.

This UST stablecoin was backed by Terra's native cryptocurrency Luna. Yes, you heard that right. A crypto token called Luna (Kwon's invention) was the collateral for the stablecoin.

In accordance with the algorithm, Luna's supply would fluctuate to maintain UST's peg to the dollar.

If UST's price dropped below $1, more Luna coins would be minted by the algorithm. If UST's price rose above $1, Luna coins would be burned.

In order to attract investors, Terra's lending protocol, called Anchor, offered 20 percent annual interest rates to investors.

Anytime an entity is promising you a guaranteed 20 percent yearly return on your money, just assume it's a Bernie Madoff style scam. No further research needed.

Well, predictably, it appears some big investors started getting some bad vibes, so started selling their Luna coins. Or perhaps this was a planned "rug pull" scam all along.

The instant result: UST lost its peg to the dollar and started crashing too.

To maintain UST's peg to the dollar, the algorithm automatically minted new Luna coins at tornado speed.

In less than 24 hours, the supply of Luna tokens increased from

300 million to 7 trillion coins. In other words, a monetary system way worse than Venezuela's and North Korea's

Panicked investors were blocked from getting their money out of the system. They watched in horror as the Luna token price dropped from a high of $116 to $0.000059 in a matter of days, most of the drop within hours.

The only reason Luna didn't collapse to $0 in minutes is because crypto exchanges locked investors out of their accounts.

Terra's so-called UST stablecoin also crashed from $1 to $0.00847. So there was nothing "stable" about Do Kwon's UST stablecoin.

The reason people buy stablecoins is they are told they are stable relative to the fiat currency they are pegged to – backed by collateral that's solid. Many, probably most, retail investors are under the impression stablecoins are risk-free.

Imagine the shock of UST stablecoin holders when $1 suddenly became $0.00847.

When Luna was flying high, Do Kwon liked to call Luna holders "Lunatics" on Twitter. He might wish now he had selected a different name for his tribe of followers.

It turns out Do Kwon was also one of the pseudonymous co-founders behind another failed algorithmic stablecoin called Basis Cash (BAC). Kwon launched this stablecoin in 2020. It failed in January of 2021, initially crashing from $1 to $0.30 in a matter of hours, before going to $0.0.

Basis Cash worked the same way as his subsequent UST-Luna stablecoin scheme, involving two linked tokens. BAC was supposed to remain stable, pegged to the dollar. The second coin that fluctuated in value was called Basis Share (BS). The so-called "seigniorage algorithm" increased the supply of BS or burned BS to keep the BAC price stable.

Kwon appears to have a great sense of humor to have named his token BS. His stablecoin BAC was literally backed by collateral that he himself called BS.

So, is it fraud if Kwon himself calls his own coin BS?

On December 29, 2020, Kwon's BS coin hit a market cap peak of $52.5 million -- $945 per coin. Incredibly, BS continues to trade today for a price of $0.29 per coin. And you can still buy Basis Cash for $0.006036. But it's no longer called a stablecoin.

Will Kwon go to prison?

Probably not. The government must prove criminal intent. Kwon might have honestly believed in his projects.

As George Costanza famously said in an episode of *Seinfeld*: "Jerry, just remember. It's not a lie if YOU believe it."

Is Do Kwon finished? Is he on the run from the law?

Apparently not. Less than 30 days after the collapse of UST-Luna, he announced on Twitter the launch of LunaX on Terra 2.0

"Rise to the challenge," Kwon tweeted on June 18, 2022. "Or capitulate - but be honest whether you are fighting for a sovereign future or for higher numbers."

The new stablecoin he's offering is called Luna2 USDT "with up to 25X leverage supported," Kwon tweets.

And there appears to be no shortage of interest in Kwon's new Terra 2.0 platform and tokens. Kwon retweeted this announcement from Binance: "Binance will list Terra 2.0 $LUNA in the Innovation Zone and will open trading for LUNA/USDT and LUNA/BUSD trading pairs at 6am UTC on May 31."

What is Binance?

Binance is a crypto exchange headquartered in the Cayman Islands. In 2021, the U.S. Justice Department and IRS announced investigations into Binance on allegations of money laundering and tax offenses. Binance is not permitted to operate in the United States. According to a report by Reuters in April of 2022, Binance shares client data with the government of Russia.

Reuters reports that Binance has been an important vehicle for helping Vladimir Putin finance his war on Ukraine.

"Binance's trading volumes in Russia have boomed since the war began, data from a top industry research firm shows, as Russians turned to crypto to protect their assets from Western sanctions," reports Reuters.

Binance was launched in China in 2017. Its founder and CEO is a software engineer named Changpeng Zhao, also known just as "CZ".

So these are the kinds of folks we're dealing with in the so-called "altcoin" market.

Now back to young Do Kwon's impact on the market from his perch in South Korea. Do Kwon is just age 30. And he's already cost investors more than $40 billion.

But the cost to investors has rippled out, multiplying losses in Crypto World.

Kwon's UST-Luna fiasco played a big role in the collapse of a large crypto hedge fund in Singapore called Three Arrows Capital, which invested $200 million in Kwon and Luna, according to *The Wall Street Journal*.

"The Terra-Luna situation caught us very much off guard," Three Arrows co-founder Kyle Davies told the WSJ. Davies said the firm's $200 million was "vaporized."

There was initially some hope that Three Arrows might be saved by an angel investor. Three Arrows collapsed. There's speculation that Three Arrows lost far more than the $200 million it had invested in Kwon and Luna.

A large crypto broker called Voyager is also teetering on the brink of bankruptcy, as of this writing. Voyager, a publicly traded company, had some $650 million tied up in Three Arrows, which was taken down by the Kwon-Luna implosion and other speculations.

Celsius is yet another so-called DeFi lending platform that imploded like a house of cards. It was launched in 2017 by tech entrepreneur Alex Mashinsky with the help of $864 million in venture capital.

According to a report by CNBC, Celsius, at its peak in October of 2021, had $26 billion under management. By June of 2022, the value of its token (CEL) had lost 97 percent of its value.

Celsius is built on the Ethereum blockchain. It's collateral is largely "staked ether" (stETH). These are ether coins that stakeholders invest in the Ethereum platform.

Staked ether is locked on the Ethereum platform for 1-2 years, or until Vitalik Buterin gives you permission to cash out.

If you want to be a stakeholder (similar to a shareholder) in Ethereum, you buy and stake your ETH. The amount you stake determines your power (votes) on the platform.

Celsius staked about $400 million on Ethereum.

Similar to Do Kwon's Anchor lending platform, Celsius was paying 18 percent annual interest rates to attract investors. Again, promising absurdly high 18 percent guaranteed returns on money is surefire evidence of scam.

stETH is traded on the open market through an outfit called Lido, which takes investors' ether and puts it in staking pools being created to secure Ethereum when it becomes a proof-of-stake blockchain at some point in the future.

Staked ETH (stETH) generally trades at a 10 percent or more discount to regular ETH.

The price of Ethereum and all crypto assets started crashing in the wake of the Luna collapse. Suddenly, out of the blue, Celsius announced on June 13, 2022 that investors would not be able to withdraw their money from the Celsius platform for an undefined period of time.

Celsius explained it this way: "We understand that this news is difficult, but we believe that our decision to pause withdrawals, swaps, and transfers between accounts is the most responsible action we can take to protect our community." Oh.

Another crypto lending the trading platform called CoinFlex announced in June of 2022 that it was freezing all customer withdrawals. CoinFlex CEO Mark Lamb said in a statement that CoinFlex had run into "liquidity" problems because Roger Ver (AKA "Bitcoin Jesus") had defaulted on a $47 million margin call.

Yes, this is the very same Roger Ver who claimed to be following the true Satoshi vision by launching of Bitcoin Cash.

Ver claims he didn't default. But Lamb tweeted what looks like solid evidence that Ver is the holder of the account in default.

Headquartered in the Seychelles (which is a speck in the Indian Ocean off the coast of Somalia), CoinFlex then announced it was launching a new token called "Recovery Value" in a "Hail Mary!" effort to recoup the alleged $47 million default by Bitcoin Jesus.

If you think it's a good idea to lend $47 million to someone who calls himself "Bitcoin Jesus," you need to check yourself.

To incentivize investors to buy its Recovery Value USD token, CoinFlex (from its perch on a small island in the Indian Ocean) was offering a preposterous 20 percent guaranteed interest rate. Lamb claimed the 20 percent yield would come from recovering the lost $47 million from "Bitcoin Jesus," plus a "financing charge."

Oh. Really?

The unfortunate truth is Bitcoin's success has attracted all manner of con artists, grifters, and scammers, to include multi-billion-dollar hedge funds, who have no understanding of, or appreciation for Bitcoin, but who know how to use leverage to manipulate prices.

The cascading collapse of sham "DeFi" crypto projects sent the crypto market into a tailspin in May and June of 2022.

Ethereum crashed from $3,500 a coin to about $950 a coin during this period. Even Bitcoin dropped from around $35,000 per coin to $17,500 in May-June of 2022.

Nothing had changed fundamentally in Bitcoin. More users were added to the Bitcoin network every day during this period. The hash rate continued to go up.

Investors were just running away from the overall crypto market because of all the bad headlines. Within a few days, Bitcoin's price stabilized and headed back up again.

But here's the bottom line point. These so-called "Decentralized Finance" and "Decentralized Applications" projects are in no way decentralized.

They are venture capital projects, with investors and marketing teams. They are companies. They are all owned and controlled by someone or some small group. They aren't transparent or auditable. Almost all are outright scams.

These outfits have nothing whatsoever in common with Bitcoin, which truly is decentralized. But the media continues to call it all just "crypto," to include Bitcoin.

Bitcoin is not crypto. Bitcoin is just Bitcoin.

Bitcoin should not be lumped in or even compared with the others. There is no comparison. Bitcoin is its own category.

Bitcoin was not launched with venture capital. Bitcoin is not owned or controlled by anyone. Bitcoin is an open source software protocol in cyberspace that distributes a synchronized ledger of transactions to more than 1,000,000 computers (miners and nodes) worldwide, and to anyone who wants to download the software.

All transactions can be monitored and tracked as they occur, in real time. The entire Bitcoin blockchain can be audited back to the first block, the Genesis Block, mined on January 3, 2009.

Nothing like this happens with any other crypto asset.

CHAPTER 15

Bitcoin's Structure Is What Makes It Work

There have been more than 19,000 cryptocurrencies and assets since Bitcoin's launch in 2009.

Many thought they could create better versions of Bitcoin. Many of these "altcoins" are or were essentially copies of Bitcoin with slight differences – mostly adjustments in the protocol to speed up transactions.

My contention is that Bitcoin was discovered more than invented in the same way that math was discovered, not invented.

Math always existed. But it had to be figured out by humans over time. Bitcoin is similar.

The building blocks existed. They just had to be assembled into the right structure and in the right balance. All the incentives in the network had to align perfectly to protect and strengthen the network.

If the incentives are out of balance in one direction or another, the system could collapse.

The perfect (or near-perfect) alignment of incentives in every part of the Bitcoin network is what makes Bitcoin work.

Why Satoshi Chose "Proof of Work" to Secure Bitcoin Over "Proof of Stake"

Satoshi could have chosen a proof-of-stake (PoS) security protocol over proof-of-work (PoW) if he had wanted to. But he chose PoW.

Why?

The main argument for PoS is that PoW uses a lot of electricity. Bitcoin mining uses more electricity than Austria and small countries.

To many, that seems wasteful. PoW is also slow. PoS is able to process transactions faster because it's not spending time and computational power in a contest among miners to solve a complex math problem.

With PoS, transactions are validated by stakeholders. When using PoS, new coins are minted, not mined.

The way PoS works is to randomly assign blocks to stakeholders to validate in accordance with how many coins the stakeholder owns.

Under PoS, those who have staked the most get to validate the most blocks and continue to accumulate the most coins. This has the effect of always increasing the power of the largest stakeholders over the network. The tendency of a PoS system is for the network to become more and more centralized over time.

PoW is far more secure than PoS.

In PoW, an attacker would need to acquire more than 50 percent of the computing power of the entire network to carry out a "51 Percent" attack. In a PoW mining system, all computers have approximately the same computing power. It's the individual ASIC computer that solves the math puzzle and wins the privilege of mining the next block.

So even with a large corporation that has a building full of ASIC bitcoin mining computers, it's just one computer that solves the puzzle and mines the next block, not a human stakeholder.

In PoS, an attacker would simply need to acquire more than 50 percent of the staked currency within the system – something that could be achieved quite easily by a country like China, a large corporation, or a cartel of billionaires.

Someone like Elon Musk could easily take over a PoS network if he wanted to.

In a PoS system, a major human stakeholder can be bribed, blackmailed, or tortured to sabotage the network.

In Bitcoin's PoW system, the mining is automated – undertaken by a vast network of computers. Only one random mining computer worldwide can win the privilege of mining the next block.

Remember what PoW was originally designed for – to prevent spam attacks by increasing costs to spammers.

The way PoW does this is to require email senders to solve a puzzle, which requires computational power. This increases cost to the spammer.

In the Bitcoin protocol, the difficulty of the math puzzle that must be solved to mine the next block increases as the network's computing power increases through the previously described "difficulty adjustment."

The difficulty adjustment occurs about every two weeks (every $2,016^{th}$ block) to ensure that blocks are mined every 10 minutes on average, so as to keep block mining on schedule with Satoshi's timetable.

Because there are more than 1,000,000 bitcoin mining computers competing to solve the puzzle to mine the next block, the combined computing power of the network is enormous. An attacker would need to overcome all of this computing power to undertake a successful 51 Percent attack.

In Bitcoin's PoW system, single-purpose ASIC computers are required to mine bitcoin. These computers can be used for no other purpose. So, in addition to the enormous power that would be needed to overpower Bitcoin's network, a 51 Percent attacker would need to acquire more than 50 percent of this specialized computer hardware.

In his White Paper, Satoshi Nakamoto describes how the system works this way:

> The proof-of-work involves scanning for a value that when hashed, such as with SHA-256, the hash begins with a number of zero bits. The average work required is exponential in the number of zero bits required and can be verified by executing a single hash. For our timestamp network, we implement the proof-of-work by incrementing a nonce in the block until a value is found that gives the block's hash the required zero bits. Once the CPU effort has been expended to make it satisfy the proof-of-work, the block cannot be changed without redoing the work. As later blocks are chained after it, the work to change the block would include redoing all the blocks after it. [21]

Proof-of-stake (PoS) systems are especially susceptible to denial-of-device (DoS) attacks. This is a directed spam attack where web robots (autonomous software bots) flood a system with fake transactions, bogging down the system, so it can't operate.

---

[21] bitcoin.org/bitcoin.pdf

Legitimate transactions are then denied service.

A DoS attack is like a crowd of non-customers blocking the entrance to a store, so real customers cannot get in.

Criminals often target businesses and sites using DoS attacks and require ransom to be paid to halt the attack. Ethereum has been the target of multiple successful DoS attacks.

In August of 2021, hackers used a DoS attack to steal $8.3 million in MakerDAO collateral on the Ethereum platform.

Attackers swamped Maker with fake spam transactions which paralyzed Maker's mempool of pending transactions. This allowed hackers to win zero-bid auctions for ETH on MakerDAO.

The crypto platform, Solana, which operates using a proof-of-stake model, has suffered multiple disruptions from DoS attacks.

On September 14, 2021, Solana went offline for nearly a full day after a surge of transactions caused the network to fork. A dispute among validators then ensued over which chain was the right one.

On January 4, 2022, Solana went offline for more than five hours, they say because of a "denial of service" (DoS) spam attack on the network.

Solana aims to compete with Ethereum in the decentralized applications business. Solana is even less decentralized than Ethereum, which is not decentralized.

A mature PoW network makes it very difficult to pull off a denial-of-service attack.

PoW was specifically engineered to prevent DoS attacks by increasing the cost (in terms of computing power) needed to conduct a successful DoS attack.

With 1,000,000 computers competing to solve a math puzzle to win the privilege of mining the next block, this process is costly.

This cost prevents DoS spammers from getting to the block to invalidate the block or to flood the block with fake transactions.

But even if an attacker were to succeed once to prevent a Bitcoin block from being mined (completed), that block would just drop back into the mempool for remining. It would only cause a slight delay for that block of transactions.

The DoS attackers would need to deploy an unfathomable amount of computing power to win the race against 1,000,000 worldwide bitcoin mining computers to solve the math puzzle not just once, but for many times in succession every ten minutes for a sustained period of time to cause any significant disruption to an enormous PoW network like Bitcoin.

If that could be done, it would have been done by now.

Example of Proof-of-Work

For Block #660000 that was mined on December 4, 2020, the hash output was:

```
00000000000000000008eddcaf078f12c69a439dde30
dbb5aac3d9d94e9c18f6.2
```
[22]

The required number of introductory zeros tells the mining community the puzzle was solved, and that this block's hash number is correct. The losing miners then begin work on the next block of transactions while the winning miner adds the block to the blockchain.

The winning miner receives a block reward of 6.25 bitcoins (about $200,000 currently) for solving the puzzle.

This particular block (#660000) will always contain 745 transactions with a bit more than 1,666 bitcoins, plus the header of the previous block. Once blocks are entered into the blockchain ledger, they can never be modified. If someone tried to change anything in this block, the network would instantly see and reject the fraud attempt.

Nothing similar happens in a proof-of-stake model, which is subjective, not subject to an ironclad mathematical protocol, and is not decentralized. With proof-of-stake, the stakeholders with the most coins have the most validating votes, mine the most blocks, accumulate more and more coins through this process, and gain more and more power over the network – resulting in centralized control for a small group.

That's why Satoshi chose a proof-of-work model over a proof-of-stake model. Bitcoin is built for security more than speed.

Starting in 2019, Amazon, seeing how effective PoW is at protecting the Bitcoin network, began using a proof-of-work model to protect its own system from DoS attacks. That is, Amazon chose proof-of-work as the best defense for protecting its system from spam bots swamping Amazon's system with fake transactions.

Why?

---

[22] blockchain.com/btc/block/660000

Because proof-of-work is the most secure model ever developed, and Amazon is run by smart people. Amazon is a centralized system, but chose proof-of-work to secure its network.

Bitcoin is Secured by Energy

Bitcoin is secured by a proof-of-work (PoW) protocol that requires the expenditure of energy – specifically electrical energy in the form of computational power.

You prove you've expended this energy by competing to solve the complex math puzzle required by the algorithm.

Some say this process is wasteful. But anything of value must be protected. This protection requires expenditure of energy.

What follows is a key insight by MIT software engineer Jason Lowery, now serving with the United States Space Force.

Lowery points out that we have an enormous military industrial complex that protects us from attacks – attacks from foreign enemies. We expended enormous energy to defeat Hitler and Imperial Japan in World War II. We expended enormous energy again to win the Cold War against the Soviet Union.

We're expending enormous energy right now to protect our country and civilization from Communist China, Russia, and worldwide terrorist organizations.

We expend enormous energy on police and law enforcement to protect our property and assets. The building of civilization and protecting it requires massive expenditures of energy.

Countries are carved out of the land and borders established by the use of energy in the form of military force. Wars are fought for territory. The Roman Empire, Genghis Khan, the British Empire, the Aztecs, the Inca, the Greeks, the ancient Egyptians all acquired their empires by using violent kinetic energy – military force.

The group that can deploy the most violent kinetic energy, notes Lowery, wins the fight for territory in the physical world.

Stones work better than fists. Spears defeat stones. Bow-and-arrows defeat spears. Guns defeat bows and arrows. Bombs defeat guns. Nuclear bombs defeat conventional bombs. The threat of a nuclear counterstrike deters a first-strike nuclear attack.

In a battle between you and the government, the government wins because the government can deploy more kinetic energy than you can. Whoever can deploy the most kinetic energy wins in the physical world.

In the digital world, what wins is computational power, which is electrical energy, says Lowery. In terms of energy expended, says Lowery, there's no difference between kinetic energy and electrical energy. If you touch an electric wire with current running through it, it will shock you. It will kill you if there's enough electric current.

Proof-of-work uses electric energy, computational firepower, to protect your digital assets. Proof-of-stake is a poor substitute for brute force computational power in the digital world.

The way you project power in the physical world is with kinetic energy – guns, bombs, planes, Naval fleets, control of space.

The way you project power in the digital world is with electrical energy in the form of computational power – "brute force" computing. The more computational power you use to protect your digital assets, the more secure your digital assets are.

And it's far better if all this computational power is distributed over a vast worldwide network of computers than if it's all just located in one place or a few places.

If all the computers on the Bitcoin network were located in just one place, the network could be destroyed by physical kinetic military force. The fact that it's so decentralized is what makes the Bitcoin network so difficult to attack. Plus, it's protected by a massive and growing wall of encrypted energy that's very difficult for attackers to surmount . . . because of the proof-of-work algorithm that requires enormous computational power.

The Bitcoin network protects your life's savings. This protection requires energy. Your money, your wealth, your savings represent your life's work, which required a tremendous expenditure of your time and energy to accumulate. Your money and your assets are where you store your life's work so perhaps you can leave something to your children. The government is stealing your life savings by way of inflation and manic money printing.

Using computational power to protect your life savings from theft is not a waste. It's actually the most cost-effective and peaceful way to protect yourself and save civilization from corrupt politicians and governments. Owning Bitcoin is another form of exercising your Second Amendment right to gun ownership.

Inherent in the Second Amendment is the right to self-defense.

Bitcoin extends this right to the digital world. The Bitcoin network is your worldwide guerrilla army of miners who are incentivized to protect your wealth – who get richer by protecting you.

But here's yet another key point that shows the superiority of proof-of-work over proof-of-stake in terms of incentivizing decentralization and securing the network.

Over the past year, 329,212 bitcoins were mined and put into circulation. Of these, miners were only able to keep 21,446 bitcoins. Miners had to sell to sell 94 percent of their bitcoins to cover the electricity cost needed to mine them.

At first glance, this sounds bad – sounds bad for the miners. But it's actually good for both the miners and for securing Bitcoin.

With a proof-of-stake system, there is no mining and no substantial ongoing cost for stakeholders to accumulate coins. The result is we see wealth increasingly concentrated in the hands of the richest stakeholders over time. Under proof-of-stake, the more you've staked (invested), the more new coins will flow your way. No substantial further expenditure or "work" is required.

In Bitcoin's proof-of-work system, miners still see it well worth their ongoing cost and "work" to mine even though they must sell 94 percent of their bitcoins to fund their mining operations.

This does not contradict my earlier point that bitcoin miners mine for one purpose: to acquire and accumulate more bitcoin. They have no choice but to sell bitcoin to fund their mining operations. But the bitcoin the miners manage to hold, they tend to hold forever.

These miners would not continue to mine if not profitable.

But the fact that they must sell 94 percent of their bitcoins to continue mining incentivizes distribution of wealth and more decentralization – so is yet another element of Satoshi's brilliant design. This also suggests these miners believe the value of one bitcoin is likely to increase exponentially over time.

They have staked their livelihoods on this conviction.

Why Bitcoin Succeeds and the Other Cryptos Fail

Bitcoin is often lumped with the other 19,000 crypto assets, as if they're all the same. The reason Bitcoin works is because of its structure. To say Bitcoin is similar to other cryptocurrencies would be something like saying an hourglass is similar to a jar of sand.

Both include sand and glass – are made from the same materials. But a precisely engineered hourglass keeps perfect time because of the way these materials are structured.

Bitcoin works as intended because Satoshi used existing building blocks, the key ones developed by the U.S. national security apparatus, to create indestructible perfect money.

Bitcoin is not trying to be anything else. It's not trying to have lots of features. When you add features, you add vulnerabilities.

When you add transaction speed, you also create vulnerabilities.

From 2015 to 2017, there was a battle among the early Bitcoiners about Bitcoin's block size. Satoshi, in his protocol, set the maximum block size as 1 megabyte (MB). This size was increased to a maximum block size of 4 MB as part of the 2017 "Segregated Witness" (SegWit) update, approved by more than 95 percent of miners and nodes.

Some Bitcoiners complained that the small block size made transactions too slow. A larger maximum block size was needed to allow for more and speedier transactions, some argued.

The crusade for a larger block size was led by an early Bitcoin investor from Silicon Valley named Roger Ver.

Recall from the previous chapter that Ver, in June of 2022, allegedly defaulted on a $47 million margin loan to CoinFlex, which contributed to crashing the entire crypto market.

So it's not surprising that back in 2017, we see the omnipresent Roger Ver causing chaos in Bitcoin World. Chaos and confusion seem to follow Ver wherever he goes.

Ver was claiming to be the true follower of the Satoshi vision. He was calling himself "Bitcoin Jesus."

Ver had been buying bitcoins since 2012 when the price was less than $1. So he had amassed a sizable fortune, and had quite a bit of influence with a faction of miners, mostly from China.

Ver and his group were able to establish a hard fork in the Bitcoin blockchain in 2017 to create Bitcoin Cash, which would have a maximum block size of 32 MB – eight times the size of Bitcoin's maximum block size. [23]

Transactions would be speedier and cheaper. So that sounded

---

[23] Much of the information here comes from the book *The Blocksize War: The Battle Over Who Controls Bitcoin's Protocol Rules*, by Jonathan Bier (2021).

good. But larger block sizes make full nodes more expensive to operate because larger block sizes require more disk space, more RAM, more computing power.

This leads to fewer people being able to run full nodes, which leads to more centralization. A key pillar of Bitcoin's security structure is to maximize the number of miners and full nodes to make the network less vulnerable to a 51 Percent attack.

Large block sizes also make the network more vulnerable to denial-of-service (DoS) attacks because large blocks can more easily be bombarded and clogged with fake spam transactions. The computational power needed to solve the proof-of-work puzzle is lowered per transaction. The network then becomes less secure.

There is always a trade-off between security and speed.

So Ver and his group of miners managed to establish a hard fork in the blockchain to create Bitcoin Cash.

Hard forks were more possible to establish in 2017 when Bitcoin's network was much smaller than it is today. But a breakaway hard fork established by rebels is not fatal to Bitcoin. The market then simply follows the fork they want to follow, which is exactly what Satoshi envisioned.

Satoshi believed forks would develop, but that the market would follow whichever fork was in the best interest of the network. It turns out that people value Bitcoin for its decentralization and security and didn't care that much about transaction speed. Bitcoin Cash continues to exist, but is less than one percent the size of Bitcoin.

Satoshi's structure emphasizes both security and decentralization.

The miners are the guardians of the network. By protecting the network, they stand far more to gain than they do by attacking the network. The reason they mine for bitcoins is to accumulate more bitcoins. They certainly don't want to destroy the value of their bitcoins by destroying the network.

Bitcoin is also very difficult to mine. The miners' reward for solving the puzzle that gives them the right to mine the next block is 6.25 bitcoins. That's a powerful incentive.

Miners are incentivized to protect the network rather than to attack the network. The miners are incentivized to protect your bitcoin because they are trying to protect their own bitcoin, plus accumulate more bitcoin through mining.

If there were ever a double-spend or if there were ever a

successful attack on the underlying technology or structure of the network, the value of bitcoin would crash, might crash to zero.

How "Game Theory" Secures Bitcoin

"Bitcoin" is a "Zero Trust" system because no trust is needed, which is what makes the Bitcoin network 100 percent trustworthy.

Some have called the perfect alignment of incentives for every member of the Bitcoin community to protect the network "game theory." We might also call this "herd theory."

A herd of animals knows it's stronger and safer if it acts as a group. Each member of the herd is incentivized to stick with the herd and contribute to protection of the entire herd. A herd moves and acts as one integrated unit. Satoshi describes how this dynamic works in Bitcoin against an attacker:

> We consider the scenario of an attacker trying to generate an alternate chain faster than the honest chain. Even if this is accomplished, it does not throw the system open to arbitrary changes, such as creating value out of thin air or taking money that never belonged to the attacker. Nodes are not going to accept an invalid transaction as payment, and honest nodes will never accept a block containing them.
>
> An attacker can only try to change one of his own transactions to take back money he recently spent. The race between the honest chain and an attacker chain can be characterized as a Binomial Random Walk. The success event is the honest chain being extended by one block, increasing its lead by +1, and the failure event is the attacker's chain being extended by one block, reducing the gap by -1. The probability of an attacker catching up from a given deficit is analogous to a Gambler's Ruin problem. [24]

When reading this passage from Satoshi, remember that the longer chain always determines the true chain because the longer chain represents the most proof-of-work (computing power).

Remember also that computers solve the proof-of-work math puzzle randomly. The odds of solving the math puzzle are in direct proportion to the computing power expended; but also the puzzle can only be solved by an individual computer. So an attacker would

---

[24] bitcoin.org/bitcoin.pdf

need to win the right to mine the next block many times in succession to cause much if any disruption.

But even if the attacker succeeded, the herd would establish a hard fork in the blockchain. The herd would then follow the valid blockchain, not the fraudulent chain.

The Bitcoin network can also be likened to an ever-expanding hornet's nest. MicroStrategy's founder Michael Saylor says "Bitcoin is a swarm of cyber hornets exponentially growing ever bigger and stronger behind a wall of encrypted energy."

The bigger the Bitcoin network grows, the more secure it becomes.

CHAPTER 16

Won't Better Technology Replace Bitcoin?

In the world of tech, better technology always comes along and replaces the old technology.

Cars replaced horse-and-buggies. Mobile phones replaced hardline phones. Smartphones replaced flip phones. Netflix and video streaming replaced Blockbuster video stores.

So won't a better technology come along and replace Bitcoin?

Won't another technology come along that does exactly what Bitcoin does, but better?

The answer is: Sure.

It's probably already happened.

But how will this new technology that does exactly what Bitcoin does gain 150 million users – achieve the network effect that makes Bitcoin valuable?

Someone can probably create better social media technology than Facebook. That's certainly possible and has likely already happened.

But Facebook's value is its three billion users. Apple's value is its one billion iPhone users. That's what's hard to compete against.

Bitcoin is also the most decentralized crypto asset. Transactions must be approved by a consensus of 1,000,000 miners spread around the globe.

How does something else rebuild this network of users?

Bitcoin is not an application. It's where 150 million people are storing their wealth.

These 150 million Bitcoin users would need to be persuaded that this hypothetical new technology is not just slightly better than Bitcoin, but exponentially better for Bitcoin's users to switch to something else – because people won't switch to a new technology until they see it's obviously better.

Upwards 19,000 cryptocurrencies and assets have tried to

dethrone Bitcoin. None have succeeded.

#2 Ethereum is not decentralized. It's under the control and direction of its inventor, Vitalik Buterin.

Ethereum is also transitioning from a proof-of-work system to a proof-of-stake system to speed up its functionality. Ethereum needs lightning-fast functionality if it's ever to become an alternative to the internet – what they are now calling "Web3."

No one knows how this transition from a proof-of-work to a proof-of-stake system will work out.

Satoshi was well aware that a proof-of-stake system could be used for Bitcoin. He (or they) chose a proof-of-work system because proof-of-work is far more secure.

Bitcoin's primary goal is security before speed. As Bitcoin Cash's failed fork demonstrated, people want security more than speed for storing and preserving their wealth.

Most people are using Bitcoin to store wealth, not for daily transactions.

And because Ethereum is trying to build an operating system for applications, competition in the applications arena is always intense.

Ethereum's competitors include Cardano, Solana, Polygon, Avalanche, and others.

The winner of this race will be decided by the developers. Which platform will developers choose for building their applications?

The platform that developers choose will be the one that's fastest and cheapest – which means the most centralized.

Competition in the applications business tends to dilute network effect. These projects and companies are competing in the same space for the same developers.

Bitcoin is not an operating system platform on which developers build applications. It's a protocol. It's a decentralized monetary system, an incorruptible money network.

Bitcoin is not in the applications business. It's not trying to be all things digital. It's not trying to be an alternative internet. It's just trying to be honest money. That's it. Nothing more.

I believe Bitcoin has already won the race to be the world's premier decentralized digital money.

Bitcoin is a protocol – just like the internet is a protocol.

There are many companies and projects that are built on the internet. Yet the protocol never changes. The protocol is standardized – the same way that electric sockets in your house are standardized.

Could the internet protocol have been different?

Sure. The light sockets in your house could have been designed with five prongs instead of two or three. But we settled on a standard. This standard makes life easier and more efficient.

We could not have a modern civilization if every house was built with a different standard for electrical wiring, electric sockets, and light switches.

Society could not function well if every gas station had different size gas nozzles at the pump.

What if you could only fill up your car at one gas station because all the other gas stations had different nozzle sizes at the pumps?

We need standards, or nothing works. Without standards and protocols, we'd all be living in mud huts.

Perhaps we can imagine better railroads than we have now. Perhaps if we made the tracks six inches wider so we could have wider railroad cars that can carry more cargo, that would be better in theory.

But then you would have to rebuild the entire network of railroads, plus replace all the railroad cars so they would fit on the new tracks that are now six inches wider.

That would be a lot of trouble, take a lot of time, and be very expensive.

For decades, I was told the U.S. was transitioning to the metric system. We would be moving away from feet, yards, inches and miles because the rest of the world was on the metric system and because the metric system made more sense. The metric system is superior in every way, in theory.

We've given up on that project because Americans are used to our system. They don't want the metric system. Once people are used to doing things a certain way, it becomes very difficult to change their habits and behavior.

This is just as true in the world of tech. Maybe a better search engine will come along than Google. But that's not likely to happen within the next ten years.

There are better office and business software applications than Microsoft's. But everyone's using Microsoft – which is established as the standard for most everyday office applications.

So far, the applications built on Ethereum and the other blockchain platforms aren't very good. And I'm not seeing anything that's likely to replace bitcoin as digital gold – the primary reason being the enormous and powerful network effect that's already been built among Bitcoin's 150 million users.

The more users there are, the more the price per coin goes up because of its fixed supply. This intensifies the Network Effect.

Once the Network Effect (Metcalf's Law) reaches critical mass, it becomes very difficult to undo and replace it with something else. It becomes like a snowball that gathers size and speed exponentially, much like Facebook.

It appears people want honest money, not the fake confetti money the Fed is printing.

Many professional athletes are now insisting on being paid in Bitcoin.

This makes sense. If an athlete is signing a multi-year contract, would you rather be paid with dollars that are declining in value, or in bitcoin that's appreciating in value over time?

I can see a day in the not-too-distant future when most people will want to be paid in bitcoin, not fiat currency. This is how adoption builds.

Facebook has become a $500 billion-dollar company by monetizing "likes" and reactions. "Likes" and reactions on social media are addictive. That's the Facebook business model – addict people to "likes" and "loves."

How much more valuable is money than "likes"?

Bitcoin is the Facebook of money.

The Power of the Bitcoin Brand

Bitcoin has also established a strong brand in the public mind.

A brand is enormously valuable.

Take the Coca-Cola brand. Coca-Cola is considered one of the most valuable brands in history.

There's nothing especially unique about Coca-Cola. It's just sugary water.

Its value is its brand.

In all blind taste tests in the early 1980s, people said they liked New Coke better than the original Coke. So Coca-Cola launched

New Coke in 1985. This turned out to be one of the biggest product launch disasters of all time.

Even though people liked New Coke better in blind taste tests, the market wanted the old Coke because that's what people were used to. So Coca-Cola brought back old Coke in the form of Coca-Cola Classic; and discarded New Coke entirely.

There was room for one competitor to Coke and that was Pepsi. There was almost no room for a third competitor in the cola space – which was RC Cola. Not sure if there is even a fourth-place cola drink.

Even though most people prefer Pepsi in blind taste tests, Coca-Cola remains by far the bestselling soft drink in the world. Seven times more Coca-Cola is sold than Pepsi.

Diet Coke is the #2 selling soft drink. Coke also launched Coke Zero. In all blind taste tests, people prefer Coke Zero over Diet Coke. But hardly anyone buys Coke Zero even though Coke Zero is objectively better tasting than Diet Coke.

That's the power of a brand.

Once a brand is carved out in people's minds, it's very difficult to dislodge.

Kleenex is synonymous with tissue paper. I can't even think of another brand of tissue paper off the top of my head, although there are many. Even if it's another brand of tissue paper, I call it a Kleenex.

I can't think of any brand of bleach other than Clorox.

There are others. I just can't think of them. We always buy Clorox.

I've used Crest toothpaste since I was a kid, probably because that's what my mom bought.

I'm sure there are other perfectly good, perhaps better, toothpastes out there.

But Crest is good enough. I would need a very good reason to consider changing to another brand of toothpaste.

It would require too much mental energy to consider other brands unless the difference is obvious.

That's the power of habit. Brands are built on human habits. There are other search engines, but people always say "Google it."

There aren't many more valuable things in this life than a strong brand. Bitcoin now has a strong brand.

So sure, another better technology will come along and probably already has. But how many people can even name another cryptocurrency?

Most people can only name one cryptocurrency – Bitcoin.

That's powerful.

How Dominant is Bitcoin in Crypto World?

The media often talks about "Bitcoin Dominance" in Crypto World.

If Bitcoin Dominance hits 50 percent of the market, that's said to mean Bitcoin is doing well. If Bitcoin Dominance drops below 40 percent, this is bad for Bitcoin, says the media.

Bitcoin dominance tends to drop during bubbles, as speculators try for bigger gains with so-called "altcoins."

Remember, "Altcoins" are crypto assets other than Bitcoin, but not stablecoins.

During manic altcoin buying bubble peaks, Bitcoin dominance drops as the casino gamblers FOMO into the market right before the blow-off top.

FOMO stands for "Fear of Missing Out."

These are the retail casino gamblers who rush into the altcoin market near the peak, only to be slaughtered – fleeced, sliced, and diced, like in *Silence of the Lambs*. It's sad to watch, but so predictable.

When the crypto market drops, Bitcoin's price drops too. But Bitcoin's market dominance rises. It's a predictable pattern. While Bitcoin's price fluctuations certainly look wild to the uninitiated, Bitcoin is the Rock of Gibraltar in terms of price stability compared to "altcoins."

The media often lumps Bitcoin in with the other 19,000 crypto assets out there. These include gaming tokens, art auctions (NFTs), sketchy lending platforms, online gambling, lotteries, and all other manner of garbage.

If we include all 19,000 cryptos, Bitcoin accounts for about 45 percent of the market. But that's the wrong measuring stick.

Correctly measured, Bitcoin is 95 percent of the market.

When assessing the merits of a project or product, we must compare apples to apples.

It makes no sense to say Microsoft Word is better than McDonald's. They are completely different. What makes sense is to compare McDonald's to Burger King and other fast-food restaurants. You compare a product to its competitors in the category.

Of the 19,000 cryptos out there, only nine coins are actually trying to compete with Bitcoin as a decentralized medium of exchange (money) that uses a proof-of-work consensus algorithm.

The proof-of-work algorithm is the only way to create any kind of decentralized governing or transaction validation structure. And it's the only way to secure a decentralized monetary network, as we've seen.

If money is not decentralized, if money is under the governance of a few who control its supply, it's not honest money. It's not real money. It's fiat money. It's confetti helicopter money that will be diluted to zero, as happens with all fiat money.

Proof-of-stake systems are centralized by definition. Proof-of-stake money systems are fiat money systems – exactly the opposite of Bitcoin.

Stakeholders in proof-of-stake models are like stockholders in a corporation. Those with the most stock (or who have staked the most) have the most votes and the control. Elon Musk owns 17 percent of Tesla stock, so has the most control over the company.

That's how proof-of-stake works with crypto projects. There's nothing decentralized about them. They are governed and controlled by humans, who are prone to corruption and greed.

Nothing wrong with profit. That's what corporations are supposed to do – make money.

But that's not the role of money. The role of money is a unit of measurement. It's a unit of account. It's a way of exchanging value, storing value, and keeping track of who paid what to who when. Bitcoin is an automated ledger. That's all it is. It's not a for-profit operation. It's not a company. It's just a way to track money accurately and honestly.

So proof-of-stake money networks are just fiat money networks. The government's fiat money system is actually far better and far more secure than unauditable black box centralized proof-of-stake money networks, most of them products of scam artists and con men.

Satoshi found a way to remove humans from monetary policy, to automate the money system with fixed rules.

If we exclude venture capital projects with Initial Coin Offerings (ICOs), stablecoins, and proof-of-stake or other centralized projects, Bitcoin is 95 percent of the cryptocurrency market – because the others don't even purport to be currencies.

The only nine coins even claiming to compete with Bitcoin as honest money are:

> Litecoin (LTC)
> Bsv (BSV)
> Bitcoin Cash (BCH)
> Monero (XMR)
> DASH (DASH)
> Zcash (ZEC)
> Bitcoin Gold (BTG)
> Dogecoin (DOGE)
> Decred (DCR)

I exclude Ethereum from this list of competitors to Bitcoin because:

1) Ethereum is not trying to be money. It's trying to be a decentralized internet for decentralized applications, such as gaming and art auctions.
2) It's transitioning from a proof-of-work to to proof-of-stake system, which makes it even more centralized.
3) Ethereum always was a centralized project, from inception.
4) Ethereum was launched with venture capital and an Initial Coin offering (which is like a public stock offering).
5) There was a massive premine prior to Ethereum's ICO, in which more than 50 percent of today's supply was only available to a small circle of founders.
6) Ethereum has always been under the control of one person, Vitalik Buterin, so doesn't qualify as immutable money with a fixed set of rules.
7) Ethereum's rules are a moving target, constantly changing.
8) No one knows how many ether coins exist.
9) Ethereum is unauditable.

So Ethereum, in no way, qualifies as money.

We exclude stablecoins as a competitor to Bitcoin because stablecoins are just tokens pegged to the value of the dollar or a fiat currency, similar to casino chips. You can exchange your casino chips for fiat money after you're done playing.

Stablecoins are a tool with a specific use, to enable easy, cheap cross-border transactions. They are akin to checks, an extension of fiat currency, or an inexpensive substitute for Western Union and wire transfers. The top two stablecoins (USDT and USDC) are products of companies.

The other stablecoins are mostly scams, such as Do Kwon's previously discussed projects, and so many others.

So stablecoins are not competitors to Bitcoin because they are not decentralized, not trying to be a currency. They are just digital tokens pegged to the value of the dollar or other fiat currency.

Once we narrow down the field to projects that are actually attempting to compete with Bitcoin as honest decentralized money with a fixed set of rules, Bitcoin is 95 percent of the market.

The above-listed nine currencies that qualify as competitors to Bitcoin are all attempting to be faster versions of Bitcoin.

Dogecoin was actually started as a joke in 2013, as a parody of Bitcoin to show that anyone can create digital money. That's true. Anyone can. It's open source code. Anyone can just copy the code.

But a secure proof-of-work network requires an enormous network of miners who are expending vast amount of computing power to solve complex PoW math puzzles and processing transactions.

The miners and nodes are the guardians of the network.

It's this vast network of 150 million bitcoin users and 1,000,000 miners and nodes, growing every day, that makes bitcoin valuable – Network Effect or "Metcalf's Law."

So depending how you wish to count, Bitcoin is either 70 percent or 95 percent of the crypto asset marketplace it competes in. By any measuring stick, Bitcoin is the 800-pound gorilla of crypto.

And it's really more like King Kong.

Central Bank Digital Currencies - CBDCs

Government central banks are now starting to issue their own digital currencies. They are called CBDCs (central bank digital currencies).

Some say governments issuing their own digital currencies will be a fatal blow for Bitcoin.

"How will Bitcoin compete with government digital currencies?" CNBC's commentators ask. And won't governments do everything possible to shut down Bitcoin, so that Bitcoin doesn't compete with them?

The answer is "yes." Central banks are issuing digital currencies because they're so worried about Bitcoin. But these government-issued digital currencies don't compete with Bitcoin.

In fact, government-issued digital currency is one of the greatest threats to freedom out there.

A CBDC is the exact opposite of Bitcoin.

Bitcoin protects the sovereignty of the individual. Bitcoin protects your freedom by safeguarding your assets.

In stark contrast, CBDCs are a digital prison.

A government-issued digital currency means total surveillance. With CBDCs, government will be able to track every penny flowing in and out of your bank account. Government will be able to seize your money by just pushing a button.

In fact, with CBDCs, there will be no further need for private banks.

Not that I'm any fan of J.P. Morgan Chase and Bank of America. They've benefitted enormously from the corrupt fiat money system. The banks borrow new money the Fed prints at 1 percent interest and then lend it out at 3-5 percent interest. This is how banks make money.

CBDCs eliminate the need for private banks – eliminate the middleman.

On one level, this change might sound good. Sounds cheaper and more efficient. But that change won't cut your interest rate. The interest rate will just be charged by the government, and there will be no competition.

There will be only one source for money – the central bank.

So the government will be able to charge whatever it wants for the loans it issues. Access to loans will only be available to the politically connected. At that point, the entire economy will be centralized. We'll be Communist China, or worse.

Bitcoin is the only counter to CBDCs. Bitcoin is your off-ramp from the coming nightmare of CBDCs.

The Lightning Network

Critics of Bitcoin often say it's not very useful for small transactions, so doesn't really work as a daily currency.

But this really isn't a problem. I don't consider bitcoin a currency and neither does the U.S. government. The U.S. government sees bitcoin as a commodity, similar to gold.

Similar to gold, bitcoin is a scarce commodity.

Most people don't and won't use the main Bitcoin blockchain to buy their groceries or coffee at Starbucks.

That's because Bitcoin is the base layer of the monetary network, much the way gold used to be the base layer for the dollar when U.S. paper dollars were gold certificates, redeemable at banks for gold.

Paper currency became the Layer 2 solution, built on top of gold, to make daily transactions easier and more efficient than carrying gold around.

In a similar, but 21st Century way, the Lightning Network is being built on top of the Bitcoin network to enable quick, cheap micro-transactions off the blockchain.

The Lightning Network is not a currency and does not have its own native currency. It's a network overlayed on top of the main Bitcoin blockchain that enables users to transact in fractions of a bitcoin (satoshis) for little or no fee.

Lightning was conceived by two developers, Thaddeus Dryja and Joseph Poon, in 2015. Their paper was titled "The Bitcoin Lightning Network: Scalable Off-Chain Instant Payments."

The Lightning Network enables users to send satoshis to one another using digital wallets. A payment channel is opened between users who want to transact with each other, much like Venmo or Cash App. A path is established on the network similar to routing packets on the internet.

This path is a Layer 2 separate ledger but is not a blockchain.

Remember, blockchain technology is slow.

Using a wallet that's set up for Lightning, you establish a channel with someone you want to transact with. You load a small amount of bitcoin (satoshis) into a digital vault on the channel. Only you and the person you are transacting with can access this digital vault.

Each of you must sign off on a transaction for funds to be moved from one address to another.

So it's still a "zero trust" system with no middleman, no intermediary.

The main chain tracks how much of your bitcoin left the chain for the channel you opened with your fellow transactor on Lightning; and then how much came back to the main chain when you close your Lightning channel. Transactions happen instantly on Lightening, just like on Venmo or Cash App.

With Lightning, the main chain is not clogged with your microtransactions. Costs on Lightning are free or almost free. There is a transaction cost for moving some of your bitcoin to the Lightning channel you open, about $2. But transactions on your Lightning channel are free or almost free at that point.

The Lightning channel you open with your fellow transactor operates as a separate ledger, off the main blockchain.

The only transactions that are recorded on the main Bitcoin blockchain are when you open and close a Lightning Network channel with your fellow transactor.

For example, you might set up a Lightning channel with your local coffee shop. You can keep this channel open indefinitely. Your money is held in escrow in a digital vault – which is an address. Every morning, you swing by to pick up your coffee. You then release the agreed-on amount from your digital vault to the coffee shop.

Payment is enforced using a smart-contracts script that verifies you have the funds in your digital vault for the coffee – then either validates the transaction . . . or rejects it if you don't have the funds. If the transaction is validated and accepted by the coffee shop, the funds move from your address to the coffee shop's address. Sign-offs by both you and the coffee shop are needed to move money.

No miners are involved. It's just you and the coffee shop operating on this payment channel.

So long as you have some bitcoin in your digital vault on the payment channel you've established with the coffee shop, you can keep buying your coffee. You can have as many transactions as you want with that coffee shop, spanning many years.

If you could move your fingers fast enough, you could theoretically conduct millions of transactions per day with this coffee shop. You're not slowed down by block mining or by the transaction needing to be validated by a worldwide consensus of nodes and miners.

If you and the coffee shop sign off using your digital signatures, the transaction is instant.

Only the opening and closing of the channel is recorded on the main blockchain.

This solves Bitcoin's "scalability" issue. On the Bitcoin base layer, the main chain can only process about 7 transactions per second compared to 4,000 transactions per second by Visa.

Visa says it can scale up to 65,000 transactions per second.

Visa is able to do this because it's a centrally administered system that can provisionally approve transactions instantly.

The Lightning Network makes Bitcoin infinitely scalable. Your payment is instant and almost free on the Lightning channel you've established with the coffee shop.

There's no limit to the number of transactions Lightning can handle per second. So it can actually be more scalable than Visa – and significantly cheaper, especially for the merchant.

Visa and the credit card companies charge significant transaction fees – 2-3 percent plus 30 cents per transaction typically. This is a big chunk of the cost of your coffee – part of why your coffee at Starbucks costs $3, $4 or more.

Transactions with legacy credit cards are only convenient from the perspective of the buyer, not the merchant. Transactions are not instant for the merchant with Visa, but are settled later – much later. With Visa, Mastercard, AmEx and legacy credit cards, transactions are never final.

Visa and the credit card companies reserve the right to reverse the amount paid to the merchant at any time in the future – called a chargeback. This accrues more fees to the merchant. It really means the merchant is never paid because transactions are never truly final.

Merchants must keep reserves on hand for chargebacks.

From the merchant's perspective, credit card transactions are inconvenient, slow, and expensive.

Merchants are also terrified of being cut off from accepting credit card payments by the credit card companies. The credit card companies have the power to shut down a business at any time.

So it's a hostage situation.

Bitcoin with the Lightning Network fixes this.

The Lightning Network also includes a "time lock" function that allows you to set the release of payment to some time in the future. This acts as an escrow function. So you can make payment conditional on receipt of the goods or services you are paying for.

With the "time lock" function, you can halt payment if the product or service isn't delivered, is defective, or unsatisfactory. The escrow, or "time lock" function, is simple "smart contract" code.

So there's no need to read a lengthy agreement on the back of your Visa statement that no one reads anyway. The agreement you sign off on every time you use Visa protects Visa, not so much you or the merchant. Lightning handles this with the "time lock" function.

Of course, all parties will want to honor whatever they agreed to. Businesses want good ratings from customers, and customers don't want reputations for being difficult. Uber allows drivers to rate customers.

No customer wants a bad rating with Uber out of fear of not being able to use the ride service. By the way, you can check your rating with Uber. Rating and review systems help keep everyone honest.

So there's no need for an intermediary, like Visa, to handle transactions. With Bitcoin and Lightning, the need for an intermediary is eliminated.

You can also set up payment channels on Lightning with more than one party operating in the same channel. Or you can have separate channels with people. As Lightning development continues to progress, more functionality will be added.

As merchants get set up with Lightning and accustomed to accepting payments from their customers via Lightning, this could spell the end for the legacy credit card system.

Why give Visa a 3 percent transaction fee if you don't have do? Why worry for months about chargebacks? And why give Visa the power to shut down your business?

One of the easiest ways for newbies to use the Lightning Network is with a digital wallet called Strike. You can use Strike to buy Bitcoin, then hit the Lightning Network tab to start using Lightning.

You can then send bitcoin to anyone set up on Lightning instantly.

You can also buy, send, and receive bitcoin on Jack Dorsey's

Cash App. Dorsey says Cash App will soon be integrated with Lightning.

Strike and Cash App are custodial solutions, which means you must trust them with your Bitcoin. But buying or loading small amounts of bitcoin (satoshis) on these apps is fine for your daily purchases. You can also convert bitcoin to fiat currency with these apps.

Two of the most popular self-custody wallets are Electrum and BlueWallet. These wallets are for Bitcoin purists and can only be used for Bitcoin. They are user friendly and good for beginners. Both are integrated with Lightning. You can download them from Bitcoin.org or from the Google Play store.

I use Electrum. So it's the one I'm familiar with. It's been around since 2011. Both Electrum and BlueWallet are known for security. Both allow you to convert your bitcoin to fiat currency.

Most people and businesses in the United States are not yet set up for using bitcoin on the Lightning Network because the U.S. dollar is still relatively stable by world standards. U.S. dollars work on an acceptable level for daily transactions in the minds of most.

People in the United States and the developed world are also used to using legacy credit cards. But Bitcoin and the Lightning Network have taken off in the Third World. Many Third World countries have inflation rates of 50 percent or more. In these countries, bitcoin is now the preferred money.

El Salvador is the first country to make bitcoin official legal tender. Use of the Lightning Network is now common in El Salvador.

El Salvador launched its Chivo wallet for Bitcoin and Lightning on September 7, 2021. Within three months, one-third of all El Salvadoran adults were using the Chivo wallet.

Though the Chivo wallet was issued by the government, so is custodial, it has fast-tracked the people of El Salvador onto the Bitcoin and Lightning networks. For any El Salvadoran who downloaded the Chivo wallet, the app came with $30 worth of bitcoin preloaded.

As a result, the number of users in El Salvador with access to Lightning payments increased from 87,000 users in August 2021 to 9,700,000 users in September – an 11,164 percent increase in one month.

Lightning is just getting started, but is quickly gathering speed, especially in the Third World.

The United States and developed world will be the last to catch on to Bitcoin and Lightning because hyperinflation hasn't quite hit here yet. It's 7 percent as of now, according to the U.S. government's CPI numbers. In reality, the number is likely significantly higher.

If inflation ticks up another few points, Americans will feel like hyper-inflation has arrived.

An annual inflation rate of 7 percent is still horrendous. Most people don't want a 7 percent cut in pay every year. Nor do they want to pay an extra 7 percent tax on their money, which is what inflation is. Think of inflation as an extra tax – a regressive additional 7 percent tax each year that hits lower-income people hardest.

Five years from now, everyone in the world will be transacting in Bitcoin and using the Lightning Network. Fiat currency, legacy credit card companies, and banks will be artifacts of history. Meetings of the U.S. Federal Reserve Board of Governors will no longer make the news, if they're still holding these meetings.

We'll wonder why anyone put up with the fiat money and legacy banking system at all.

CHAPTER 17

More on Why Dishonest Money is So Destructive

The true inflation rate is significantly higher than the official rate given by the U.S. Bureau of Labor Statistics.

There is an ongoing debate over how much higher the true inflation rate really is.

Economist John Williams at Shadowstats.com says the annual inflation rate would be 7 points higher if the U.S. Bureau of Labor Statistics (BLS) were still using the same methodology it used in 1980. In a long article for TheStreet.com, the economist, Ed Dolan, disputed Williams' calculations, saying CPI understates the inflation rate by 2.45 percent, not 7 percent

Either way, CPI is understating inflation significantly. Based on Williams' number, true inflation is about 14 percent. Using Dolan's number, true inflation is in the 9-10 percent range, not the 7 percent inflation rate reported by the U.S. government.

The U.S. government has a strong incentive to understate inflation with its official CPI number. This allows the Fed to keep interest rates (bond yields) artificially low so the U.S. government can keep up with interest payments on its $30 trillion national debt (heading soon to $100 trillion).

Right now, the interest rate the U.S. government pays on its national debt is about 2 percent per year – much lower than the interest would be if the free market was allowed to operate properly.

In 2019, the U.S. government paid $575 billion in interest on its debt out of a $4.4 trillion budget, or 13 percent of the federal budget.

But the interest rate the government is paying on the national debt is an absurdly low 2 percent per annum. This is an insanely low interest rate given that the government's own CPI report tells us inflation is 7 percent.

How can interest rates be lower than the official CPI inflation number? Interest rates should be higher than the inflation rate in a free-market economy.

If the government wasn't overriding the free market, it would be paying an interest rate of at least 10 percent on the national debt . . . or substantially more if John Williams at Shadowstats.com is correct and if the government measured inflation by the same standard it was using in 1980.

True market-based interest rates would consume most or all of the federal budget. There would be no money left for national defense, roads, courts, Social Security, Medicare, welfare programs, or anything else. The entire federal budget would be interest payments.

Also, by keeping the official inflation rate artificially low, the U.S. government can keep cost-of-living increases (COLAs) low for Social Security recipients. Inflation is an especially brutal tax on people living on fixed incomes, such as those on Social Security.

Social Security is the largest item in the federal budget. If the U.S. government had to increase Social Security benefits in accordance with the true inflation rate, the entire U.S. budget would become Social Security payments.

The Fed really has no choice but to keep interest rates artificially low, while the U.S. government also understates true inflation. If it didn't, the entire U.S. budget would implode into a black hole of interest payments on the debt.

Fed economists push back against the claim that the official CPI number is understated by design. They say the reason they must keep changing the way CPI is calculated is because technological improvements keep pushing costs for products and services down.

So the cost of your iPhone and your TV don't go up much. And there were no iPhones in 1980 or 1990. Technological progress makes manufacturing more efficient, makes all of us more productive, so has the effect of pushing the cost of living down.

Government economists will say CPI has to keep adjusting its formula to take technological progress into account.

But keeping the "cost of living" stable (or increasing slightly each year) is not the correct objective. Because of technological progress, Americans should be living much better than they are. Americans, including lower-income Americans, should be living lives of abundance.

171

For perspective, consider this.

My dad bought our family house in Vermont in 1971 for $20,000. It included 12 acres of land and a beautiful view of the Ompompanoosuc river.

Today, that house is valued at more than $1,000,000 by Zillow. The address of my childhood home is 261 Rt 132, Norwich, VT. Check it out.

This house had five bedrooms and 4,500 square feet. We had a ski hill, a ski tow, lights for night skiing. We also had plenty of room for our four horses to run.

Our mom was a stay-at-home mom with four kids. We weren't rich at all. Our Dad was an English Literature professor at Dartmouth College earning a college professor's salary, probably earning about $17,500 per year at that time. Today, his salary as a full professor at Dartmouth would be $235,000 per year.

This means there's been a 93 percent devaluation of the dollar since 1971, if we use the college professor salary measure.

Gold was $35 per ounce back then. Today one troy ounce of gold will cost you $1,800. This means there's been a 98 percent devaluation of the dollar since 1971 if we use gold as the measure.

Why did we go off the gold standard?

The reason is our government needed more money to fund the Vietnam War and President Lyndon Johnson's Great Society welfare programs without raising taxes. This, by the way, also shows how inflation funds war.

The only way to fund war is to print a lot of money. Massive fiat money printing is how all wars are funded. Without inflation, we would be far less likely to get involved in expensive wars – that is, if we had to pay for war with real money instead of confetti money.

But still, you might counter, America appears to be much wealthier today and living better overall than in 1971. So perhaps it's good we went off the gold standard. Perhaps all this money printing has been positive. Maybe this "new economics" is correct.

It is true Americans today are living better overall than in 1971 (in some ways). But that's not because we went off the gold standard. It's because of advances in technology, science, and overall human progress.

Good Deflation Versus Bad Deflation

When the U.S. Bureau of Labor Statistics releases its inflation data each month, what it calls its Consumer Price Index (CPI), it often sounds like the overall inflation number is pretty reasonable.

For the past decade, we've seen annual inflation, as measured by the Consumer Price Index, in the 2-3 percent range.

Since the Covid pandemic began and all the extra money printing that ensued to prop up the economy, we've seen the annual official CPI inflation number rise to 7 percent-plus.

But, again, remember what the Consumer Price Index measures. It measures price increases in the goods and services consumers buy regularly – cost of living.

Constant technological advances and more efficient mass-production push costs and prices down steadily. We've found more efficient ways to mass-produce food, furniture, houses, cars, drill for oil, and produce everything we need now than was possible back in 1971.

The U.S. Federal Reserve tries to calibrate its money printing to keep the prices of things you buy and need to live relatively stable – plus tack on an extra 2-3 percent cost of living per year.

Prices go up, but not so much each year that it causes a revolution.

People think that 3 percent or even 5 percent inflation each year is bad, but most think we can live with this. It doesn't sound like a lot in the grand scheme of things.

But the inflation rate is really much more than the official number if you factor in technological innovation that would be pushing prices down dramatically if we had honest money. Most of the things we buy would be getting cheaper every year, not more expensive every year.

Instead of paying an average $40,000 for a car, you should be paying more like $1,000 for a nice car, or perhaps less – if we were still on the gold standard.

We have also been conditioned to believe that deflation is bad because if we have deflation people will hoard money – won't spend it, won't invest in new businesses, so there won't be much economic activity.

The velocity of money would slow down, or so we're told.

We're told this was what happened to prolong the Great

Depression. We had deflation because people were hoarding their money.

This is false history.

There is good deflation and bad deflation.

Bad deflation is created by uncertainty, which causes people to hoard their money and not take risks, such as starting a business.

Here's the real history.

The United States had been on the gold standard since the 1830s. Paper money denominations were gold certificates that could be exchanged at banks for actual gold. Until 1933, gold certificates were used in everyday commerce.

But monetary policy started to change with the creation of the Federal Reserve centralized banking system in 1913.

Under this new law, the Federal Reserve would be required only to hold gold equal to 40 percent of the value of the currency it issued. Still, anyone could go to a Federal Reserve bank branch and exchange their paper currency for gold at a fixed price of $20.67 per troy ounce.

Gold the Federal Reserve held in excess of 40 percent was called "free gold."

The Federal Reserve could increase its stock of "free gold" by encouraging people to bring their gold to the bank in exchange for interest. The depositor would then receive a gold certificate, called a Federal Reserve Note.

When the Fed wanted or needed more gold in reserve, it would increase interest rates to encourage gold deposits, as well as encourage foreigners to invest in the United States. When the Fed lowered interest rates, this would cause gold to flow out of the Federal Reserve System.

When the stock market crashed in September of 1929, at first it was seen as just another recession, not much different from other recessions the country had recovered from usually within about 18 months.

But the fact that the Federal Reserve was only required to back gold certificates by holding 40 percent of their value in gold accelerated the public's rising distrust of the banking system, which in turn generated a run on the banks. People wanted gold, not paper money.

In March of 1933, the Federal Reserve Bank of New York could no longer honor its commitment to convert currency to gold. This created a panic. President Roosevelt then declared that people could no longer bring their paper money (gold certificates) to a Federal Reserve bank branch to exchange for gold.

On January 30, 1934, Congress passed and Roosevelt signed the Gold Reserve Act that outlawed the ownership of gold, except for jewelry and collector coins. This law required all owners of gold to show up at a Federal Reserve bank branch and exchange their gold for paper money.

Also under this law, the value of the dollar would be pegged to $35 per troy ounce of gold instead of the $20.67 it had been pegged at under the Gold Standard Act of 1900.

This change amounted to an instant 41 percent devaluation of the dollar. People who failed to turn in their gold for the new currency were also prosecuted.

The constant changing of the rules, the uncertainty, and the constantly shifting sands in the money system are what deepened and prolonged the Great Depression, causing people to hoard their money, bury it, not buy things, not start businesses.

This lack of economic activity in the 1930s caused deflation, the bad kind of deflation.

A thriving economy needs a fixed set of rules – including a fixed monetary policy.

The deflation we saw during the Great Depression was bad deflation. That deflation was caused by lack of economic activity, which was largely created by changing the rules of money – specifically by devaluing money overnight by 41 percent.

How could uncertainty like this not deepen and prolong the recession, turn a relatively routine recession into a decade-long Great Depression?

But there's also a good kind of deflation.

Good deflation is created with technological progress.

Are you going to avoid buying an iPhone this year because you know the same model will be cheaper next year?

Some might make this calculation. Still, people always want the newest and best technology because the newest and best technology makes us more productive, makes life easier, and more fun.

If the dollar value of gold had remained pegged at $35 per ounce (as it was until 1971), you would be paying $1,000 for a great car instead of $40,000.

Would the fact that you would only pay $1,000 for a car instead of $40,000 for the same car make you less likely to buy that car?

Of course not. You need the car. You want the car. So you buy it if you can afford it.

Money is a unit of measurement. We could not have engineering without fixed units of measurement.

A millimeter is always the same. It never changes.

We could not build skyscrapers, bridges, and rockets without precise units of measurement that never change, that everyone understands.

If we didn't have standard precise units of measurement, we would still be living in mud huts.

This is what money is supposed to be, a unit of measurement, a unit of account.

It can also be a notation on a ledger. Money is a convenient way for people to exchange value over space and time.

If I perform a job, provide a service, or make a product that's useful, I'm paid money.

I can then use that money to pay others to do work for me. Or I can use the money to buy food, a place to live, and products that I need or want.

By constantly adding new money to the system, the government is stealing my labor, my creativity, my energy, my time, and my life.

But we tend not to notice how much money is really being devalued by all this money printing because technological progress is a powerful deflationary force. Technology allows us to make things much more efficiently, allows for much more productive use of time.

Because of technological progress, everything should be getting cheaper over time.

Instead of the CPI rising 7 percent, we should be experiencing CPI decreases of 2-3 percent per year because of advances in technology, including AI-powered robotics. Most farming today is automated. Fertilizers are better. We don't have food shortages anymore the way we did in the 1970s and 1980s.

We don't see millions of people starving to death anymore – a horror that was common two decades ago. Food is plentiful today because of technological advances in farming.

So why do food prices continue to go up? Why aren't food prices dropping?

The answer is all the money printing.

The money supply has been increasing at a rate of about 25 percent per year since the start of the Covid pandemic in March of 2020, up from about 7 percent per year before the pandemic. But the money printing press is not likely to throttle back much.

The most we hear from the Fed is they might start to "taper" the supply of new money. This just means a slight reduction in the rate of increase.

The problem with stopping the money printing or even moving the supply of new money entering the system back to 7 percent per year instead of 25 percent is it would cause the stock market to collapse. That would cause a cascading domino effect. Heavily leveraged financial institutions would collapse.

We would see a replay of the 2008 financial collapse, but ten times worse.

Interest rates would zoom skyward if the Fed was to throttle down its money printing. This would make it impossible for the U.S. government to make interest payments owed on the $30 trillion national debt, even if interest rates were only to tick up only a little.

In 2021, U.S. federal spending totaled $6.82 trillion. But tax revenue totaled only $3.86 trillion.

So tax revenue barely covered half of federal spending. We're $3 trillion short . . . every year!

The rest must be covered by money printing. We call this more federal "borrowing." This is what happens when Congress "raises the debt ceiling."

But the government is just borrowing money from itself.

The way it does this is to print more money.

The Fed's money printing press is a lot like crack cocaine. You need to do more and more of it to keep the high going and keep from crashing.

Imagine if you had a money printing press in your basement that you could just turn on.

It would be very hard to resist. But at the level the U.S. government is spending money and the Fed is printing it, at a certain point this house of cards Ponzi scheme collapses in on itself.

Inflation is a hidden tax that hits poor people and people on fixed

177

incomes hardest. Inflation is the real source of wealth inequality in America. And it can be traced back to when we abandoned the gold standard completely in 1971.

Some people at the top are also getting very rich from this corrupt fiat money system.

People with excess cash put their cash into assets that appreciate when measured against a rapidly devaluing dollar. They buy beachfront property in Miami. They buy tech stocks. They buy rare art. They buy Bitcoin.

Low-income people don't have excess cash to buy appreciating assets like real estate or put money in an S&P 500 or Nasdaq 100 index fund.

Inflation is actually a massive money redistribution program from the poor to the rich. Inflation is a regressive tax on low-income people, and people on fixed incomes.

Inflation is theft. Money represents your life energy, your labor, your ingenuity. Inflation steals some of your life work and energy from you every minute of every day, like termites eating your house.

Termites don't seem that bad at first. But then your house collapses.

Of course, "appreciating" assets are largely an illusion too because people are in the habit of measuring their stock market returns against the dollar. But the dollar is a very inaccurate measuring tool. That's why it's so difficult to retire these days.

Retirement at age 65 used to be the norm. People could live on the 4 percent return they were getting from their life savings.

Now people can't afford to retire because the value of the dollar goes down every year. They need 20 percent annual returns from the stock market just to stay even.

This creates boom-and-bust asset bubbles, like what happened in 2000 and again in 2008.

Inflation (even 3-4 percent per year) forces people to stay on the work treadmill until they die.

Why do people work so hard all their lives?

Most people work hard all their lives so they can raise a family and one day enjoy retirement – have a few golden years at the end of their lives.

It's almost impossible to retire today because we really don't know what the cost of tomorrow will be. How much fiat money will we need to live five years from now or ten years from now?

Even if you have a net worth of $10 million, that might not be much in five years or ten years, much less in 20 years, because the Fed's money printing press never stops.

The money printing must continue at faster and faster rates to keep the Ponzi scheme going.

China has stopped buying U.S. Treasury bonds because there's no yield. The 10-year Treasury bond pays a 2 percent interest rate. That's nothing given the real inflation rate. China would be far better off buying beachfront property in Miami, which is exactly what China is doing.

So who is buying U.S. debt?

The Fed is.

The Fed bought about $120 billion in government bonds each month throughout 2021.

Where does the Fed get the money to buy all these government bonds?

ANSWER: The Fed simply prints the money.

So a government bond (Treasury bill) is just an IOU that the U.S. Treasury prints up and puts in one drawer. The Fed then prints more money to pay that IOU. So it's printing both the bonds (IOUs) and the money to pay the bonds.

Of course, the average person is actually the one paying for all this through a hidden tax called inflation. Though inflation is a regressive tax that hits those at the lower end of the economic ladder hardest, it ultimately sinks most of the rich too . . . because the entire financial ship goes down.

If your net worth is $10 million, that might sound pretty good today, but it might not be worth much in ten years.

So you have to keep working to stay ahead of the Fed's money printing press, which will continue printing money at faster and faster rates in order to prop up the system a bit longer – at least until the next election.

Most people are sensing that something has gone very wrong in society. We are seeing rising crime, rising mental illness, rising suicide rates. We see the rise of the "lie flat" movement. This is a fad that started in China – a fad that's moved here and where young people opt out of the system by simply "lying flat" all day.

They lie flat on the floor, or in their bed, or on the sofa.

They do this because they sense working is futile, that economic advancement really isn't possible.

They believe their future will be like Sisyphus, the figure in Greek mythology who was sentenced by the Gods to roll a boulder up a hill for eternity for no purpose. The boulder keeps rolling back down.

Many young people are now living in their parents' basements until they're 40, or older. They see their future as just watching Netflix and playing video games. Their life lacks purpose.

People are anxious. People feel insecure about their future. This anxiety, this insecurity is produced by this massive money printing by government. People know in their gut something is wrong.

People think 7 percent inflation is bad, but maybe not that bad. They feel they can live with it – that maybe it's not worth launching a revolution over. But that's a 7 percent pay cut per year every year. Or it's a 7 percent hidden tax every year.

But it's really more like a 10 percent pay cut or more for reasons I've stated here.

Because of constant technological progress, the cost of living should be going down every year – not up. We should be paying less and less, not more and more. Americans should be enjoying secure lives of abundance, not lives of panic and desperation.

People have been conditioned to believe that one solution to this problem is to buy real estate – buy rental properties, buy desirable beach front property, buy property in midtown Manhattan.

Buying real estate has been a pretty good bet. It will likely continue to be a decent bet as long as the system continues to function at some acceptable level – if we don't have total societal collapse.

But real estate could crash in value quickly if people cannot afford to rent it or buy it. Real estate isn't valuable if there's a Communist revolution and the regime just seizes it.

I own a number of rental properties. We have homes in Chicago and Fort Lauderdale.

Overall, the real estate bet has been a good one for us.

The value of these properties increased 40 percent over 24 months from the start of the Covid pandemic in 2020 – in large part because of all the money printing, also because people were fleeing rampant crime in the cities for the suburbs, and because people were losing their jobs so they needed cheaper places to live.

So our apartment rental business did very well during the pandemic.

There are also some tax advantages to real estate. You can depreciate rental properties over 27 years. You can deduct the cost of maintaining rental properties on your taxes. Then, in theory, the value of the property increases over time, as measured against the dollar. So property has been a good hedge against inflation.

There's only a finite amount of desirable property. So, in theory, it goes up over time if it's in the right location.

Location, location, and location are the three most important rules of the real estate business.

But there are some drawbacks to owning real estate.

My real estate holdings are subject to impairments and ongoing costs. Property taxes are always rising.

Tenants who stop paying rent are difficult to evict. It can take 90 days or more to get a non-paying tenant out – someone who has decided to "lie flat" instead of work. There are maintenance and insurance costs.

Whatever the value of your property, just figure you need to add 5 percent per year to pay the tax on it and maintain it. Then if you have a mortgage on the property, add the interest you must pay.

Make sure you factor in the true interest rate because the interest owed on a 30-year mortgage is frontloaded. In the early years of your 30-year mortgage, almost your entire mortgage payment is interest.

Most people don't keep their mortgage for 30 years. If you refinance or sell the property within 10 years, your real interest rate might be more like 15 percent per year because the interest owed was front-loaded.

And then, if all Hell breaks loose and there's a revolution, perhaps there will be a Socialist takeover such as what happened in Venezuela. I can't move my real estate. I can't carry my real estate out of the country.

Gold is no good in this kind of situation because you can't carry gold bars very easily across borders.

At this point, you'll want Bitcoin.

I wouldn't put all my assets in Bitcoin because maybe we won't have a Socialist or Communist revolution, and my real estate holdings will be fine. So I currently have about 15 percent of my assets in Bitcoin. Bitcoin is my escape hatch, my ejector seat if all Hell breaks loose here.

How We Got Here

We have been conditioned to believe that deflation is the worst thing that can possibly happen, that part of the Fed's job is to prevent deflation. The Fed does that by printing money.

I learned in my economics classes at Dartmouth that we need 2-3 percent inflation per year to prevent people from hoarding money.

We are told that people hoarding their money (due to bank collapses) was a big part of what caused the Great Depression. The lack of economic activity then created deflation, which deepened and prolonged the Great Depression.

The theory is that some inflation is needed to keep people producing, to keep people on the economic treadmill, to keep people running. Also, injections of new money into the system are needed to stimulate the economy.

In addition, some modest deficit spending is fine to keep the economy humming along – often what is called "stimulus."

This is called Keynesian economics as expounded by the early-20th Century British economist John Maynard Keynes.

To support this thesis, people point to the explosion of economic activity in America that flowed from World War II.

Massive deficit spending was required to fund World War II.

Following World War II, the United States became the supreme economic superpower of the world.

Therefore, as the thinking goes, all this deficit spending produced tremendous economic prosperity in America following the war.

I would argue that America reigned supreme following the war because the rest of the world was destroyed by the war. The war was not fought here. The war was fought in Europe and we dropped two atomic bombs on Japan.

Europe and Japan were both destroyed. The British Empire was no more. So the United States was able to prosper compared to everywhere else.

The U.S. also held most of the world's gold supply by the end of World War II. So the rest of the developed world adopted the dollar standard as a proxy for the gold standard.

Whichever country has the dominant currency and dominant military has the dominant economy.

So even though the U.S. had a massive debt from the war, we were still in far better shape than every other country. We had the dominant currency, the dominant industrial base, and the dominant military.

The massive debt from the war was viewed as temporary.

Winning wars is how countries have always gotten rich. Empires gain wealth by conquering territory.

That's how the Romans did it. That's how every empire does it. That's how every country became a country. They won a war fought over territory at some point.

The United States became the world's #1 economic superpower by winning World War II. Plus, we had a wealth-creating capitalist system.

However, the myth is that massive deficit spending created this prosperity.

The national debt after World War II in 1945 was $285 billion – which would be about $4.3 trillion in today's dollars. That compares to our $30 trillion debt today.

What did we buy for this $285 billion debt we had in 1945?

Well, we won World War II, defeated Hitler, defeated Imperial Japan, and emerged as the dominant economic and military superpower of the world.

So we bought quite a lot with this $285 billion.

There's good debt and bad debt.

Some types of debt are productive. Other types of debt are destructive.

Taking out a mortgage to buy a home or taking out a loan to pay for an education or to start a business might make sense, depending on circumstances.

Debt to feed a gambling addiction is destructive debt.

$25 trillion of our $30 trillion national debt has been racked up since 2000. So almost all this debt has been added recently. What have we bought with all this money?

Well, we've seen the rise of the "Lie Flat" movement among young people because we've been paying able-bodied people not to work when there are 11 million job openings.

So is this $25 trillion in additional debt our government has racked up from 2000 to 2022 productive debt or destructive debt? You decide.

CHAPTER 18

How the 19th Century Austrian School of Economics Provides the Framework for Bitcoin

In 1871, an economist from Vienna, Austria named Carl Menger published his *Principles of Economics* that outlines his theory of value. Though the title of the book sounds ordinary, the concepts Menger outlined were revolutionary. Menger believed that value is subjective and determined by the consumer.

This is in contrast to Karl Marx, who believed value is determined by utility. So water and food have more value than diamonds because people need water and food to survive.

Menger and the Austrian school believed the market determines value. In a prosperous economy where water and food are plentiful, people will pay more for diamonds. So diamonds are more valuable under these conditions because the market says so.

The market is objective.

But if water and food were to become scarce, their value would rise in the minds of people. Value is determined by the laws of supply and demand.

Karl Marx's concept of utility to determine value is subjective. Price signals from the market are an objective measure of value.

The Austrian school viewed economics as science. Menger saw the market as providing ongoing feedback in the form of price signals to determine value and enable the most efficient allocation of capital.

If the people are desperate for water, the market will quickly find a way to produce water in abundance. Water then becomes less expensive as the profit motive creates competition to produce water in abundance at the lowest possible cost.

Conversely, when government bureaucrats decide how capital is allocated instead of price signals from the market, taxpayer money is misspent because government bureaucrats don't have the information they need to make good decisions.

Plus, if government bureaucrats make poor decisions on how money is spent, there's no consequence for failure. The government agency never goes out of business for making bad decisions. Instead, the government agency tells us the reason it's failing is lack of money.

"If we just had more money, we could solve the problem," the bureaucrat tells us.

So the solution is always to get more money from the taxpayer by force (taxation), or to print more money.

Government's incentive is to use its monopoly on force (taxation) to enrich itself and increase its power. Politicians and government bureaucrats are primarily incentivized to protect their positions in government, not to make good decisions on how taxpayer money is spent . . . because it's not their money.

When government officials decide how money is spent, they usually just dole out to their cronies and the politically connected. This produces corruption.

So centralized economic planning by government bureaucrats (socialism) always produces shortages, hampers innovation, and halts economic progress. Capitalism and market-based economies, by contrast, incentivize innovation and entrepreneurship, which creates broad prosperity.

But Menger's most revolutionary insight was his thesis that money is not a creation of government. Instead, money is a commodity, like sand, silver, gold, water, or many other things. The value of a commodity as a unit of exchange is determined by the market, not government.

In his 1892 classic *The Nature and Origin of Money,* Menger wrote:

> Money is not an invention of the state. It's not the product of
> a legislative act. Even the sanction of political authority is
> not necessary for its existence. Certain commodities came
> to be money quite naturally, as the result of economic
> relationships that were independent of the state.

Menger posited that money emerged naturally on its own through trial and error. "This transition did not take place abruptly," wrote

Menger, "nor did it take place in the same way among all peoples."

This is true. Gold and silver were not created by government, but were discovered by ordinary people thousands of years ago as useful for transmitting value in exchange for goods and services. Both gold and silver had been used as money for at least 4,000 years. Money was nationalized later by governments, starting about 600 B.C.

Governments wanted to control the money. Government, most notably the Roman Empire, needed money to fund war. As the Roman Empire spread and became expensive to maintain, the government in Rome had to debase the currency to pay its soldiers and fund its war machine. Instead of pure gold and silver coins, the Roman government paid soldiers with diluted coins.

At first the soldiers didn't notice. But eventually the debasement of the currency was so total that the soldiers could wipe the silver finish off coins with their thumbs.

Many Roman soldiers rebelled over being cheated out of their pay and joined the barbarian hordes invading the empire. This debasement of the currency accelerated the collapse of the Roman Empire.

The only way government can fund war and bigger government is by debasing the money, for the simple reason that the people won't put up with taxes constantly going higher.

So fiat currency systems always impose a hidden tax called inflation that most people don't notice – at least for a while, until the inflation is out of control, which usually happens suddenly.

Debasement of the currency always eventually leads to the collapse of nations and empires.

The two most famous Austrian school economists in the 20th Century were Ludwig von Mises and Friedrich A. Hayek, who built on the ideas of Carl Menger.

In his book *Money and Credit*, published in 1912, Mises also showed that it's unlikely gold and silver were immediately recognized by people as money. Gold and silver were competing among many other possibilities as mediums of exchange. Gold and silver just worked best.

Mises said further that central banks were not necessary, hinder economic progress, and that the market can determine the best form of money.

The Liberty Fund has published an excellent library of some of the best passages from Mises. This text from Mises' classic work *Human Action,* published in 1949, summarizes much of his theory of money and liberty:

> Freedom, as people enjoyed it in the democratic countries of Western civilization in the years of the old liberalism's triumph, was not a product of constitutions, bills of rights, laws, and statutes. Those documents aimed only at safeguarding liberty and freedom, firmly established by the operation of the market economy, against encroachments on the part of officeholders.
>
> Government is a guarantor of liberty and is compatible with liberty only if its range is adequately restricted to the preservation of what is called economic freedom. Where there is no market economy, the best-intentioned provisions of constitutions and laws remain a dead letter. [25]

So where there is no free market economy, there can be no liberty.

That was the view of the Austrian school. Also, money is a product like other products. The free market, if allowed to function, will produce the best money, just as the free market produces the best products in all other areas of the economy.

In a 1928 essay, Mises noted that the reason classical economists of the 19th century favored gold as money, or as the base layer for paper currency (gold certificates redeemable for gold), is this preserved the money (gold) as "independent of any direct manipulation by governments, political policies, public opinion or parliaments."

Mises explains in *Human Action*:

> The gold standard was the world standard of the age of capitalism, increasing welfare, liberty, and democracy, both political and economic . . . everywhere destroying the fetters of age-old prejudices and superstitions, sowing the seeds of new life and new well-being, freeing minds and souls, and creating riches unheard of before. [26]

Mises' *Human Action* is an enormous and dense work. Fortunately, Liberty Fund has pulled the best passages, which you

---

[25] oll.libertyfund.org/quote/mises-on-the-interconnection-between-economic-and-political-freedom-1949

[26] oll.libertyfund.org/quote/mises-on-the-gold-standard-as-the-symbol-of-international-peace-and-prosperity-1949

can find in Liberty Fund's "Online Library of Liberty." [27]

Mises thought the gold standard enabled tremendous prosperity and economic progress, but also thought we could do better than gold, but not through government.

He argued that "we have always had bad money because private enterprise was not permitted to give us a better one."

Mises advocated a system of privately created money, most likely based on baskets of commodities, though the market would decide the best money.

Again, free your mind from the idea that money is a government creation. Free your mind from the idea that money must be controlled and administered by government.

Open your mind to the idea that money is a product like any other and that the market will discover or invent the best money, much the way the market creates language. It develops naturally.

What would Mises think of Bitcoin if he could see it?

Bitcoin was exactly what Mises was talking about.

The Nobel Prize-winning economist Friedrich A. Hayek was also in the Austrian school of economic thought. Hayek was a colleague and friend of Mises.

Hayek immigrated from Austria to London in 1938 as Hitler was ramping up. Mises immigrated to the United States from Austria in 1940 as Hitler was sweeping across Europe. So these great thinkers witnessed totalitarianism first hand.

Both warned about the corrupting influence central banks have on money. They showed how expansionary credit policies (money printing) by central banks leads to inflation, boom and bust business cycles, and fuel the growth of government.

Hayek's great book *The Road to Serfdom*, published in 1944, was aimed at a general audience, isn't academic. In this book, Hayek warns about "the tyranny that inevitably results from government control of economic decision-making through central planning."

He argued that fascism, Nazism, Communism and all forms of socialism have their origins in a belief in central economic planning and empowering the state over the individual. *The Road to Serfdom* has sold more than two million copies and has been translated into more than twenty languages.

---

[27] oll.libertyfund.org/person/ludwig-von-mises

Similar to Menger and Mises, Hayek saw the price system as emerging naturally, through human interaction, to produce a peaceful spontaneous order.

What's more peaceful than lawful commercial activity?

Hayek wrote a book titled *The Denationalization of Money* (1972) which argued that government should have no role in money at any level. Hayek believed there needs to be a complete separation of money from state. Again, that's Bitcoin.

Think about how the free market works to produce exponential improvements in products.

Look how quickly the market was able to go from smoke signals to the pony express, to the telegraph, to the crank phone on a wall, to the dial phone, to the mobile phone, to the iPhone. We see this progress in every area of human life where the market is allowed to function.

We could see this kind of progress in medicine and health care if we allow the market to do its work.

We see what a disaster government-run education has become.

Everything under the control of government gets worse – whether it's health care, education, or the money.

In the view of Menger, Mises, Hayek and the Austrian school of economics, money is a product, like any other, that can be continuously improved if the market is allowed to operate.

Human innovation, through trial and error, creates better products, including better money.

That's what happened with Bitcoin.

CHAPTER 19

Why Much of the World Wants to Get Out from Under the U.S. Dollar

With the end of World War II, the dollar emerged as the world reserve currency. The dollar maintained its status as the world reserve currency even after moving completely off the gold standard in 1971.

The reason the U.S. went off the gold standard in 1971 was so it could be unrestrained with its money printing. Since then, the price of one ounce of gold has risen from $35 per troy ounce to more than $1,800 an ounce. So the dollar has lost 98 percent of its value in relation to gold since 1971.

This is really the entire reason for Bitcoin – to be digital gold. Bitcoin has many of the properties of gold. There's a fixed supply. But it's easy to transport. You can carry your wealth anywhere on your phone, or in your head if you can remember a 12-word phrase. It's also a borderless currency. You can transact business with anyone in the world with a few keystrokes.

Unlike with a bank or credit card company, there is no central authority that can stop your bitcoin transactions. Your account can't be frozen or seized, so long as you hold your private keys – so long as you aren't trusting someone else with your private keys. Bitcoin allows you to be your own bank.

This development is causing much of the world to wonder if they should be on the dollar standard.

The dollar is used in more than 40 percent of the world's transactions. In cross-border transactions, the dollar is used in about 80 percent of transactions.

As a result, countries tend to buy dollar-backed securities, such as U.S. Treasury bonds, to increase trust in their own currencies.

But this is becoming less and less attractive as inflation rates soar and the 10-year U.S. Treasury bond yields an interest rate of just 2-3 percent.

One of the big privileges for the U.S. dollar being the world reserve currency is this allows the United States to have the rest of the world pay our debt.

Here's how that works.

If the official inflation rate in the United States is 7 percent, but the U.S. government only pays 2-3 percent annual interest on its debt (the yield on 10-year U.S. Treasury bond), this is a 4-5 percent negative spread.

This means if you buy a 10-year bond from the U.S. Treasury, you will lose 4-5 percent per year on your investment. This assumes the official CPI inflation measure is accurate – which few believe it is.

True inflation is likely running at more like 10 percent or more per year. For countries that peg their currencies to the U.S. dollar, this means they are effectively paying a 6-10 percent tax per year in the form of inflation to monetize (pay for) the national debt of the United States.

This negative spread is unlikely to change for the simple reason that the United States cannot afford to pay a market-based interest rate on its $30 trillion national debt – rapidly heading to $100 trillion.

So most of the world is effectively paying for America's national debt – is subsidizing America's lavish lifestyle. Much of the world is starting to question this arrangement.

The Petrodollar System

But there's more that's causing the world to question the benefits of sticking with the dollar standard.

Most people don't know about the "petrodollar system."

This was another outgrowth of the post-World War II Bretton Woods agreement of 1944 that replaced gold with the U.S. dollar as the world reserve currency.

Remember, the rest of the world was destroyed by the war. The United States held most of the world's gold reserves. So since the U.S. dollar was pegged to the price of gold at the time, it made sense for the rest of the advanced world to peg their currencies to the dollar.

But when President Nixon took the U.S. dollar off the gold

standard in 1971, this sent the price of commodities, such as oil, skyward. Oil is essential for powering civilization. Without oil, civilization collapses.

This led to the creation of the petrodollar system in the early 1970s when Saudi Arabia agreed to peg oil prices to the U.S. dollar. Other OPEC countries followed the Saudis and agreed to this.

This is really a reverse of the gold standard. Gold is rare. Gold supply increases at a rate of about 1.5 percent per year. Oil is plentiful. There are oceans of oil underground.

OPEC stands for the Organization of Petroleum Exporting Countries.

Under the petrodollar system, anyone buying oil from an OPEC country must first convert their currency to U.S. dollars before a sale can be completed.

Because everyone must use petrodollars to buy oil, this creates surpluses of petrodollars. These petrodollar surpluses are used to buy U.S. Treasury bills, thus further subsidizing U.S. debt and America's standard of living. This is called petrodollar "recycling."

"Recycling" sounds good, right?

Not quite – or depends on your vantage point. This is a different kind of "recycling."

These surplus petrodollars are also divvied up ("recycled") among OPEC countries to create enormous "sovereign wealth" funds for OPEC countries.

These petrodollar surpluses amount to trillions of dollars for the treasuries of the United States and OPEC nations. Trillions of "surplus" petrodollars also flow through the banking systems of the United States and Europe.

"Flow through" also means "recycled."

So if you stumble across the phrase "petrodollar recycling," that's what's happening.

Those at the top of the world financial and political system are very skilled at coming up with phrases few people understand – phrases you have to look up and spend many hours studying.

"Petrodollar recycling" is not a phrase that's likely to come up even in a college-level course on economics.

"Petrodollar recycling" is a great racket if you are the United States or an oil producer. Not so good if you are outside the petrodollar system. If you are outside the petrodollar system, say in the Third World, you are subsidizing the standard of living of the United States, Europe, and OPEC by paying much higher prices for oil and gas than would be the case if the free market were allowed to operate.

If you often wonder why we always seem to be fighting wars in the Middle East for no obvious purpose, protecting the "petrodollar recycling" system is a big part of the reason. The U.S. decision to go to war with Iraq twice were cases in point.

Again, much of the world is starting to question this arrangement.

How the International Monetary Fund and World Bank Spread Poverty

The World Bank and International Monetary Fund (IMF) were two more institutions established by the Bretton Woods Conference in 1944. Their ostensible purpose was to help a shattered world rebuild from World War II.

The World Bank and IMF are both headquartered in Washington, DC. Taxpayer-funded institutions rarely (if ever) go away.

It's been a long time since World War II. But like all government institutions, the World Bank and IMF continue to grow and find new jobs to do.

These institutions just keep getting bigger and more powerful.

A sign at the entrance of the World Bank reads "Our dream is a world without poverty."

To achieve this, the World Bank has amassed a bureaucracy of more than 10,000 employees and some 150 offices around that world. Its annual budget is more than $1.5 billion.

The IMF's mission is similar. It's common for government bureaucracies to have overlapping missions. The IMF also has thousands of employees.

Both the World Bank and IMF say their specific job is to provide the developing world with access to capital, also to help bring a legal structure and financial stability to impoverished countries.

Okay. Well that sounds pretty good.

But what's actually happening is these international organizations are preventing economic progress in the Third World by effectively imposing socialistic bureaucracies on impoverished countries.

The problem has been that much of the "lending" from the IMF and World Bank flows to elites, corrupt oligarchs, and to governments in the Third World instead of fledgling entrepreneurs who could actually deploy capital productively.

Rarely are World Bank or IMF "loans" ever repaid.

After decades and decades of work and hundreds of billions of dollars spent, the World Bank and IMF can point few examples of success.

The World Bank's own evaluation of the effectiveness of its projects in Africa finds a 73 percent rate of failure in reducing poverty – which should have included helping these countries create legal and financial structures that would enable the developing world to advance economically.

The IMF admits that decades of focusing on short-term emergency relief and crisis management has produced little in the way of economic progress for the Third World.

Let's take Argentina as just one example. Since 1958, Argentina has received some $44 billion in loans from the IMF. Argentina has never come close to making the required payments on these loans.

So what did the IMF do?

The IMF lent Argentina another $17 billion in 2018, bringing the total owed to $57 billion.

Though the agreement calls for Argentina to pay $19 billion per year to the IMF, no one who looks even briefly at Argentina's finances and track-record of default after default believes Argentina has the intention or ability to repay anything close to this.

Argentina's annual inflation rate is running at about 51 percent. More than 40 percent are living in poverty.

But Argentina was not always an economic basket case. In the early 20th century, Argentina was among the most prosperous countries in the world.

The IMF has not helped. IMF money has just served to prop up Argentina's corrupt regimes.

When you reward corruption with more money, you'll always end up with more corruption.

This has been the track record of the IMF and World Bank throughout the world for more than half a century.

Bangladesh is the world's third largest recipient of World Bank funds. It remains one of the world's poorest countries with a per capita GDP of $1,968 in 2021. Bangladesh, with 170 million people, is also one of the world's most corrupt countries.

Most of the World Bank's money (your money) just ends up in the pockets of a few oligarchs who run Bangladesh.

Capital would flow into a large country like Bangladesh if it had a legal structure to support capitalism.

But the World Bank and IMF incentivize corruption. Yet incredibly, the World Bank boasts of its success in Bangladesh, saying: "Bangladesh has an impressive track record for growth and development, aspiring to be a middle-income country by its 50th birthday. The World Bank has supported Bangladesh since 1972, providing more than $30 billion in support."

The World Bank's website tells us: "Poverty declined [in Bangladesh] from 43.5 percent in 1991 to 14.3 percent in 2016, based on the international poverty line of $1.90 a day."

Wait. What!?

The international poverty line is an income of $1.90 per day?

The World Bank calls this success.

Now let's look at what's happening in Somalia – which owes the IMF and World Bank about $5 billion.

This is a country of 15 million people. Somalia's per capita GDP is $309 per year.

This $5 billion Somalia owes to the IMF and World Bank divided by 15 million people is $333 per Somalian – more than the per capita GDP of the country.

Where is all this World Bank and IMF money going?

Obviously, straight into the pockets of the warlords who run Somalia – of "Black Hawk Down" fame.

The IMF and World Bank not helping – most likely hurting the people of Somalia by propping up the warlords, keeping them fat and happy.

Or how about Brazil?

Brazil has received $53 billion from the IMF since 1958.

Brazil's per capita GDP was $6,795 in 2020 compared to $63,543 for the U.S. Brazil is rife with corruption. Corruption scandals have engulfed three recent Presidents of Brazil.

Socialist President Luiz Inacio Lula da Silva was convicted of taking $1,000,000 in kickbacks in 2017.

His successor Dilma Rousseff was impeached and removed from office for falsifying official government numbers in order to hide the magnitude of the federal budget deficit.

Her successor Michel Temer was arrested on charges of funneling $470 million to a criminal organization he led. He is accused of a lengthy list of crimes, including accepting $1.5 million in kickbacks from a construction company, election fraud, and campaign finance fraud.

Temer was initially arrested in connection with a massive money laundering scheme known as "Operation Car Wash" that involved former President Lula and the embezzlement of upwards of $13 billion.

So that's what's happening in Brazil. $53 billion from the IMF (your tax money) has done nothing to clean up corruption in Brazil or to help the 212 million people of that country.

We see this in country after country where the IMF and World Bank are most heavily involved.

In fact, many people in Latin America see the IMF and World Bank as an American scheme to trap these countries in poverty – much the way the welfare system in America has trapped large swathes of our population in poverty. Dependency creates poverty over the long term. When you reward (incentivize) poverty, crime and corruption, you end up with more poverty, crime, and corruption.

This is what the IMF and World Bank are doing throughout the developing world – incentivizing corruption, propping up criminals in power, and not helping these countries set up functioning legal structures that would allow honest businesses to build and prosper.

This is no way to help the people of these countries. Crime and corruption are the highest forms of taxation, and hit poor people hardest.

Wherever the IMF and World Bank go, corruption, crime, cronyism, and poverty flourish. The IMF and World Bank are like drug pushers – the drug being free money for corrupt oligarchs.

Their goal is to get poor countries addicted to this "free money" because this money really isn't free. It comes with strings. You get free money so long as you do what bureaucrats at the World Bank and IMF want you to do.

The IMF and World Bank create perpetual dependence which creates perpetual poverty. But mostly the money just goes to the politically connected.

Perhaps the IMF and World Bank are not intending to be a scheme by the United States and Europe to keep the rest of the world in poverty. But that's how it's working out. The road to Hell is paved with good intentions – assuming the intentions are good. A big assumption.

A less charitable interpretation: By exacerbating problems and creating more dependency, bureaucrats at the IMF and World Bank ensure they continue to have jobs and guaranteed paychecks for life. The last thing these bureaucrats would want to do is solve the problem and work themselves out of a job. The World Bank and IMF mostly serve as jobs programs for bureaucrats at these institutions.

Keep in mind that most of these government bureaucrats at the IMF and World Bank have never started a business, never had to survive in the private sector. They have no idea how to read a balance sheet or assess the merits of an entrepreneurial enterprise.

They have absolutely no idea how to create a product or provide a service that anyone would want to buy. They have no clue how wealth is created. They have never been held accountable for failure.

They also tend to have a socialistic, anti-capitalist mindset. All they know how to do hand out taxpayer money and boss people around.

The Director of the United Nations World Food Program David Beasley told CNN that it was time for the ultra-rich to pay more money to the United Nations and similar international organizations, saying that a small percentage of Elon Musk's fortune could solve world hunger. Beasley said he needs $6 billion to keep 42 million people from starving – "$6 billion to help 42 million people that are literally going to die if we don't reach them."

Elon answered in a tweet saying that he would happily sell $6 billion of his Tesla stock and contribute the money to the UN's World Food Program "if WFP can describe on this Twitter thread exactly how $6B will solve world hunger."

Elon went on to say that the UN's plan must include "open source accounting, so the public sees precisely how the money is spent," adding that Beasley must publish WFP's current and proposed spending plan in detail. "Sunlight is a wonderful thing," noted Musk.

Another Twitter user named Dr. Eli Gold tweeted: "In 2020

the UN World Food Program (WFP) raised $8.4B. How come it didn't 'solve world hunger'?"

In yet another tweet, Elon linked to a 2015 Express report alleging that UN peacekeepers were sexually abusing children in the Central African Republic in 2014. "What happened here?" Musk asked.

It's clear Elon is serious about his offers to contribute to real plans that make sense. For example, he has pledged to give away $150 million in prizes for technologies that remove carbon from the atmosphere.

The problem with the IMF, the World Bank, the United Nations, and government organizations in general, is they are not actually trying to solve problems.

They are out to create more problems for them to talk about, so they can get more money.

When private businesses fail, they go bankrupt and disappear.

When government agencies fail, they say it's because they don't have enough money. "Give us more money. Then we'll solve the problem," they say.

The more government programs fail, the bigger they get. But the problem is never solved. The problem always gets worse.

There's no economic incentive for these government agencies to fix the problem they were set up to fix. Their economic incentive is for the problem never to be fixed, actually always to get worse.

Government agencies are incentivized to fail.

These government agencies and international organizations really aren't trying to solve problems. They just want more power and more money. The power to give away money to their friends gives them power over people – gives them power to boss people around.

The people who receive money from the IMF and World Bank are not entrepreneurs with viable business plans. The people who receive the money are the politically connected.

After more than half a century of failure by the IMF and World Bank, many in the Third World are saying they no longer want to be part of this corrupt system. They are looking for new answers.

El Salvador, for example, is saying "Maybe one answer is Bitcoin."

El Salvador Adopts Bitcoin as Legal Tender

On September 7, 2021, El Salvador became the world's first country to adopt bitcoin as legal tender, thanks to the leadership of El Salvador's charismatic young President Nayib Bukele.

Bukele was elected President in 2016. He is libertarian-leaning who often retweets statements made by Senator Rand Paul.

As of this writing, El Salvador holds about 2,000 bitcoins.

The other official currency in El Salvador is the dollar.

By adopting bitcoin as legal tender, El Salvador appears to be charting a path for other poor countries to get out from under the U.S. dollar and out from under bureaucratic meddling by the IMF and World Bank.

In response to the news, the IMF began threatening El Salvador. The IMF issued a statement saying it had "serious economic and legal concerns" regarding El Salvador adopting bitcoin as legal tender, and suggested the move would "cloud the outlook" for further IMF support for the country, to include increasing interest rates on El Salvador's outstanding loans from the IMF.

"Adoption of bitcoin as legal tender raises a number of macroeconomic, financial and legal issues that require very careful analysis," IMF spokesman Gerry Rice told reporters in a press briefing. "We are following developments closely, and we'll continue our consultations with the authorities," Rice intoned somberly.

U.S. banks instantly increased interest rates on El Salvador's debt, citing concerns expressed by the IMF.

"We see the bitcoin headlines out of El Salvador as noise that could complicate discussions with the IMF," Citi Group's Donato Guarino told clients in a note, according to Reuters, saying Citi would "underweight the bank's exposure in El Salvador."

The blowback El Salvador received from the IMF and the banking community was ferocious, many appearing to root for El Salvador's failure for even daring to try a new approach.

In January of 2021, during the lead-up to El Salvador's adoption of bitcoin as legal tender, the President of the European Union

Central Bank Christine Lagarde delivered this unhinged rant against Bitcoin:

> It's a speculative asset by any account. For those who had assumed that it might turn into a currency, terribly sorry, but this is an asset and it's a highly speculative asset, which has conducted some funny business and some interesting and totally reprehensible money laundering activity.
>
> I think that there are criminal investigations that have taken place; I'm sure will continue to take place that demonstrate it very clearly. And there has to be regulations and this has to be applied and agreed upon. And it's a matter that has to be agreed upon at a global level because, you know, **if there is an escape, that escape will be used**.
>
> So I think it needs to be, if anything, it shows that global cooperation, multilateral action is absolutely needed whether it's initiated by the G7 and moved into the G20 and then enlarged, but it's something that needs to be addressed. [28]

The key phrase by Legarde is: "**If there is an escape, that escape will be used**."

They don't want El Salvador to leave the clutches of the IMF, the World Bank, or the "New World Order."

They want El Salvador dependent on them. Legarde and leaders of these international organizations are not the least bit curious about why El Salvador might choose this path. These bureaucrats and bankers are just furious with El Salvador for choosing freedom and independence over dependence on them.

The IMF has not let up with its attacks on El Salvador.

The IMF demanded that El Salvador dissolve the $150 million bitcoin trust fund it created and convert their bitcoin back to dollars.

It's all about the dollar, you see.

The IMF called on El Salvador to rescind its offer to give $30 worth of bitcoin to every adult citizen of El Salvador who uses the "Chivo" Bitcoin and Lightning wallet. The $30 and free Chivo wallet are aimed at educating El Salvadorans about Bitcoin and the Lightning Network.

Almost all households in El Salvador are now using the Chivo

---

[28] Transcribed from video posted by Reuters. "ECB's Lagarde Calls for Regulating Bitcoin's 'Funny Business.'" January 13, 2021.

wallet and were very pleased it came loaded with $30 worth of Bitcoin.

$30 is a lot of money for many El Salvadorans who don't even qualify for bank accounts.

So how has El Salvador's adoption of bitcoin as legal tender worked out for Bukele politically?

Well, according to the Gallup organization, Bukele is supported by 85 percent of El Salvadorans.

The IMF, however, continues to call on President Bukele to cancel El Salvador's use of the "Chivo" wallet. Or, if used, it should only be used for U.S. dollars, not Bitcoin.

"In the near-term the actual costs of implementing Chivo and operationalizing the Bitcoin law exceed potential benefits," warns the IMF.

The problem for the IMF is Chivo and Bitcoin are implemented. And El Salvadorans love it.

El Salvador's Treasury Minister Alejandro Zelaya answered the IMF by saying: "No international organization is going to make us do anything, anything at all."

Zelaya said El Salvador's adoption of bitcoin as legal tender reestablishes the "sovereignty" of El Salvador. "Countries are sovereign nations and they make sovereign decisions about public policy," he added.

Zelaya further noted that El Salvador has complied with all international financial and money laundering rules.

Meanwhile, McDonald's, Starbucks, Pizza Hut and other major U.S. corporations are accepting bitcoin as payment from customers who use El Salvador's Chivo wallet.

President Bukele told the IMF El Salvador's adoption of Bitcoin and launch of the Chivo wallet are helping many El Salvadorans who have never held bank accounts.

He also talks about increased tourism to El Salvador from Bitcoin enthusiasts and by those curious to see how Bitcoin is working in El Salvador.

El Salvador still owes the IMF $1.3 billion, which President Bukele says El Salvador will pay off with its new volcano-powered bitcoin mining operations.

At the base of El Salvador's Conchaga volcano, President Bukele says he and his government will build a new city called Bitcoin City.

The city will use the Volcano's geothermal energy to power bitcoin mining and the city's power grid. So this will be sustainable green energy. No one will be able to criticize Bitcoin City for excessive energy consumption, or for polluting the air, because nothing stops a volcano. But we can tap into a volcano for power.

The Conchaga volcano is located in southeastern El Salvador and overlooks the Gulf of Fonseca. The building of Bitcoin City will be funded with Bitcoin-backed bonds. Bukele says the only tax in Bitcoin City will be a value-added tax (VAT).

Bukele says: "Invest here and make all the money you want. This is a fully ecological city that works and is energized by a volcano."

Half of the VAT tax collected will be used to fund bonds issued to build the city and pay off the IMF, while the other half will pay for infrastructure and services such as garbage collection, says Bukele, who thinks outside the box.

Bukele estimates that infrastructure for the city will cost about 300,000 bitcoins. He believes El Salvador will become the Hong Kong or Singapore of Latin America, "but better."

The U.S. dollar continues also to be legal tender in El Salvador. The two currencies can compete with each other. The citizens can use whichever currency they think is best.

Let the market decide the best money. That's how freedom works. So it's Austrian school economics now in El Salvador. More and more, El Salvadorans are loving their country's independence.

As this book was going to press, the Central African Republic became the second country to adopt Bitcoin as legal tender.

What Countries Will be Next to Adopt Bitcoin as Legal Tender?

Bitcoin adoption is likely to gain traction in the poorest countries first – countries with shaky or collapsed economic and political systems. The most likely early candidates are El Salvador's neighbors in Latin America.

The day after Bitcoin's adoption as legal tender in El Salvador passed into law, a congressman in Panama named Gabriel Silva promised to introduce legislation to make bitcoin legal tender in Panama, saying in a press statement: "This is important. And Panama cannot be left behind. If we want to be a true technology and entrepreneurship hub, we have to support cryptocurrencies. We will be preparing a proposal to present at the Assembly. If you are interested in building it, you can contact me."

Legislation is moving now forward in Panama to make bitcoin legal tender. In Paraguay, a bill is gaining support to regulate the mining and trading of bitcoin and other crypto assets, which would be a step toward making bitcoin legal tender.

Paraguayan lawmaker Carlitos Rejala, who says he's running for President of Paraguay, is promising to make Bitcoin the official currency of Paraguay. Rejala tweeted: "Our country needs to advance hand and hand with the new generation. The moment has come, our moment. This week we start with an important project to innovate Paraguay in front of the world."

Rejala proposes using Paraguay's hydropower capabilities to mine Bitcoin.

Surprisingly, Cuba is now allowing its people to use cryptocurrencies. Citizens can use cryptocurrencies to transfer money and can even be paid for their work with crypto. One result of this is more than 400 Western Union offices have closed across Cuba. Currency exchanges are also closing.

In September of 2021, Ukraine's parliament passed a law by a near-unanimous vote to legalize and regulate cryptocurrency.

Ukraine formed a Ministry of Digital Transformation. This was before Russian dictator Vladimir Putin launched his invasion of Ukraine in February of 2022.

Quoted by *The New York Times*, Ukraine's deputy minister Alexander Bornyakov says: "The big idea is to become one of the top jurisdictions in the world for crypto companies. We believe this is the new economy, this is the future, and we believe this is something that is going to boost our economy."

As I write these words, Ukraine is fighting for its existence. On February 26, 2022, Ukraine's official Twitter account began to actively solicit Bitcoin, ETH, and crypto asset donations.

"Stand with the people of Ukraine. Now accepting cryptocurrency donations. Bitcoin, Ethereum and USDT," proclaimed Ukraine's Twitter account. It provided the following BTC wallet address:

0x165CD37b4C644C2921454429E7F9358d18A45e14

And this is Ukraine's address for ETH and USDT stablecoin

donations: 0x165CD37b4C644C2921454429E7F9358d18A45e14

Tens of millions of dollars worth of bitcoin, ETH and USDT stablecoins poured in to help Ukraine defend itself. Ukraine says the arrival of these crypto asset donations has been critical to keeping Ukraine alive.

Bitcoin is also gaining enormous traction in Africa, where there's a population of 1.3 billion people. The Central African Republic became the second country to adopt bitcoin as legal tender. Africa is the world's poorest continent, with a median per capita GDP of $1,483 in 2020.

Somalia's annual per capita GDP is $309. Because of hyperinflation, lack of access to banking, and dysfunctional economic and political systems, nearly 3 percent of all transactions in Africa are now conducted using Bitcoin. And because so many Africans are unbanked, they are used to transacting on their phones with digital wallets. So it's an easy transition to Bitcoin.

The United States will likely be last to adopt bitcoin as legal tender because we want to preserve the dollar as the world reserve currency. For reasons explained earlier, this status as the world reserve currency allows us to offload much of our national debt to the world's poorer countries – those outside the G7, G8 or G20.

But the world is growing fed up with this arrangement. El Salvador is the crack in the dam. Many other countries are following suit. A trickle is turning into a flood.

The President of the European Union Central Bank Christine Lagarde revealed herself when she warned that Bitcoin is the world's escape from the global economic prison elite bankers have been trying to build since the end of World War II. **"If there is an escape, that escape will be used,"** she complained. Exactly!

Lagarde had hoped there would be no escape. She's exasperated there is an escape. Bitcoin is an uncensorable, unconfiscatable, unstoppable, honest, borderless currency.

Bitcoin allows the struggling person in Africa, Latin America, Asia, South Bronx, or anywhere to say "F**k You!" to Christine Lagarde and what she hoped would be her New World Order.

But Legarde's New World Order is not an arrangement that helps average people. Her New World Order only helps well-positioned bankers and politicians – like her. Bitcoin fixes this. Bitcoin levels the playing field.

CHAPTER 20

But Aren't Rogue Regimes Using Bitcoin to Escape U.S. Sanctions?

An objection we often hear raised about Bitcoin is rogue regimes such as North Korea, Russia, and Iran are mining and using bitcoin to evade crippling economic sanctions by the United States and NATO.

U.S. intelligence agencies report that North Korea appears to have extensive bitcoin mining operations.

The U.S. Justice Department reports that North Korea has stolen at least $400 billion in bitcoin by hacking into cryptocurrency exchanges and computers and stealing private keys.

In all, North Korea has amassed more than $2 billion worth of bitcoin with its mining and cybertheft operations, according to a report by the United Nations.

Meanwhile, approximately 4.5 percent of the world's bitcoin mining operations are in Iran.

In late 2021, Russia's dictator Vladimir Putin declared he wants Russia to be the world's bitcoin mining capital. It's highly doubtful this will happen given Putin's invasion of Ukraine. What miners would want to relocate in Russia under Putin's murderous regime?

Though approximately 12 percent of the world's bitcoin mining is based in Russia as of this writing, I expect Russia's bitcoin miners will be looking to leave Russia for more free and civilized locations so long as psychopath Putin is running the country.

Bitcoin miners tend to go where freedom is. Bitcoin is the Freedom Machine.

But U.S. Senator Elizabeth Warren and others in Congress are calling for a ban on Bitcoin by the United States and NATO. They claim the existence of Bitcoin is a national security threat.

There's only one problem with this.

Bitcoin can't be banned. Bitcoin is a decentralized protocol in cyberspace distributed on more than 1,000,000 computers (nodes and miners) worldwide. No one owns or controls Bitcoin. So there's no owner of the network government can target. Bitcoin is governed by math and automated protocols, not humans.

Banning Bitcoin is like trying to ban air. It's very difficult to do, and you would not want to ban it if you could.

This is why decentralization is so important. With more than 150 million users and 350 million transactions taking place on the Bitcoin network each day, Bitcoin is probably unbannable at this point.

Estimates are that more than 45 million Americans own some bitcoin. Only a very self-destructive or clueless politician, like Elizabeth Warren, will want to risk alienating 45 million American voters by trying to ban Bitcoin at this point. And this number is growing every day.

The bigger and more decentralized the Bitcoin network becomes, the less bannable it becomes.

Will Bitcoin be used by rogue regimes to evade U.S. sanctions?

Certainly. And this is happening.

But tens of millions of dollars worth of bitcoin and other cyrpo assets have also poured into Ukraine to help Ukraine protect itself from Putin's invasion.

Unlike Senator Elizabeth Warren, Ukraine's not trying to ban Bitcoin or crypto. Ukraine continues to say it wants to make Bitcoin a key part of Ukraine's monetary system. Ukraine says it wants to be the Bitcoin mining capital of the world.

Does Putin also have access to Bitcoin?

Sure.

Bitcoin is a public resource anyone can access – including the dictator of North Korea and murderous thug Putin. Yes, even serial killers, child rapists, and genocidal maniacs can use Bitcoin. But I suspect, in the final analysis, Bitcoin benefits countries that aspire to be free far more than dictatorships.

I've never thought economic sanctions and blockades to be effective tools for dealing with rogue regimes anyway.

Have economic sanctions worked with Cuba?

The Communist regime established by Fidel Castro in 1959 is still in place despite the harshest economic sanctions we could impose on the island country. Sanctions hurt the people, but actually serve to entrench the regime.

Sanctions allowed the regime to point to the United States as the source of Cuba's economic problems, not the regime's Communist ideology.

There is no example in history we can point to where sanctions have succeeded in achieving what we hoped sanctions would achieve. Never have sanctions produced better behavior by the dictator, the genocidal maniac, or the sanctioned country.

Sanctions have always produced worse behavior by the regime targeted. Sanctions do hurt the people in these countries. Sanctions also hurt us because sanctions restrict trade and commerce.

Trade and commerce are what produce wealth. When people are focused on generating wealth for themselves through lawful economic activity, this tends to produce peace.

When there's poverty and economic instability, this tends to produce desperation, which produces crime and war. When people are prosperous, they don't want war because war threatens their prosperity.

So the result of sanctions is usually war.

Extreme economic sanctions against Germany following World War I produced Hitler and World War II, resulting in the death of 100,000,000 people.

President Franklin Roosevelt put extreme economic sanctions on Japan, which triggered Japan's attack on Pearl Harbor. Sanctions on Japan included the Export Control Act in July of 1940, imposed because of Japan's aggression against China and much of Asia.

Was Imperial Japan a world menace?

Absolutely. Imperial Japan was as brutal and genocidal as Hitler and Stalin.

But Japan's response to sanctions was to form an alliance with Hitler in September of 1940. President Roosevelt answered with an economic embargo against Japan in October of 1940, and then froze all Japanese assets he could get a hold of in July of 1941.

Japan's response: To attack Pearl Harbor on December 7, 1941.

Economic sanctions, embargoes, and cutting off a country's access to trade is almost always counterproductive, often leads to war. Closing the door to economic participation cannot help but produce hostility. Trade and commerce tend to produce peace and prosperity. Not always, but usually.

Objecting to Bitcoin on the grounds that Bitcoin gives North

Korea, Russia and other rogue regimes access to money is akin to complaining that Kim Jong-un and Vladimir Putin have access to air. Bitcoin is neutral. Bitcoin takes no sides.

Bitcoin is a tool, like a gun is a tool. A gun can be used for good or evil. When a criminal uses a gun to kill someone, that's not the fault of the gun. The criminal is the problem, not the gun.

Outlawing guns means only outlaws will have guns. We can't prevent criminals from having guns. The best we can do is ensure everyone has access to guns so they can protect themselves.

Bitcoin is math.

Math can be used for good or evil. Math is used by rogue regimes to build nuclear missiles. So should we try to ban math?

That's what attempts to ban Bitcoin really amount to – attempts to ban math.

Most people want to be part of the legal economy. But if the United States were ever to make it impossible for people to own bitcoin legally, people will own bitcoin illegally.

Bitcoin is now a worldwide monetary network. Bitcoin has no headquarters that can be attacked, no fortifications that can be overcome with force. There's nothing to bomb with Bitcoin.

In the United States, only daffy Senator Elizabeth Warren and a few other Luddites appear even interested in banning Bitcoin. For the most part, serious policymakers are focused on how best to incorporate Bitcoin into the legal U.S. economic and financial framework.

The Chairman of the U.S. Federal Reserve Jerome Powell has said Bitcoin can't be stopped. Powell has not expressed any interest in banning Bitcoin. His comments on the asset have been more along the lines of cautioning investors about price volatility.

The Chairman of the Securities Exchange Commission Gary Gensler taught a course at MIT on Bitcoin and is favorably disposed to the asset. He is more focused on making sure the exchanges have adequate safeguards to protect investors.

At no point has Gensler said Bitcoin should be banned. He has expressed concern about altcoins.

Gensler sees Bitcoin as an asset, much like gold.

In a June 2022 interview on CNBC with Jim Cramer, Gensler said that Bitcoin is the only crypto asset he's seen that qualifies as a "commodity" because it's the only truly decentralized asset. All the other cryptos look and behave like companies, are securities, and so fall under the jurisdiction of the SEC, says Gensler.

Since no one owns or controls Bitcoin, there's no one at Bitcoin HQ who the SEC can regulate, any more than the SEC can regulate air or sand. Bitcoin just now exists.

The SEC is suing XRP Ripple and a number of altcoins. But Bitcoin cannot be sued because no one owns or controls Bitcoin. The SEC cannot sue a mathematical algorithm or protocol that just exists on its own in cyberspace.

Bitcoin is morally neutral, just as air is morally neutral.

We don't deal with bad actors by trying to ban air, which everyone needs.

We find other ways to deal with bad actors. Trying to ban Bitcoin is cutting off our nose to spite our face.

About 35 percent of the world's bitcoin mining is in the United States, which has become the world leader in bitcoin mining since China's ban on bitcoin mining in the summer of 2021.

China's decision to ban bitcoin mining will likely prove to be a multi-trillion-dollar strategic blunder by China. But that's been good for the United States.

Bitcoin is the world's greatest force for liberty.

Bitcoin puts pressure on countries to be free, civilized places to live, or people can just carry their wealth on their phones and leave for a better place . . . or carry their wealth on a piece of paper, or in their head if they can remember a 12-word keycode recovery phrase.

The United States should feel good about being the bitcoin mining capital of the world.

Why would the U.S. want to give up this position?

Why chase Bitcoin out of the United States into the welcoming arms of Putin?

On one level, Bitcoin does threaten the position of the U.S. dollar as the world reserve currency. That's the primary concern expressed by some U.S. policymakers.

I view it differently.

Bitcoin imposes discipline on the U.S. dollar. The U.S. government cannot just keep printing money like confetti if bitcoin is the alternative money, the honest money. People are willing to put up with a certain level of inflation, perhaps 2-3 percent, to have the convenience that fiat money offers.

But when money printing by the Fed becomes too wild, the dollar starts looking less and less attractive. People start looking for alternatives.

The existence of Bitcoin puts pressure on the U.S. government to curtail its out-of-control money printing and spending. This holds out the prospect of allowing the U.S. dollar to keep its position as the world reserve fiat currency.

That's good for the United States.

By imposing discipline on the Fed's money printing press, Bitcoin actually helps the dollar by keeping the dollar honest and strong relative to other fiat currencies.

But this point is almost academic because the U.S. government cannot ban Bitcoin even if it wanted to.

There is no way for the U.S. government to stop Russia, North Korea, Iran, or anyone else from participating in the Bitcoin monetary network – anymore than we can block these countries from accessing air or math. All the U.S. government can do with an effort to ban Bitcoin is hurt American citizens.

The only way we could stop serial killers like Ted Bundy and John Gacy from accessing air and math was to execute them. But it's unlikely we can do that to the Russian dictator without launching World War III. And we can't do that to North Korea without starting a war with China – again, launching World War III.

Even if we had World War III, Bitcoin would continue to exist, would likely thrive. Bitcoin is exactly what everyone needs if there is World War III.

To access Bitcoin, all anyone needs is an internet connection. All that's needed for an internet connection is two computers talking to each other.

The only way to ban Bitcoin is to ban access to the internet.

And actually, even if the entire internet is destroyed, if one person has a computer with a complete copy of the Bitcoin blockchain ledger, Bitcoin will exist – can then be brought back online as soon as a computer network exists again.

My guess is China will soon see its ban on bitcoin mining was a serious strategic blunder, and will reverse course on Bitcoin. China has banned bitcoin mining and trading a number of times in Bitcoin's history, but then gave up.

India tried to ban Bitcoin in 2018, 2019, and 2020 – then stopped trying to ban it in 2022 because they saw the futility. India is now writing regulations to treat Bitcoin and other cryptos as assets for the purpose of taxation. So India, with its 1.4 billion people, has surrendered to the reality of Bitcoin.

Elon Musk's Space X is launching rockets into space about every 14 days. As of this writing, he has strung up about 2,000 satellites for his Starlink internet system.

This will allow anyone to access cheap high-speed internet from anywhere in the world without any need for an earth-based server.

You'll be able to access the internet from Antarctica, the top of Mount Everest, the middle of the Rain Forest, the Sahara Desert, or anywhere on earth.

This will make Bitcoin even more impossible to stop because Bitcoin is the native currency of the internet. If you have an internet connection, you have access to Bitcoin.

This reality also puts pressure on the governments of countries to make their countries attractive places to live because Bitcoin makes it so easy for people to just pack up and move somewhere else. That's why Bitcoin is the world's greatest freedom machine.

Calls by Senator Elizabeth Warren and others to ban Bitcoin have become laughably moot.

If the U.S. wants to stay on the cutting-edge of technological innovation; if the U.S. wants to be the place where free people live; if the U.S. wants to be the place where capital flows in instead of flowing out; the U.S. should be encouraging bitcoin miners to set up shop here, should welcome Bitcoin.

CHAPTER 21

Bitcoin Is Your Defense Against Big Tech's Emerging Push-Button Totalitarianism

Technology provides enormous benefits. The computer and internet age have powered exponential gains in productivity and created wealth that was unimaginable as recently as 1990. Technology enables us to achieve great breakthroughs in health, medicine, and longevity. The benefits of technology are obvious.

But Big Tech is also proving to be the greatest threat to liberty in human history.

The way technology developing, and the way its power is being consolidated into the hands of a few companies make Big Tech extraordinarily dangerous and a grave threat to our freedom.

Nation states are now being replaced by the titans of tech. Our constitutional democracy, our representative republic, is being overridden by our Big Tech overlords.

Powered by artificial intelligence (AI), Google and Microsoft are tracking every keystroke on your computer.

All your Google searches are being recorded and stored. Google knows everywhere you've been and exactly when you've been there and why. AI algorithms are constantly combing through all this data so these companies can serve us with precisely targeted ads. You are the primary product of these big tech companies. Their business model is to collect and harness data about you for profit.

How much does Google know about you?

Well, I downloaded all the data Google has on me, which Google allows anyone to do. It amounted to 3 GB of data, which is about 2.5 million pages of material.

This is the digital surveillance system that the computer engineer and cryptographer David Chaum warned us about in the 1980s.

Of course, Big Tech will counter that we sign away our privacy

213

when we hit that button that says we agree to their "terms and conditions."

Analogous to Shylock's bargain in Shakespeare's *The Merchant of Venice*, few are paying attention to the details or implications of what they are signing away when they hit the button agreeing in "terms and conditions."

People just know they are gaining access to the social media site, have a GPS that works, and are gaining better functionality of apps they want to use.

Think of the power this gives Google over us, over you.

Google knows exactly what the stock market will do tomorrow because it can track searches precisely. Google knows all your usernames and passwords. Google can seize all your assets at any time.

Google can blackmail you. Google can shut down any business with the flick of a switch. Google has the power to bankrupt the entire population at any moment.

"But government will protect us from all this," you might counter.

Google, if it wants to, can do the same to every politician, every government regulator, and all of law enforcement.

Google can shut down the power grid.

Why have we allowed one company to gain so much power?

The answer is simple. Google achieved this immense power by giving us the convenience that we all want. The same can be said of the power we've willingly given to Apple, Microsoft, Amazon, Facebook and a few big tech companies.

All these big tech companies have your usernames and passwords. They know everything about you.

Microsoft can read all your Microsoft documents stored in Microsoft's Azure cloud.

We are living in a system that Edward Snowden has called "turnkey totalitarianism."

Information is power. There is no commodity more valuable than information. If you know the combination to the vault, you can access the money.

The big tech companies (especially Google) have all the information they need to instantly destroy civilization if they want to. And they certainly have the power to control every politician, decide the outcome of any election, control the information flow across the internet, and move government policy in any direction they choose – especially when they collude, as appears to be happening.

The Panopticon

The 18th Century British philosopher Jeremy Bentham designed a panopticon prison that allowed the entire prison population to be observed and controlled by just one guard.

The basic structure involved a circular rotunda with a guard tower in the center. The cells were placed around the perimeter so the guard could easily see what was happening in each cell quickly. There was a common area in the center with no place to hide.

Although the guard could not watch all prisoners all the time, his power came from the fact that the prisoners could not tell when they were being watched. So they had to behave as if they were being watched at all times.

The word panopticon derives from the Greek word *panoptes,* which means "all seeing."

Bentham said his designs could be applied to schools, hospitals, asylums, factories, workplaces, and all of society. If people believe they are being watched, they will believe they must follow the rules.

This was a big theme of George Orwell's classic novel *Nineteen Eighty-Four*, about a dystopian totalitarian surveillance society.

Orwell wrote:

> There was of course no way of knowing whether you were being watched at any given moment. How often, or on what system, the Thought Police plugged in on any individual wire was guesswork . . . You had to live – did live, from habit that became instinct – in the assumption that every sound you made was overheard, and, except in darkness, every movement scrutinized.

Modern movies based on this total surveillance theme include *Squid Game, Cube, Minority Report, Enemy of the State, Black Mirror, Running Man, Hunger Games.*

The watchtower at the center of Bentham's panopticon prison today has become surveillance cameras in every area of life. Everywhere you go, there's a surveillance camera watching you.

Everyone has a Smart phone camera. We have security cameras in our homes to protect us from home invaders, but the cameras also watch us 24/7.

Cameras inside modern cars now monitor your behavior as you drive – alert you when you are not paying attention.

Breathalyzers are being proposed for cars to prevent you from driving drunk. Your car will administer a breathalyzer test that you must pass before you can start your car.

All this data on you -- your every movement, your every keystroke, your every communication, your every passing thought – is being collected and organized by Big Tech's AI-powered algorithms, which then will predict your future behavior.

We are now living in Steven Spielberg's movie *Minority Report*.

How Big Tech is Destroying Our Constitutional Republic

Dr. Robert Epstein, the Editor-in-Chief of *Psychology Today*, testified before the U.S. Senate's Judiciary Committee in June of 2019 about his research on the impact Google is having on elections.

Dr. Epstein has a PhD in Psychology from Harvard University. He is the author of 15 books and more than 300 articles on artificial intelligence and related topics.

"Our research leaves little doubt about whether Google has the ability to control voters," Epstein told the Senate. "In laboratory and online experiments conducted in the United States, we were able to boost the proportion of people who favored any candidate by between 37 and 63 percent after just one search session."

According to Epstein, Google is manipulating "upwards of 15 million votes" in Presidential elections with its search algorithms and information about candidates that Google chooses to present to voters, or hide from voters.

Epstein talked to the Senate committee about the "Search Engine Manipulation Effect" (SEME), which he said "is one of the most powerful forms of influence ever discovered in the behavioral sciences, and it is especially dangerous because it is invisible to people – 'subliminal' in effect. It leaves people thinking they have made up their own minds, which is very much an illusion."

Epstein testified that, according to research done by his team, "biased search results can easily produce shifts in the opinions and voting preferences of undecided voters by 20 percent or more – up to 80 percent in some demographic groups."

SEME is an example of an "ephemeral experience," said Epstein, "and that's a phrase you'll find in internal emails that have leaked from Google recently. A growing body of evidence suggests that Google employees deliberately engineer ephemeral experiences to change people's thinking."

Here are some bullet point quotes from Epstein's testimony before the U.S. Senate Judiciary Committee on June 19, 2019:

- On Election Day in 2018, the "Go Vote" reminder Google displayed on its home page gave one political party between 800,000 and 4.6 million more votes than it gave the other party. Those numbers might seem impossible, but I published my analysis in January 2019 (Epstein, 2019a), and it is quite conservative. Google's data analysts presumably performed the same calculations I did before the company decided to post its prompt. In other words, Google's "Go Vote" prompt was not a public service; it was vote manipulation.

- In the weeks leading up to the 2018 election, bias in Google's search results may have shifted upwards of 78.2 million votes to the candidates of one political party (spread across hundreds of local and regional races). This number is based on data captured by my 2018 monitoring system, which preserved more than 47,000 election-related searches on Google, Bing, and Yahoo, along with the nearly 400,000 web pages to which the search results linked. Strong political bias toward one party was evident, once again, in Google searches (Epstein & Williams, 2019).

- My recent research demonstrates that Google's "autocomplete" search suggestions can turn a 50/50 split among undecided voters into a 90/10 split without people's awareness (Epstein, Mohr, & Martinez, 2018). A growing body of evidence suggests that Google is manipulating people's thinking and behavior from the very first character people type into the search box.

- Google has likely been determining the outcomes of upwards of 25 percent of the national elections worldwide since at least 2015. This is because many races are very close and because Google's persuasive technologies are very powerful (Epstein & Robertson, 2015a). [29]

Epstein noted that he's a lifelong Democrat, but told the Senate

---

[29] Dr. Robert Epstein, Senate Judiciary Committee Transcript, June 19, 2019.

that "No single entity – especially a private company that is not accountable to the public – should have such power."

There' is little doubt about Google's partisan political allegiance.

Former Google CEO, Eric Schmidt, offered in writing to run Hillary Clinton's tech campaign in 2016.

Hillary Clinton's Chief Technology Officer was a woman named Stephanie Hannon, a top executive at Google. Google's employees and PACs have contributed $21 million to Presidential and Congressional candidates since 2019, 93 percent to Democrats.

The biggest recipient of Google's money in 2020 was Joe Biden and Democrat super PACs.

And it's not just Google.

Twitter and Facebook deplatformed the President of the United States because they disagreed with his political views. You might like or not like Donald Trump, but he was the duly elected President of the United States.

In the modern world, social media has become an essential communications tool, like the telephone.

If you don't have a social media account in today's world, you are almost a non-person. Without a social media account, it becomes very difficult to build a business, run for office, have a professional life, or maintain communication with your friends and family.

Under Federal law, Section 230 of the Telecommunications Act of 1996, social media companies are not publications, but are considered public utilities – like the telephone, electricity, and water.

Social media companies are not supposed to have editorial control, not supposed to be controlling the content of messages, not supposed to be censoring opinion. Social media is supposed to be a public square. In exchange for acting as a neutral public square, social media companies are immunized from defamation lawsuits under U.S. law.

But social media companies are not acting as public utility companies, not acting as an unbiased public square.

Instead, they are manipulating information, controlling what information we can see, shadow-banning opinions they don't like, and outright banning the accounts of people they disagree with – including the duly elected President of the United States.

If those who run social media companies see illegal activity taking place on their platforms, they should report it to law enforcement. But short of this, social media platforms are considered public utilities under federal law, like the telephone.

When the phone company provides service, it doesn't interrupt conversations it disagrees with. That's what a public utility is supposed to be – neutral.

Throughout America's history, the federal government has taken action to break up public utility companies that had gotten too big and powerful – the most famous analogous example being the breakup of AT&T in 1984 by the antitrust division of the U.S. Department of Justice.

It was considered dangerous to the survival of a free society to have one company with monopoly control of our nation's communications system.

But this is what's happened with Big Tech, but far more dangerous. At least AT&T wasn't trying to silence opinion it disagreed with. AT&T did not disconnect the phone calls of Republicans. AT&T did not prevent politicians and citizens it disagreed with from using the phone service.

Big tech companies see themselves as the ones actually running our society. Elections are for show, manipulated by Big Tech using AI algorithms.

Facebook founder and CEO Mark Zuckerberg spent $419 million of his own money to elect Joe Biden President. But far more important than the $419 million he spent was Facebook's manipulation of algorithms to shadow ban and censor opinions Mark Zuckerberg disagrees with.

Politicians have become irrelevant. They are now just compliant pawns of Big Tech.

These companies have become our overlords.

China's "Social Credit" System: A View of the Future

For a window into the future, let's take a look at China's "social credit" system.

China's social credit system is powered by Artificial Intelligence (AI) technology. In China, you are not just required to follow the law. You are expected to be a model citizen at all times. All of your activity is monitored by the state.

In China, citizens start with 1,000 social credit points.

Points are deducted if you engage in behavior the regime deems sub-optimal – such as play music too loud, loiter, be too argumentative, exceed the 40-minute daily time limit on social media, play too many video games, engage in frivolous spending, post an opinion the regime disagrees with.

You can also gain points by doing good deeds, such as contribute to approved charities.

You certainly do not want to express any concerns about human rights in China.

Those with good social credit scores gain privileges. Those with poor social credit scores lose privileges.

Those with sub-optimal social credit scores won't be able to board a train, buy a plane ticket, eat at a nice restaurant, stay at a hotel, are denied credit cards – certainly won't be able to get a good job. You can even have your dog taken away.

Punishments are calibrated depending on your score. Perhaps you'll be permitted to fly coach, but not First Class. Perhaps you'll be allowed to board a train, but not have a seat.

A teenager who is applying to universities can even be denied admission if one of her parents has a sub-optimal social credit score.

This happens!

Those with the best social credit scores are awarded privileges such as gaining access to priority health care, not having to put a deposit down for a rental apartment, get discounts on their utility bills, eat at the best restaurants, and have access to the best jobs.

If your social credit score drops too low, you end up on the government's "blacklist."

The regime encourages companies to consult its blacklist before hiring people or giving them contracts.

The social credit system even applies to dating websites.

China's biggest dating website, Baihe, encourages users to include their social credit scores in their profiles, and it boosts profiles of those with high social credit scores.

Businesses are also subject to China's social credit score system. China's corporations assist the regime in collecting and aggregating data on customers. China's corporations are effectively arms of the regime.

China first announced its plans to build its "social credit system" in 2014, hailing it as "an important component part of the Socialist market economy system and the social governance system."

A 2015 document produced by China's regime said its goal was to train people in the mindset that "keeping trust is glorious and breaking trust is disgraceful."

Those with high social credit scores are deemed "trustworthy." Those with lower social credit scores are deemed untrustworthy.

In 2018, China's Premier Li Keqiang boasted in a speech that "Those who lose credibility will find it hard to make a tiny step in society."

Social credit score rankings are compiled and maintained by China's National Development and Reform Commission (NDRC), the People's Bank of China, and China's court system.

Data is collected and aggregated from court records, academic records, medical records, credit reports, video surveillance, internet browsing history, social media posts, email and text message communications.

AI algorithms comb through all the data to assemble profiles of China's citizens.

Video surveillance is so extensive in China that the government can follow people across entire cities.

In a demonstration of its capabilities, China's officials showed the BBC how it could find one of BBC's reporters, John Sudworth, within seven minutes and follow his movements using its national network of 170 million cameras.

China's facial recognition software and AI algorithms can instantly identify a jaywalker. The jaywalker will then be fined and points deducted from that person's social credit score.

If you're arrested for an offense in China, your social credit score will be a major factor in your sentence. Human Rights Watch calls the China social credit score system "chilling."

But how bad can it get? What happens to you if you are at the bottom of China's social credit system?

Well, you end up like the Uyghur Muslims, other minorities, and political dissenters the Chinese regime deems undesirable.

Human Rights Watch estimates that upwards of two million people, mostly Uyghur Muslims, as well as other ethnic Turkic Muslims, Christians, political dissenters, and anyone who the regime doesn't like have been placed in secretive concentration camps, mostly in northwest China.

China calls these camps "vocational educational training centers." But they are actually slave labor camps. Rape of Uyghur women by guards is reported to be routine.

Uyghurs who have successfully completed "reeducation" training are rewarded by being used as slave labor at Foxconn's massive factory in Zhengzhou. Foxconn assembles most of Apple's iPhones. They also work as slave labor for many other U.S. companies, such as Nike.

These Uyghur workers are brought from slave labor camps to work in the factories and are kept in dormitories where they continue with their "reeducation." They are forbidden from practicing their religion. They are separated from their families and are subjected to brutal discipline.

China has also built the world's largest human organ transplant industry by harvesting the organs of healthy Uyghur Muslims and other political and religious prisoners – while alive, like in a horror movie.

These are the people at the bottom of China's "social credit" system. This is China's high-tech prison. China's entire population are inmates. But China's social credit system could never happen in America, right?

Well, perhaps not as horrifically as China's genocidal policies against the Uyghurs and others this regime deems socially undesirable. But elements of China's digital prison are in place and already being used in the United States.

Microsoft's China-Style "Social Credit" System

Let's take a look at Microsoft's seldom discussed program to make the criminal justice system in the United States more efficient, more effective, and more secure.

You might ask: Don't we want more efficient, more effective, more secure prions?

Sure we do. But what's more than a bit concerning are the eerie similarities between the digital prison system Microsoft has built and China's social credit system – and how easily this high-tech prison system can be extended to the rest of society, can be turned against you.

Take Microsoft's "Offender 360" program, described on Microsoft's website, which uses AI technology to "surveil, predict and analyze the correctional pipeline."

The information in this section is taken directly from Microsoft's website. Just type "Microsoft Offender 360" into Google and you'll find it. Microsoft boasts about the efficiency of the criminal justice system it's built.

This system aggregates every piece of data on an inmate – history, photos, videos, identifying marks, and behavior history to control the inmate and predict future behavior by the inmate.

Video cameras track the inmate's every movement. This data is analyzed by AI algorithms to determine where the inmate should be secured and how the inmate should be treated.

Should the inmate be put in maximum security, minimum security, or something in between?

This data is also used at parole hearings to determine whether the inmate can be released into society or is likely to become a repeat offender. Prisoners receive privileges and punishments depending on their behavior – a type of social credit score.

On one level, all this sounds fine. After all, we're talking about the prison system. But the technology and how it can be used to monitor, track and control all of society deserves our attention.

Microsoft has a similar program called "Youth 360" that collects and consolidates all data about the young offender, including school records, medical history, behavior history, family background – any and all data that can be collected. The system hosts a "Youth Assessment and Screen Instrument" to build a profile of the youth. Risk scores are created.

A third system is called "Pretrial 360."

This system offers courts case management and predictive analytics to determine a defendant's risk to the community when setting bail. Pretrial 360 centralizes data from criminal records, jails, police departments, job history, academic records, social media posts, and other data sources. This data is analyzed by AI algorithms.

A risk profile of the defendant is then produced based on that defendant's history.

Guided by AI algorithms, the courts can more quickly assess whether a defendant is likely to skip trial and commit additional crimes. Low-risk defendants can be released to supervision by a parole officer. The parole officer can then use the software to add additional information to the defendant's permanent profile.

Algorithms can also be used to calculate sentences.

The meaning of the number "360" in each of these products is that Microsoft is creating a full "360-degree" picture of each person in the criminal justice system.

This profile never goes away. You never get to start over. You never get a clean slate. Microsoft says its technology is simply making the criminal justice system more efficient. The problem is that Microsoft, Google, Facebook, and Big Tech have been using this technology on you.

They are tracking, monitoring, and collecting data on your every move, your every keystroke. Amazon and Apple can listen in on your conversations via Alexa and Siri.

These companies have created enormous profiles on you.

They also have major contracts with governments – with the IRS, FBI, CIA, and the national security state. They are the new national security industrial complex that President Dwight Eisenhower warned us about.

In 1961, President Eisenhower delivered this warning:

> In the councils of government, we must guard against the acquisition of unwarranted influence, whether sought or unsought, by the military-industrial complex. The potential for the disastrous rise of misplaced power exists and will persist. We must never let the weight of this combination endanger our liberties or democratic processes. We should take nothing for granted.
>
> The prospect of domination of the nation's scholars by federal employment, project allocation, and the power of money is ever-present and is gravely to be regarded . . .
>
> Yet in holding scientific discovery in respect, as we should, we must also be alert to the equal and opposite danger that public policy could itself become the captive of a scientific-technological elite.

The big tech companies are the modern military-industrial complex of today. They are also far more powerful than the defense industry corporations of Eisenhower's day.

The data these big tech companies are collecting on you all day every day is the product of these companies. These companies are now effectively the government. They supply and manage the technology used by the IRS, the FBI, the CIA, and the national security state to track and monitor you 24-7.

Information is the most powerful weapon there is. With the right information, you can do anything. With the right information, your power is infinite.

You are currently living in Big Tech's digital panopticon prison. We have willingly given Big Tech all this control (full access to our computers, phones, homes, and financial accounts) because we like the convenience. We have made a Faustian bargain. You traded your freedom for convenience.

And now these same companies can destroy your life in an instant by pushing a few buttons. Edward Snowden calls this "turnkey totalitarianism."

This digital prison will become more and more oppressive because those in power almost always crave more power. People love money, but they crave power more. Power equals money, but power is far more valuable than money. Those in power begin to see themselves as God over the rest of us.

Most tyrants don't see themselves as evil. They see themselves as virtuous. They see their tyranny as for the overall public good. To make an omelet, you must break some eggs, right?

The great early 20th Century writer C.S. Lewis put it this way:

> Of all tyrannies, a tyranny sincerely exercised for the good of its victims may be the most oppressive. It would be better to live under robber barons than under omnipotent moral busybodies. The robber baron's cruelty may sometimes sleep, his cupidity may at some point be satiated; but those who torment us for our own good will torment us without end for they do so with the approval of their own conscience. [30]

That's the Big Tech panopticon.

Freedom is the Exception in Human History

Ninety-nine percent of human history is the story of tyranny. Most of the 20th Century was characterized by tyranny: Hitler,

---

[30] C.S. Lewis, *God in the Dock: Essays on Theology* (1970).

Lenin, Stalin, Mao, Pol Pot, and more. Tens of millions of people died at the hands of the Communist and Nazi tyrants of the 20th Century.

Why would we think the 21st Century will be much different?

Except now our high-tech rulers have Big Data and Artificial Intelligence (AI) to control the population. There's no need anymore to kill millions of people. You just control their minds and their lives.

Big Tech can exert control by using a "social credit" system or its equivalent.

Let's not forget that Twitter, Facebook, Google, and Apple deplatformed the President of the United States.

That's almost unthinkable. But it happened. They did not think twice about it. They had the power, and so they did it. What's even scarier is that there was nothing the President of the United States could do about it.

In October of 2020, Twitter froze the account of *The New York Post* to prevent circulation of a story on Joe Biden's son Hunter because Joe Biden was Twitter's preferred candidate.

Twitter users could not share this story. The accounts of Twitter users who tried to share this story were locked or cancelled.

The story was about what was found on a laptop computer that Hunter Biden had abandoned at a computer repair shop in Delaware. We learned from the contents of this laptop that the Bidens in 2017 were pursuing a lucrative deal involving China's largest energy company called CEFC China Energy.

This deal included 20 percent for Hunter, which totaled $850,000 and 10 percent "for the big guy," who was Joe Biden. This meant that Joe Biden would be getting about $425,000 from this deal with China.

Another email, sent by Hunter Biden on August 2, 2017, detailed a deal with CEFC China Energy's Ye Jianming, where Hunter would become the 50 percent owner of a new holding company they were creating. This deal was expected to pay Hunter $10 million per year for three years – a total of $30 million paid to Hunter Biden to provide "introductions" to the Chinese.

On Hunter's laptop is a text message conversation with his daughter where Hunter says Joe Biden was taking 50 percent of everything Hunter was paid. "I hope you all can do what I did and pay for everything for this entire family for 30 years," Hunter wrote in a 2019 text message to his daughter Naomi. "It's really hard. But don't worry, unlike Pop [Joe], I won't make you give me half your salary."

Twitter did not want this story to get out before the 2020 Election. This information was also buried by Google search.

About the only way you could find this information was by going directly to *The New York Post* website.

Voters certainly have a right to know if the potential President of the United States is a business partner with Communist China, America's primary adversary in the world. Voters should have been able to see and assess this information before voting.

The arrogance of Big Tech will only continue to increase, as their wealth and power become even more immense. We must also assume they are partners with China's regime.

America's biggest and most advanced tech companies all have extensive business operations in China

Microsoft operates its Azure cloud business through a partnership with China's 21Vianet Group – which means it is partnering with China's regime.

For these companies to operate in China, they must abide by China's corporate "social credit" system. If you are too critical of China on Facebook, Twitter, YouTube, and social media, your post will be deleted. You also risk having your account shut down.

So Big Tech is now a propaganda arm for China's Communist regime. If Big Tech doesn't like what you are saying, they will deplatform you, as they did to President Trump.

If they don't like your business, they will shut down your website, your ad campaigns, and your access to payment processors. They will deny you the means to make a living. They are now doing this to the NRA and American gun manufacturers.

They did it to political commentator Alex Jones. His accounts have been deleted by YouTube, Facebook, Twitter. The only way you can find Alex Jones is to go to his website InfoWars.

The issue is not whether you agree or disagree with Alex Jones or Donald Trump.

If these companies can cancel Donald Trump, the NRA, and Alex Jones, they can cancel you. They can prevent you from earning a living, and worse. They can disappear you from society.

These big tech companies are now multi-trillion-dollar, all-seeing entities, powered by AI. They can track your every keystroke, your every movement, your every communication, your notes on Microsoft Word or notepad.

Big Tech is a new kind of oligarchy, a new kind of high-tech feudalism. They are in the business of mining your personal data, tracking and cataloging your behavior – which means they control YOU.

Data is power. Data about you is power over you and your life.

Big Tech has modern punishments to keep society in line, to keep society and politics flowing in the direction Big Tech wants society and politics to go. There's no need anymore to boil you in oil, strap you on the rack, or to skin you alive. Big Tech can just deplatform you and prevent you from functioning.

Just the threat of being deplatformed, canceled by Big Tech, having your business shut down, or not being able to get a job due to a suboptimal background check are enough to keep most people in line.

As AI and robotics continue to advance, more and more wealth and power will flow to these Big Tech oligarchs – a handful of people at the very top of the tech pyramid.

The rest of the population is trapped in a digital maze, herded in one direction or another, like mice responding to stimuli.

We believe China's social credit system can't happen here. But it is happening.

With the push of a button, one employee at Google can make you disappear from digital life.

Social Media is a Weapon of Mass Destruction (WMD)

One of Big Tech's most dangerous weapons is AI-powered social media. Social media is a giant data collection machine – data about you. Social media is also an addictive drug that rewires the human brain – especially a child's brain that is still forming.

Instead of changing people's brains with chemicals, social media rewires people's brains using powerful AI social media algorithms.

AI powered social media is digital crack cocaine, especially for young people.

For many defined tasks, modern AI, such as Google's DeepMind, only needs to be given an objective. It's then able to figure out how to achieve the objective in the fastest, most efficient way possible.

In games like chess, Google DeepMind just needs to be told the objective is to win.

With no prior knowledge of the game and only a few hours of playing millions of games against itself, Google DeepMind learns and can defeat world champion chess players with ease.

A world champion chess player has not been able to defeat a top-level computer since 2005. It's no longer a contest.

But suppose the AI deep learning algorithm is told the objective is to addict humans to computer screens and social media. Let's say the best way to do this is to create massive social conflict, get people to hate each other, and create warring political tribes.

AI can learn how to do exactly this on its own, with little human input. AI-powered social media can potentially destroy civilization this way, easily and quickly.

The mission AI has been given by Mark Zuckerberg and Big Tech is to addict humans to social media and computer screens because that's how Facebook and Big Tech make money.

Teens are spending an average of nine hours a day on social media. Children ages 8-12 spend six hours a day on social media on average.

Since the rise of social media, the suicide rate among teens increased 60 percent between 2007 and 2018 according to the Centers for Disease control. The suicide rate was 6.8 per 100,000 in 2007. By 2018, it had risen to 10.7 per 100,000.

From 2000 to 2007, the youth suicide rate was relatively stable.

A 2019 Youth Behavioral Risk Factor Surveillance System survey reported that 18.8 percent of high school students have seriously considered suicide and 8.9 percent have actually attempted suicide.

Mental health experts agree that social media is a major factor for the rise of just about every form of mental illness – including depression, anxiety, loneliness, insecurity, poor self-image, anger, self-absorption, eating disorders, sleep disorders, and mood swings that can become a bipolar disorder.

Social media makes money by selling ads. The more time users spend on social media, the more money these companies make.

The goal of social media companies is to create addicts. Social media creates addicts in the same way slot machines in casinos create addicts.

Slot machines create addicts by handing out small rewards to trigger surges of dopamine to the pleasure centers of the brain.

The rewards come in the form of periodic wins when change or tokens drop into metal trays, often accompanied by loud bells and sirens that declare you a winner. You feel a rush of excitement. You want more of this pleasurable rush of dopamine bathing the pleasure centers of your brain. So you keep playing.

When I watch players at the slot machines, most interact with no one. They just stare at the screen blankly. Hours can pass without the player even realizing it. This is how all those multibillion-dollar casinos and Vegas are built.

Social media companies are built in the same way. But instead of rewards coming in the form of coins or tokens falling into your metal tray at the slot machine and bells going off, you are rewarded with "likes," "loves," comments, interactions, and an increasing number of "friends" and "followers" you will never meet.

If you stick with this "game," you can gain a big following and feel like a mini-celebrity. A major goal for many young people today is to become an "influencer" on social media.

Young "influencers" can become rich. Advertisers pay "influencers" who have big followings to mention and recommend products. Social media's AI algorithms are designed to create and intensify social and political conflict because conflict is exciting, so it is addictive to users, creates engagement, and is thereby profitable for social media companies.

Extreme statements tend to attract the most reactions (positive and negative). It is addictive to the provocateur and attracts like-minded provocateurs. Politics is no longer a rational debate about policy. It is now characterized by warring tribes.

Twitter is a cesspool of hate. Reports have found that about 15 percent of Twitter users are bots (fake accounts) that post two-thirds of the links on the site. These bots are AI-driven autonomous computer programs, designed to trigger users on hot-button political and social issues.

This activity triggers more engagement.

The fuel of social media is hate, conflict, self-absorption, and young people trying to become famous.

Children are bullied and shamed on social media as a form of amusement. People post videos of themselves committing horrific acts, such as the "knockout" game. This is a game where a friend of the thug videos him walking up to a random person on a street and knocking him out.

The video is then posted and goes viral, which becomes profitable for the social media company.

Throughout 2020, we saw anti-police riots in cities across America, fueled by social media. Buildings were torched and burned to the ground, and dozens of people killed. Mobs blocked interstate highways, dragged people out of their cars, and beat them at random.

All this is great for big social media corporations – creating more user engagement and, therefore, more ad revenue. But it's horrible for society and horrible for people.

China's Trojan Horse

Tik Tok is a social media company that has taken the use of AI to create social media addiction and pathology to an entirely new level. Tik Tok's parent company is Byte Dance. Headquartered in Beijing, Byte Dance is one of the most influential companies in China.

Tik Tok has been referred to as China's Trojan Horse – a seemingly benign, but powerful, weapon of mass destruction aimed at the United States and the free world. Its focus is on destroying the lives and minds of children.

The Tik Tok app has been downloaded on three billion devices worldwide. There are at least 100 million Tik Tok users in the United States.

Tik Tok is a social media platform used for sharing short videos. Tik Tok is primarily used by young people to express themselves through singing, dancing, comedy, and lip-syncing. This sounds fine at first.

Tik Tok also provides tools that allow users to create and edit videos on the fly with their phones. Anyone who has used Tik Tok for even a few minutes will see how addictive it is.

As soon as you sign up, Tik Tok starts collecting data about you – including all your contact information, your location, gender, and age. To get full use of the Tik Tok app, you must grant Tik Tok complete access to all contacts on your phone.

A Tik Tok user must agree to its "terms of use," which means you grant Tik Tok the right to collect "faceprints" (for facial recognition), "voiceprints," and biometric information.

Why does a giant company in China need all this information on teenage girls – the primary users of Tik Tok?

President Trump attempted to ban Tik Tok as a national security threat because China's regime requires China's tech companies to share all data they harvest on users with the regime.

Many believe China's regime is using Tik Tok as a tool to collect the most sensitive data on America's citizens and people of the free world, especially on vulnerable young people.

When Trump lost reelection in 2020, the Biden Administration reversed Trump's ban on Tik Tok.

Biden's decision was a disaster, in my view.

Tik Tok is primarily interested in addicting users to the app. For the most part, you don't pick what to watch. Instead, Tik Tok serves you videos in an endless stream.

The video stream you are fed is called "For You."

Tik Tok's AI algorithm learns the kinds of video content you like by tracking your reaction to what the app shows you. The algorithm is fine-tuned in accordance with how long you watch each video. Tik Tok very quickly learns your preferences, so it then serves you more of what you like.

The video content served is also continuous.

Everyone's initial Tik Tok experience begins the same way. When you open the app, you will immediately see videos streaming one after the other on your "For You" page.

Tik Tok begins by showing the most popular videos, curated by Tik Tok moderators, that are cheerful and happy. Tik Tok claims "Our mission is to inspire creativity and bring joy."

The videos Tik Tok shows in its first introduction are pleasant, often funny, always eye-catching, very engaging. Before you know it, you've been watching for an hour. Nothing bad has happened yet. You've been entertained.

But if you linger even briefly on a piece of content, this tells the AI algorithm something about you. Every second you pause to watch, or back up to watch again, empowers Tik Tok's AI to learn your hidden desires, emotions, motivations, and interests.

Within a few hours, Tik Tok's AI knows more about you than you know about you.

Tik Tok is then able to lead you down a rabbit hole of addictive content, often content that becomes extreme and dark in nature. This content you are served tends to reinforce your worst insecurities, phobias, and pathologies.

So young girls interested in fitness and healthy living end up feeling ashamed of their own bodies.

They are shown videos of girls who had bodies almost exactly like theirs but were able to change their bodies into a model of unreal beauty through some kind of radical diet, fitness regimen, surgery, or combination.

Tik Tok has also has augmented reality cameras and beauty filters that allow girls to change the shape of their body in videos they create, and adjust the shape of their face and skin color to create an unreal model of beauty. Young girls can present themselves as looking like supermodels in videos.

A popular hashtag on Tik Tok is #WhatIEatInADay. This hashtag features thousands of videos with billions of views of teenage girls boasting about what they ate that day – which often is almost nothing, perhaps a few pieces of lettuce.

It's hard to know whether these videos are real bodies and real faces, or whether their appearance has been enhanced by Tik Tok's beauty editing tools.

The result is Tik Tok has triggered a pandemic of eating disorders among teenage girls.

Jonna is a 17-year-old who lives in Pennsylvania. She told *The Guardian* that she believes her anorexia eating disorder was triggered and intensified at age 15 by social media.

Her symptoms grew more intense when Instagram's AI algorithms served her endless videos about diet and exercise featuring beautiful girls her age.

The algorithm then led her to more posts on extreme dieting and ultimately to content that explicitly promotes anorexia, including tips on how to hide eating disorders from parents.

Her anorexia became so serious she had to be institutionalized. She spent several months in a recovery and rehabilitation facility.

Jonna says she thought she had gotten her eating disorder under control.

But then she downloaded the Tik Tok app and was quickly introduced to the same kind of content, which retriggered her eating disorder.

"Everyone was sharing about how skinny they were, about how they weren't eating, and I started to feel left out," she told *The Guardian*. "I wanted to stay recovered, but I started to get in this mindset that I wasn't good enough if I didn't look like that." [31]

Jonna says her anorexia was retriggered by the unrealistic standards of beauty being pushed by Tik Tok.

In 2020, Tik Tok policy documents were leaked showing that Tik Tok suppresses posts featuring any people Tik Tok considers "ugly, poor, or disabled."

Tik Tok's internal documents say videos are excluded from feeds that feature people who are "chubby or obese" with "ugly facial looks … like too many wrinkles … or facial deformities … and other disabilities."

So Tik Tok's young users are getting the sense that the world is mostly full of unrealistically beautiful people, not people who look the way most people look. Tik Tok's AI algorithm appears designed to create and magnify all kinds of insecurities, phobias and psychological disorders, especially in young girls.

According to a report by *The Wall Street Journal*, Tik also feeds sexual content and promotes drug use to children as young as thirteen. The *Wall Street Journal*'s investigation in 2021 found that Tik Tok was introducing 13-year-old users to sexually explicit content even when the user's profile said the user is 13. The more the child lingered on sexual content, the more sexual the feed became.

When I started watching video content on the app, at first it was very pleasant and amusing. But then the content gradually became darker.

Because I had researched the app and knew what I was dealing with, I could see that the AI algorithm was selecting my content based on what it was learning about me from my subtle reactions to

---

[31] The Guardian.com. "It Spreads Like a Disease': How Pro-Eating-Disorder Videos Reach Teens on Tiktok." October 16, 2021.

the videos Tik Tok was showing me, essentially one video after another of extremely sexually provocative young girls who were dancing. I started to wonder if I was a bad person.

It was certainly not content I would choose on my own. But Tik Tok was delivering these videos to me, one after the other. I felt like I was encountering Satan, some strange evil intelligence that was trying to mold and shape my brain with video after video.

How then would video content like this affect the brain of a 14-year-old boy with raging hormones? What kind of distorted view of the world is this creating for our kids?

This question brings up another aspect of Tik Tok that makes it quite different from other social media.

Tik Tok is not really promoting interaction with others. It's more about having an interaction with yourself. Tik Tok's AI algorithm is trying to learn everything about you – your hidden secrets, your innermost motivations, desires, and impulses – so it can feed you more tailor-made video content that is designed just for you.

That is very different than, let's say, watching a movie created for the general public.

You interact personally with Tik Tok's AI algorithm, which means you are really just interacting with yourself because the Tik Tok algorithm is attempting to hold up a mirror to your inner life and thoughts.

Tic Tok tends to play to and reinforce one's darkest impulses. If Tik Tok's algorithm detects your political interests, it won't be long before you are shown extremist videos from the left or right, depending on your leanings. Tik Tok will take you down a dark rabbit hole of extremism.

A tech advocacy organization called Reset Australia ran some experiments to find out what happens if a 13-year-old indicates any racist inclinations. It's not long before racist videos will swamp the 13-year-old's Tik Tok feed.

Lawmakers in India have been trying to ban Tik Tok from that country for pushing racist content and hate speech on children. Tik Tok has streamed videos that deny the Holocaust ever occurred and even served up propaganda created by the ultra-violent terrorist organization ISIS.

Tik Tok's AI algorithm incentivizes destructive, dangerous and antisocial behavior because these kinds of videos attract the most views and the most personal engagement.

Popular on Tik Tok are dangerous "challenge" hashtags.

One of these is called #pennydrop. With this hashtag, you are treated to endless videos of kids plugging a charger into the wall part way. The kid then drops a penny between the charger and the wall on top of the partially plugged-in metal prongs. Sometimes this causes an electrical fire or an explosion.

If the child were to hold the penny while touching the prongs (instead of dropping it), this challenge could lead to electrocution. So far, no one's been killed, but several electrical fires and explosions have occurred requiring the arrival of firefighters.

Another hashtag is #BlackoutChallenge.

If you hit this hashtag, you will see endless videos of kids choking themselves, hanging themselves, or otherwise restricting their airflow until they blackout.

Permanent brain damage is likely to occur if the brain is deprived of oxygen for just 3-6 minutes.

A 9-year-old boy named Matias died from attempting this #BlackoutChallenge. He was found hanging from a tree with a garden hose around his neck.

A 12-year old boy from Colorado named Joshua Haileyesus also died from trying this challenge. He spent 19 days on life support before dying. Another 12-year-old boy from Oklahoma also died trying the #blackout challenge. In June of 2021, a 9-year-old Tennessee boy named TJ Smith died from the #blackout challenge.

Other dangerous new challenges are also trending all the time on Tik Tok. Kids engage in these stunts because they get a rush from seeing the views and reactions of others to their videos. They love the worldwide attention they get from their videos.

The big goal for many kids is to become a Tik Tok star. That is achieved by engaging in the most extreme, dangerous, and incendiary behavior. Of course, young girls garner the most attention by dancing in as sexually provocative a way as possible. This then becomes a magnet for predators.

Medical professionals worldwide are also reporting an outbreak of a syndrome similar to Tourette's among teens, especially among girls. Psychiatrists point to excessive use of Tik Tok as the likely cause.

Tourette's is a nervous system disorder characterized by uncontrollable repetitive movements or unwanted sounds (tics), such as repeatedly blinking eyes, shrugging shoulders, contorting faces, uncontrolled muttering, or blurting out curse words.

Dr. Caroline Olvera specializes in these kinds of disorders at Rush University Medical Center in Chicago.

She told *The Wall Street Journal* : "We were seeing a lot of girls in their late teens for the very first time, which is abnormal. They had developed these tics very abruptly — sometimes the week before we would see them in clinic, which is also an unusual situation." [32]

Dr. Olvera and her colleagues published a paper in the journal, *Movement Disorders Clinical Practice,* in July of 2021 after studying more than 3,000 Tik Tok videos produced by people who said they had Tourette's syndrome. They found that 19 of the 28 most popular influencers had developed tics as a result of all the time they were spending on Tik Tok.

Psychiatrists don't think this disorder is actually Tourette's syndrome because Tourette's typically starts developing gradually when children are young. Also, boys are four times more likely to have Tourette's than girls.

Medical professionals report that this outbreak of tic cases worldwide is happening more among teenage girls and not as much with boys. This outbreak has also been sudden, explosive, and widespread.

The young women report difficulty doing simple tasks, such as cooking, driving safely, doing the laundry, or even reciting the alphabet.

Psychiatrists are comparing this tic disorder to PTSD that soldiers suffer from time spent in war zones. Doctors believe this outbreak of Tourette's-like symptoms in teens is the result of psychic distress caused by Tik Tok's powerful AI algorithms that are aimed precisely and calibrated perfectly to engage the eyeballs and psyches of

---

[32] *The Wall Street Journal.* "Teen Girls Are Developing Tics. Doctors Say TikTok Could Be a Factor," by Julie Jargon. October 19, 2021

children and teens so strongly that it becomes almost impossible for the child to disengage their attention from the screen.

This is why I call Tik Tok China's weapon of mass destruction (WMD). And it's a weapon aimed primarily at children of the free world.

Now imagine what the metaverse will do to the minds of our children. Will they even know what reality is anymore?

The metaverse will be social media on steroids. It will fry their brains. Mark Zuckerberg is the world's richest social media digital drug pusher. He's so excited about the metaverse that he's changing the name of his company from Facebook to Meta.

We tend to think of the big AI threat as robot killing machines taking over the world and exterminating humans, like we see in the movie *The Terminator*.

But AI-powered social media is likely far more dangerous and sinister. Few people know more about AI than Elon Musk. Tesla is on the cutting edge of using advanced AI to create full self-driving cars and robotaxis.

"I am really quite close, I am very close, to the cutting edge in AI, and it scares the hell out of me," Elon told a tech conference in Austin, Texas in 2018. "It's capable of vastly more than almost anyone knows and the rate of improvement is exponential."

Elon added: "I think the danger of AI is much greater than the danger of nuclear warheads by a lot."

AI is being used to scoop up enormous troves of data about you. Big tech companies use this data primarily to give you more targeted ads. Google, the social media companies, and corporate media use the data they collect about you primarily to make money.

But money and power are indistinguishable. Those who have the money have the power. Those who have the power get the money. Power is addictive.

These big tech companies are using all this data they collect about you to set up a push-button tech tyranny.

Right now, it's a soft tyranny and seems almost friendly. It's a tyranny that's giving you convenience in exchange for access to your data and control over your computers and digital devices – which means control over your life.

Of course, this soft tyranny can quickly become a hard tyranny, as we see in China.

As the 19th Century thinker Lord Acton put it, "Power corrupts, and absolute power corrupts absolutely."

There is no doubt Big Tech believes it's using its immense power for the public good. They see themselves as virtuous. Twitter, Facebook, Amazon, Apple, and Google conspired to deplatform the President of the United States out of good motives, right?

It was for the public good that we could no longer hear from the President of the United States because of his abhorrent views, they told us. Never mind that President Trump had the support of roughly half the American people.

But we, the plebes, were no longer permitted to hear from the President, according to the thinking of our Big Teach masters.

Big Tech sees people as mice in a maze, to be steered and manipulated for profit by AI-powered algorithms, also for their own amusement . . . because power is fun.

Inflation helps Big Tech because gross profit margins for Big Tech are in the area of 60 percent.

Once you've built the software and created the algorithms, the rest is mostly profit. All that's left for them to do is tweak the algorithms. Their enormous profits are used to expand market share and increase Big Tech's control over the political system and population.

How can this possibly NOT end very badly?

So what's the answer?

I only see only one hope for escaping this Big Tech's global digital prison. And that's Bitcoin. Bitcoin is the only counter to the Big Tech oligarchy – our only real defense.

Bitcoin cannot be controlled by Big Tech because Bitcoin is not located on a centralized server. Bitcoin is a ledger that's distributed on more than 1,000,000 computers (nodes) around the globe. This means Big Tech cannot shut down Bitcoin.

So long as there is an internet somewhere off the Google, Amazon, and Microsoft cloud platforms, Bitcoin will exist.

So long as one computer somewhere has a copy of the distributed ledger, Bitcoin will exist. And so long as you can remember a 12-word seed phrase, you will be able to recover your Bitcoin.

Bitcoin protects the sovereignty of the individual, empowers the individual, protects the individual from the push-button totalitarianism of Big Tech and corrupt political systems.

So long as a central authority controls your money, that authority controls you.

Bitcoin allows you to be your own bank. No one can confiscate your bitcoin. No one can stop you from transacting in bitcoin

No one can erode the value of your bitcoin with inflation.

Bitcoin frees you from being dependent on any central authority. Bitcoin is borderless. Bitcoin allows you to live off the grid, if necessary.

Instead of technology being used to track and control populations, Bitcoin uses technology to free people from the Big Tech oligarchs and corrupt governments that are now owned and controlled by Big Tech.

Bitcoin is your escape hatch from this totalitarian digital prison.

CHAPTER 22

Bitcoin Is an Extension of the American Idea

The most important feature of the Constitution of the United States is decentralization – specifically the decentralization of government power.

Most people will say the Bill of Rights is what's most important.

But the Bill of Rights cannot protect freedom by itself. What protects our freedom is the Bill of Rights plus decentralized (distributed) political power.

The more decentralized political power is, the more secure your liberty.

For legislation to become law, both chambers of Congress must approve – requiring a simple majority vote in the House plus a three-fifths super-majority vote in the U.S. Senate.

This then must be signed into law by the President. The law can then be challenged in the Supreme Court as a potential Constitutional violation.

In addition, most of the governing in America was supposed to be carried out at the state and local level. The federal government was only empowered to carry out certain defined functions, as outlined in the Constitution. The Constitution is a protocol – meaning a set of rules.

The Tenth Amendment to the U.S. Constitution states:

> The powers not delegated to the United States by the Constitution, nor prohibited by it to the States, are reserved to the States respectively, or to the people.

James Madison, the primary author of the Constitution, initially opposed adding a Bill of Rights to the Constitution because this could imply that our rights come from government, also implies these might be our only rights.

Madison wrote the Tenth Amendment to make it clear that the U.S. government would have no authority to exercise any power not explicitly given to the U.S. federal government by the Constitution.

Unless power is explicitly granted to the federal government by the Constitution, the federal government does not have that power. That power is reserved to the states or the people. That's what the Tenth Amendment says.

The federal government's primary jobs are to . . .

1) Provide for the common defense.

2) Ensure domestic tranquility (law and order).

That was it. Ninety percent or more of the governing was supposed to take place at the state and local levels. For the most part, individuals and families were supposed to govern themselves.

Most state constitutions are similar to the U.S. Constitution.

So the system of government established in the United States was very decentralized – the most decentralized governing structure on earth for a major country.

There would be no king in America, no dictator. In America, the President would be a weak office.

This decentralized system of governance led to tremendous freedom and prosperity in America.

This attracted the attention of many, including the French writer Alexis de Tocqueville, who arrived in America in 1831 to learn the secret to America's stunning prosperity. Tocqueville's observations of America's political structure and life were chronicled in his classic two-volume work *Democracy in America*.

Tocqueville admired America's decentralized social and political structure.

America's political system is often criticized as too sluggish. It's difficult for government to get much done. But that was the point.

This decentralized structure, this sluggishness, this difficulty for government to get much done, is what protects the individual.

Decentralized political power protects liberty. Under the American system, government isn't supposed to do much – certainly isn't supposed to be able to do much of significance quickly.

America's founders set up our governing system this way on purpose – the most important feature being decentralization.

In 1788, James Madison, the primary author of America's Constitution, wrote:

> If Men were angels, no government would be necessary. If angels were to govern men, neither external nor internal controls on government would be necessary. In framing a government which is to be administered by men over men, the great difficulty lies in this: you must first enable the government to control the governed; and the next place, oblige it to control itself. [33]

The primary mechanism the founders used to achieve this was decentralization (separation of powers) – distributing political power as widely as possible.

The U.S. Constitution was not perfect of course. Centralization did occur. The natural tendency of government is always toward centralization of power in the executive, especially in times of war.

We had enormous centralization of power in the Presidency during the Civil War, then again during World War I, then massively during World War II when FDR was empowered by one-party control of Congress to do just about whatever he wanted to do.

Once the central authority acquires that kind of power, there's usually no going back.

Bitcoin seeks to bring the principle of decentralized, distributed power to the digital realm – with the specific purpose of fixing the money system.

Bitcoin is the software upgrade, the reboot, of the original American idea. Bitcoin takes the American idea and modernizes it for 21st Century technology.

America's founders, of course, could not have foreseen technology as powerful and sinister as Google and Big Tech. Powerful countermeasures were needed to tip the balance of power back toward the individual.

Bitcoin primarily addresses the problem of corrupt money and how centralized power inevitably leads to corruption of money,

While fixing the money doesn't fix everything, it fixes a lot. It fixes one of the big worries in life: Where we can store our life's work, our life savings without having it stolen by politicians and central bankers.

---

[33] *Federalist Papers*, Number 51 (1778)

The mechanism Satoshi and his band of cryptographers devised was an uneditable ledger of transactions distributed live to a worldwide network of 1,000,000 nodes and miners.

The integrity of this ledger is protected by this network of nodes and miners, the proof-of-work consensus protocol, plus military grade SHA-256 algorithmic cryptography.

A 95 percent super majority of nodes and miners is required to approve upgrades to the Bitcoin software (which is open source) or adjustments to Bitcoin's protocol.

The "separation of powers" principle is also integral to Bitcoin's governing structure. Miners do the work and are paid in Bitcoin. Nodes oversee and validate the work of miners. Developers work on patches and upgrades to the open-source software. Upgrades must be approved by 95 percent of nodes and miners to be adopted.

So change is possible, but must be obviously good for the network and in everyone's best interest to be approved.

The Segregated Witness (SegWit) upgrade in 2017 increased Bitcoin's maximum block size from 1 MB to 4 MB to allow for speedier transactions, while still protecting decentralization.

Computers are always improving, so had advanced to a point, in terms of computational power per device, where a typical laptop computer was capable of being a full node. The block size could be increased without sacrificing decentralization.

But even modest changes and upgrades to Bitcoin can take years to implement because Bitcoin's primary attraction is its security, stability, and immutability.

There will never be more than 21 million bitcoins. We can be 100 percent certain that number will never change. The number 21 million, however, is not so much what matters here.

Most likely, it would not have mattered if Satoshi had set the cap at 18 million or 23 million or 30 million bitcoins. What matters is there's a definite cap. What matters is the money supply is fixed. What matters is this number can never change. What makes Bitcoin valuable is its immutability.

Bitcoin is often criticized as being too difficult to change.

This was Vitalik Buterin's criticism, which is why he left *Bitcoin* magazine to launch Ethereum – to try to build a new kind of decentralized internet for decentralized applications.

Bitcoin was too conservative, he thought. Now Ethereum is being challenged by other "more progressive" blockchains that are faster. They are faster because they are even more centralized.

Bitcoin's immutability is its strength and its value proposition. The strength of Bitcoin is the rules don't change. They are fixed. Bitcoin is like the sun. We know exactly when the sun will rise tomorrow. We know exactly when the sun will rise on this day 100 years from now or 1,000 years from now. That's Bitcoin. That's what honest money is supposed to be.

There will be tweaks and upgrades to Bitcoin as needed if the upgrades are obvious improvements and agreed to by 95 percent of miners and nodes.

The upgrades will be to further secure the fixed 21 million bitcoin cap or to make the network easier to use and more accessible to the public. Nothing fundamental to the protocol will change.

If all change is impossible, that also creates vulnerability. If quantum computers come on the scene suddenly, countermeasures might need to be taken if Satoshi's "difficulty adjustment" is insufficient. But it should be sufficient because the miners will also have increasingly powerful computers, including quantum computers, to guard the network as we move into the future.

If an attack on Bitcoin is ever successful, the worldwide army of miners, nodes and Bitcoin developers have the capacity to reverse that attack and repair any vulnerability.

The 95 percent supermajority vote by nodes and miners required to approve upgrades ensures nothing will be approved that puts their own bitcoins at risk – bitcoins they've worked so hard to accumulate.

These 1,000,000 miners and nodes are your army, distributed worldwide, guarding your bitcoin because, by protecting your bitcoin, they are protecting their own Bitcoin. Your interests and the interests of all the nodes and miners in the world are in perfect alignment.

The structure of Satoshi's brilliant design appears to be just about perfect. Without decentralized and widely distributed power, there is no security because humans crave power and are prone to corruption. In a fiat money system, central bankers have the power because they control the value of the money.

Whoever controls the money, holds the power.

Thomas Jefferson foresaw this weakness in our Constitution. He noted that our Constitution does not address corruption in banking

– banks being the issuers and custodians of the money. In a letter to his close friend John Taylor, Jefferson wrote this in 1816:

> The system of banking we have is both equally and ever reprobated. I contemplate it as a blot left in all our constitutions, which, if not covered, will end in their destruction, which is already hit by gamblers in corruption, and is sweeping away in its progress the fortunes and morals of our citizens . . . And I sincerely believe, with you, that banking establishments are more dangerous than standing armies; and that the principle of spending money to be paid by posterity, under the name of funding, is but swindling futurity on a large scale. (*Works of Thomas Jefferson*, volume 11. Correspondence and Papers, 1808-1816)

This is the problem Bitcoin seeks to address – corruption in banking and dishonest money, which is also corruption in government. This corruption ultimately leads to the loss of liberty and the collapse of civilization.

No other cryptocurrency or crypto asset even claims to address this problem – the problem of securing your life savings and your liberty in a digital vault that is far more secure than Fort Knox; that no one can access but you; and that will allow you to carry your assets with you on your phone or on a piece of paper if all Hell breaks loose where you live, so you can quickly move to a freer, more civilized situation with your life savings.

Bitcoin levels the playing field – puts the average person on equal footing in terms of power with politicians, puts the people back in charge of government.

Bitcoin does this by imposing free-market forces on government to improve, to get better . . . or people will just pack up and leave. Bitcoin is the great freedom and prosperity machine for the world.

That's what Bitcoin does.

How to Start
Bitcoin Resources

To get started with Bitcoin, you need to know where to go and what to do. Here are some resources to get you launched.

Wallets

Wallets are needed for buying, selling, and trading bitcoin. There are "Hot Wallets," which are connected to the Internet.

There are also "Cold Storage" hardware wallets that are not connected to the internet. "Cold storage" hardware wallets are the most secure way to store your bitcoin. You should also have more than one hardware wallet for backup. You should have both.

Popular Self-Custody Hot Wallets:

Electrum (can only be used for Bitcoin). Founded in 2011. Most secure hot wallet. Includes two-factor authentication and multi-signature support. Includes access to the Lightning Network. Integrates with the most popular off-line "cold storage" wallets, such as Ledger, Trezor, and KeepKey. Electrum is available in both the Apple and Google Play stores.

BlueWallet. One of the best wallets for mobile phones and is available for desktop. BlueWallet is self-custodial, and can only be used for Bitcoin. It includes access to the Lightning Network and all the latest Bitcoin features. Integrates with Cash App. BlueWallet is available in both the Apple and Google Play stores.

Mycelium. First launched in 2008 (before Bitcoin), this is the oldest crypto wallet. User friendly and feature-rich. Integrates with the top crypto exchanges. Is compatible with the most popular cold-storage hardware wallets, such as Ledger, Trezor, and KeepKey. Compatible with Android and iOS mobile device users. Strong focus on security, with several layers of pin protection. Available in both the Apple and Google Play stores.

Muun Wallet. Pronounced "Moon," this wallet is used by many early Bitcoiners, including Max Keiser. Munn got more attention when Block and Twitter founder Jack Dorsey started tweeting about it. He's a fan. Muun is a simple and clean wallet with strong security. Muun is completely self-custodial. It's integrated with the Bitcoin Lightning Network and includes multi-factor identity authentication. Muun prides itself on making it easy to take sole custody of your bitcoin. Muun says: "Your money is safe. Two keys are needed to spend it, and one is your phone." Muun is available in both the Google Play and Apple App stores.

Cold-Storage Hardware Wallets

Cold-storage hardware wallets are where you store your private bitcoin keys off-line out of reach from hackers. Your keys never leave your hardware wallet unless you export them.

Good hardware wallets come with two-factor identity authentication, and software applications that allow you to use and manage your funds when connected to your online device.

Hardware wallets are also protected by passcodes, so if someone steals it, the thief won't be able to access your bitcoin. However, if someone does steal your hardware wallet, quickly move your bitcoin to a new address on a back-up hardware wallet that will have a new private key.

Keep multiple back-up wallets and multiple addresses in secure locations.

Popular Hardware Wallets:

Ledger Nano X. Secure off-line storage. Connects with devices via USB. Includes software interface for your devices, similar to wallet apps you probably have. Ledger works on laptop, phone, and tablet. Protected by stainless steel case. Provides randomly generated seed words for your 24-word seed phrase, which is then used to generate your keys. Is compatible with Fido U2F two-factor identity authenticator. Includes good instructions for getting started. Compatible with Coinbase and other major exchanges. This is the "cold storage" hardware wallet I use.

Trezor Model T. Secure off-line storage. Nice touch screen, which makes it easier than Ledger for beginners. Connects with devices via

USB. Includes software interface for your devices. Trezor offers the option of a 12 or 24 word seed phrase to generate your keys, as well as to recover your private key if you lose it. Ledger only provides randomly-generated 24-word seed phrases. 24 words is the standard. Some think 12 words is enough security, so Trezor provides that option. Trezor than uses your seed phrase to generate the private and public keys. Similar to Ledger, Trezor supports the Universal Second Factor (U2F) method, which is a widely supported standard for two-factor authentication, developed by Google and Yubico, with a help from NXP Semiconductors, and hosted the FIDO Alliance. As always, just follow the product instructions carefully.

KeepKey. Includes the biggest screen of the three options described here. It's also bigger in size than the above described Ledger and Trezor devices, so not as good if you want to tuck it in your front pants pocket. Protective metal case. It's the least expensive of these three. Connects with devices via USB. Works with exchanges. KeepKey is compatible with Electrum and Mycelium wallets. It produces a 12-word seed phrase to generate your keys, not a 24-word phrase that I prefer. KeepKey is designed more for beginners. It's user friendly, with nice interface for use with your laptop, phone, or tablet. All these wallets are PIN number secured. I have not used KeepKey. But it receives favorable reviews.

I only keep a small amount of bitcoin on anything that's touched the internet, to include these hardware wallets. A hardware wallet you disconnect from your devices is more secure than a hot wallet. But for true security, you'll want to read the "Hardcore Security" section below.

Bitcoin Exchanges

The two cryptocurrency exchanges approved in the United States are **Coinbase.com** and **Gemini.com**. Both are custodial, follow "know your customer" (KYC) rules, and must operate according to the laws of the United States. They are subject to oversight by the Securities and Exchange Commission (SEC). These exchanges operate much like E-Trade, Charles Schwab, and other exchanges.

Both Coinbase and Gemini allow you to off-ramp easily to self-custody of your bitcoin.

Coinbase. I use Coinbase to buy my bitcoin. I then move most of my bitcoin off Coinbase to my Ledger hardware wallets (multiple back-ups). Coinbase is a publicly traded company, so must be hyper-careful to follow all SEC rules. I like the fact that Coinbase stock is publicly traded. This allows me to track Coinbase's quarterly financial reports so I can monitor the financial health of the company.

You do not want your money on an exchange that goes bankrupt. In the event of an exchange going bankrupt, your coins could be frozen as the company goes through bankruptcy proceedings. You might even lose your coins.

Coinbase is my recommendation for beginners who are making their first bitcoin purchase of $1,000 or more. You can then graduate to self-custody for your bitcoin later. If you want to make a smaller purchase, say $100, see **Cash App** below.

As you become a more advanced Bitcoiner, you will want to move your Bitcoin off of exchanges and third-party custodial solutions. You will want to self-custody, be your own bank.

Gemini. This exchange was founded by the Winklevoss twins of Facebook fame, central characters in the movie "The Social Network" about the founding of Facebook. The Winklevoss twins sued Mark Zuckerberg and Facebook, accusing Zuck of stealing Facebook from them when they were all students at Harvard. The Winklevoss twins secured a $65 million settlement from Facebook in 2008.

The Winklevoss twins have been involved in crypto since the early days. They started buying bitcoin in 2011 through Winklevoss Capital for as little as $10 per coin. In 2012, they revealed they owned about one percent of the bitcoins in circulation at the time. They are said to have amassed a $6 billion fortune. They founded the Gemini crypto exchange in 2014.

I have no reason to think Gemini is anything but solid and honest. My concern about Gemini, as of this writing, is it's not a publicly-traded stock. So you can't track the company's quarterly financials.

This makes Gemini a bit of a black box, though as a U.S. financial institution, it must comply with the laws of New York state and U.S. laws governing custodial financial institutions. The laws of New York state are quite tough.

If you are a U.S. citizen, do no use an exchange outside the United States.

Good Custodial Wallets

Some people just are not comfortable with self-custody. They prefer to trust someone else with their Bitcoin keys. They want to be able to call customer service in case they forget their password or need assistance. They're accustomed to using a bank and traditional financial services. That was me for a while, until I realized that trusting someone else to secure my bitcoin really isn't secure at all. But for those who just want to start by purchasing a little bitcoin in the way you are accustomed to operating, here are some good options:

Cash App. Buying bitcoin on Cash App is super easy and a great option if you are just buying a small amount of bitcoin. If you don't have Cash App, just head on over to Google Play or Apple Store and download it. Get set up. Connect it with your bank or debit card. Load in some fiat money. Then tap the "Buy BTC" tab in the app. Presto. You're done. You've bought your first satoshis. Then if you want to take full custody of your bitcoin, Cash App allows this. Just install "BlueWallet" (described above). Hit the "BlueWallet" tab in Cash App. Follow instructions. Cash App is a product of Block, founded and run by Bitcoin maximalist Jack Dorsey, who quit as CEO of Twitter to dedicate his life to giving the unbanked and impoverished of the world easy access to bitcoin (money).

Strike. This is a custodial wallet launched by pro-freedom Bitcoin maximalist Jack Mallers. Though Strike is custodial, it allows you to take custody of your Bitcoin keys and is fully interoperable with self-custody Bitcoin wallets. It also provides access to the Lightning Network. Mallers' goal is similar to Jack Dorsey's: To make it as easy as possible for beginners and merchants to get launched on Bitcoin. Strike has launched in upwards of 200 countries. Strike is easy to use for beginners and is a bridge between Bitcoin and the fiat money system.

Coinbase. This is the largest crypto exchange in the United States. It also includes a wallet for mobile devices. It's easy for beginners.

Gemini. Similar to Coinbase, Gemini is the second biggest crypto exchange in the United States. It also has a downloadable wallet for mobile devices, easy for beginners.

Hardcore Security

Buy a military dog tag metal stamping kit for about $29, and stamp your private key code on stainless steel tags. For more detailed information on this, go on YouTube and type "store bitcoins on steel military dog tags" or "stamp military dog tags" or "emboss military dog tags." Lots of videos will come up.

Buy some stainless steel credit card holders or wallets. Place your stamped dog tag in a stainless steel credit card holder case, and bury it somewhere on your property. Just remember where you buried it. Do this several times, burying your tags in different locations.

Your buried stainless steel tags will survive corrosion, flood, fire, and thermonuclear war. This is where you store your emergency fund, for when all Hell breaks loose and socio-economic collapse ensues.

How to Generate New Keys and Wallets Securely

The hardware wallets described above include tools that generate random words for your seed word phrase. Use this hardware wallet tool off line to perform this task.

Seed word phrases are used to create your keys. Write down your seed word phrase. Words must be in the proper order.

You can also find a tool online for generating random seed word phrases at bitaps.com/mnemonic

Download this page onto your laptop. Disconnect from the internet. You can then use the tool.

Hit whether you want a 12, 15, 18, 21, or 24 seed-word phrase. When the random words appear, hit load. Your new keys will appear along with your seed words. Print page. Keep this page hidden and stored somewhere safe until you've had a chance to imprint the codes on steel dog tags for burial.

Never let your seed word recovery phrase fall into the wrong hands. Anyone who gets a hold of your seed word phrase (whether online or offline), and who knows what they are doing, can instantly empty your bitcoin wallet.

If this happens, instantly move your bitcoin to an uncompromised wallet. New wallets can be created in seconds with these methods outlined here.

Bitcoinaddress.org

Another method of generating a new set of keys is to head on over to bitaddress.org

Follow the instructions.

The instructions tell you to download the page that comes up.

Again, disconnect from the internet.

Pull the page up that you've just downloaded on your laptop

Start using the tool by moving your mouse around the computer screen randomly for about 20 seconds. This tool tells you when it has enough information (random movements from your mouse) to generate your new public and private keys with accompanying QR codes. Print the page before connecting to the internet.

Also, delete the bitaddress.org page from your computer before reconnecting to the internet. Head on over there now to try it out. It's quite amazing.

But be careful when visiting sites. There are fake clone sites that look real, but are criminals setting traps to steel your private keys.

Whenever I set up a new address, I move just some bitcoin in. I then leave it there for a while and watch what happens. I do this many times over a substantial period.

Once I feel comfortable the address has not been compromised, I'll move larger amounts into a wallet.

NOTE: Private key codes cannot be used to find your seed phrase. This system does not work in reverse. Remember, information in cryptography flows in one direction only, which is what makes it secure.

Don't worry yet. If you lose your seed word phrase, you still have your bitcoin so long as you have your private key code. You will just have to do without a seed word recovery phrase for that wallet.

If having a seed word recovery phrase is important to you, you will need to generate a new wallet with new keys and move your bitcoin to that wallet.

For your most secure wallet, the one with codes stamped on military dog tags and buried in the ground, you should go without a seed word recovery phrase or QR code. You can generate a QR code from your private key code.

IMPORTANT: Practice taking full custody of your bitcoin using small amounts – so if you make mistakes, it's no disaster. If you make a few mistakes and lose a few bucks here and there, that's how you learn. Taking full custody of your bitcoin is like learning how to swim. It's scary at first, but becomes second nature with practice. And it's really a lot of fun. You'll feel empowered.

Purism Laptop

I use a Linux-based Purism Librem laptop to conduct all my financial transactions. There's no Microsoft Office, no Google Chrome loaded on this laptop. The operating system is PureOS, designed for privacy. No tracking.

This laptop is only connected to the internet when I need to conduct financial activity. I use another laptop for surfing the Web, watching YouTube, and general use.

I am especially a fan of the Purism Librem laptop's PureBoot, which enables you to verify if the software on a Librem laptop has been tampered with in any way. When files in the /boot directory change, the Librem Key's red LED will flash. The Librem Key can also be used to encrypt and decrypt storage.

IMPORTANT: I do NOT store important keys and passcodes on the Purism laptop – and especially not my keys with the bitcoin motherlode. Just assume the entire world (criminals, the NSA, China, Russia, Iran, everyone) is rifling through your regular laptop around the clock. And you know Google, Microsoft, and all the Big Tech companies have all your pass codes and key codes, or can get them if they want to. Nothing is 100 percent secure. But do what you can so it's at least not easy to fleece you for everything you have. Hackers can steal your house out from under you if you're waltzing through life unaware.

Very Suboptimal Options for Buying Bitcoin

Robinhood. Launched the trend to no-fee trading in stocks, which forced most stock exchanges to adopt the same practice. Robinhood is popular among young people. Also includes a wallet for mobile devices and allows cryptocurrency purchases. With bitcoin purchases on Robinhood, you cannot transfer your bitcoin to cold storage. You don't own your private keys, therefore don't really own your bitcoin. You can sell your bitcoin on Robinhood, pocket the money, then move your fiat money off the exchange.

Venmo. PayPal's Venmo app allows you to buy bitcoin, but Venmo also keeps custody of the key and does not allow you to move your bitcoin off the app. This means you don't really own your bitcoin. Similar to Robinhood, you can cash out your bitcoin and move your fiat money off the app.

Venmo and Robinhood are suboptimal options for buying bitcoin. They are okay if you just want to do some trading or HODL small amounts. Nothing wrong with that.

But Robinhood and Venmo are not off-ramps from the corrupt political and financial system.

A Final Note

With this book, you have just scratched the surface of how to buy, use, and secure your bitcoin. For further study, YouTube is a tremendous resource. For some of the best "How to" Bitcoin channels on YouTube, I recommend **Dan Held** and **Andreas Antonopoulos**.

For the more philosophical underpinnings of Bitcoin, follow **Michael Saylor** (Hope.com), **Robert Breedlove**, **Nic Carter**, **Lyn Alden**, **Anthony Pompliano**, **Matt Odell**, **Jeff Booth**, **Greg Foss**, and **Peter McCormack**.

Take **Gary Gensler's** MIT course on Bitcoin and crypto assets. It's 24 classes, online, free, and available to everyone. Just Google "Gary Gensler MIT Bitcoin course." It's easy to find.

Read Satoshi's 8-page white paper. Download the PDF from bitcoin.org/bitcoin.pdf

You should not buy any bitcoin until you've read Satoshi's white paper at least five times.

Gensler is the SEC Chairman, as I write this. He says Bitcoin is the only "commodity" in Crypto World. All the other cryptos are securities and under the jurisdiction of the SEC because they aren't decentralized, says Gensler. They operate and function like private companies.

Fascinating to me are interviews on YouTube with the likes of **Adam Back**, **Nick Szabo**, and **David Chaum** -- all founding fathers of Bitcoin. One or all of them might even be Satoshi. These are people well worth listening to. All this should get your safely on board the Bitcoin train and moving down the Bitcoin rabbit hole.

For the most part, avoid the price predictors and chartists who have daily podcasts. To me, Bitcoin's short-term price fluctuations is the least interesting aspect of Bitcoin.

I'm quite confident about the direction Bitcoin's price is heading long term. But there will be 50 percent and even 70 percent price drops along the way . . . because it's still an emerging technology and asset.

These price predictors and chartists on YouTube don't know anymore about Bitcoin's price next week, next month, or next year than you do. They're just trying to get views and sell products. So don't waste your time listening to them. And avoid those who hold themselves out as experts on all things "crypto."

Bitcoin is not "crypto."

Bitcoin is Bitcoin.

Glossary of Bitcoin Terms

Altcoins: These are cryptocurrencies and assets other than Bitcoin. There are upwards of 19,000 other crypto assets in circulation. Only a few altcoins have any substantial following. The largest altcoin is Ethereum. It's the #2 crypto asset behind Bitcoin in terms of market cap – about half the size of Bitcoin. Altcoin prices tend to crash hardest when crypto is in a bear market.

ASIC – or Application-Specific Integrated Circuit: This is a computer chip designed for a specific purpose. Bitcoin miners use ASIC computers to solve math puzzles generated by SHA-256 algorithms. Whichever computer (miner) solves the puzzle first wins a reward, currently 6.25 bitcoins, plus the privilege of mining the next block and inserting that block into the immutable blockchain. Bitcoin mining computers can be used only for mining Bitcoin, no other purpose.

Austrian School of Economics: A set of economic theories originating in Vienna, Austria in 1871 when Carl Menger published his *Principles of Economics* that outlined his theory of value. In summary, Menger believed that value is determined by the consumer and the laws of supply and demand. The most famous economists from the Austrian school in the 20th Century were Ludwig von Mises and Friedrich A. Hayek. They were advocates of the free market as the mechanism for determining capital allocation. They opposed central planning of economies by governments (socialism, communism, and fascism) because government central planners don't have the signals needed from the market to know how to allocate capital efficiently and productively. In simple terms, government programs don't go out of business if they fail. Instead, government programs and agencies tend to keep growing despite failure. Austrian school economists also oppose subjective fiat money creation (printing) by governments, which distorts price signals. They strongly favored the gold standard for money over fiat money printing. But they preferred government not be involved in the creation and management of money at all. They believed the best money would emerge on its own if the free market is allowed to operate properly. Bitcoin is often said to be the embodiment of the

257

Austrian school of economics.

Bitcoin Address: This is a string of numbers and letters that represent the virtual location where bitcoin can be sent. People often publish their Bitcoin address on their website, sometimes in the form of a QR code, so people can pay them in bitcoin.

Bitcoin Core: This is the original Bitcoin source code created by Satoshi Nakamoto. All other implementations and upgrades to the Bitcoin protocol and software look to Bitcoin Core for guidance and to keep Bitcoin pure. Bitcoin Core is open-source software, meaning anyone can view it, download it, and propose upgrades. Bitcoin Core provides software for both nodes and wallets. There are alternatives to Bitcoin Core. Most nodes continue to use Bitcoin Core, while third-party software is used for most wallets.

Bitcoin Maximalist: This is someone who buys only bitcoin, no other crypto asset. One of the most outspoken Bitcoin "maximalists" is economist Max Keiser. He calls all other cryptocurrencies and assets "shit coins." He is especially critical of Ethereum. Other prominent Bitcoin maximalists include tech titans Jack Dorsey (founder of Twitter and Square, now called Block) and MicroStrategy founder and Executive Chairman Michael Saylor.

Bitcoin Network: The Bitcoin network is a worldwide network of computers that broadcast and maintain the Bitcoin blockchain ledger of transactions. Bitcoin transactions are distributed live and in real time to the Bitcoin network. Transactions are confirmed by a consensus of Bitcoin nodes and miners who also guard the network.

Block: A block is a batch of bitcoin transactions. It's a data structure, or virtual container. Blocks of transactions are grouped together (mined) every ten minutes on average. Once a block of transactions is confirmed as valid by the network, the block is closed and inserted into the immutable blockchain. Then a new block is created for new transactions to be validated.

Block Header: The metadata in a block is summarized in the header. This summary includes the timestamp, hash representation of the block data, block height, difficulty, nonce, Merkle root, and the hash of the previous block.

Blockchain: A blockchain is a type of shared database. In Bitcoin, the blockchain is a ledger distributed to a worldwide network of computers. Blocks are data structures (blocks of data) that are linked together with cryptography. Once a block is filled with data (transactions), it's inserted into the blockchain. A new block of transactions is then worked on for the next block. Once a block is inserted into the blockchain, it can never be removed from the chain. Blockchains preserve transactions in chronological order.

Block Reward: This is the reward a bitcoin miner receives for winning the worldwide race among miners to solve the math puzzle generated by the SHA-256 algorithm. The winning miner currently receives a reward of 6.25 bitcoins, plus the privilege of assembling the next block and inserting it into the blockchain. This function is a key pillar of securing the Bitcoin network.

Block Size: This refers to the maximum amount of data a block can hold. Originally, the maximum block size for Bitcoin was set at one megabyte of data. This was increased to a maximum of 4 MB of data in 2017 in order to increase transaction speed. More accurately, the block unit of measurement was increased from a maximum of 1 weight unit (WU) to 4 weight units, which is slightly different from megabytes. But most people say megabytes. Block size has been a contentious debate in Bitcoin's history and created a type of civil war in Bitcoin World, detailed in a book titled *Blocksize War*, by Jonathan Bier. This book was crucial in helping my own understanding of why Bitcoin's structure is so brilliant.

Central Bank: A central bank governs a nation's money. It creates new money and sets the rules for a country's monetary (money) and banking system. Central banks are usually governed by a board of governors and are theoretically independent. In the United States, the central bank is called the United States Federal Reserve System. For more information on this see "**United States Federal Reserve System**" section below.

Central Bank Digital Currency (CBDC): A digital form of a fiat currency issued by a central bank. Instead of printing money, the central bank issues electronic tokens backed by the government. CBDCs can be built on blockchain technology or not. CBDCs are not to be confused with stablecoins, which are pegged to fiat currencies, but are creations of private entities, but are not backed by government.

Coinbase: This is the first transaction in each Bitcoin block. The coinbase also distributes the reward to the winning miner. It's thereby also the mechanism for putting new bitcoins into circulation. The coinbase in each Bitcoin block is not to be confused with the crypto-asset exchange called Coinbase.com

Confirmation: A bitcoin transaction that is approved as valid by the network, and therefore qualified to be included in the next block. Confirmation of transactions ensures no double-spending. Each transaction is unique with its own cryptographic signature.

Cryptography: This is the science of creating codes, based on mathematical concepts, for secure communications. For Bitcoin, cryptographic algorithms are used to secure funds, and enables Bitcoin users to transact freely without funds being intercepted by a malicious actor.

DAO – or Decentralized Autonomous Organization: This is an organization that, at least in theory, can run autonomously via "smart contracts" without management by a human administrator. "Code is law" is a phrase we often hear in connection with DAOs. Ethereum is attempting to create a platform for DAOs – a decentralized internet for DAOs and decentralized applications (DAPPs). So far, this effort hasn't created much in the way of decentralized applications or organizations that would be useful to the public.

Decentralized Applications (DAPPs): These are applications (such as games) that claim to be decentralized – that is, owned by no one and controlled by no one. This is the promise of Ethereum and its competitors. DAPPs are supposed to be governed by algorithms and automated protocols. So far, no successful DAPPs exist, as of this writing.

Decentralized Finance (DeFi): These are supposed to be

decentralized financial services, such as lending platforms, banking, insurance, stock market and crypto exchanges, auctions, etc. These also are supposed to be governed by protocols and algorithms ("smart contracts"). So far, no successful DeFi projects exist. Tens of billions of dollars have been lost to scammers on DeFi platforms. Perhaps the most famous is the Terra-Luna collapse of 2022 that cost investors $40 billion.

Denial-of-Service Attack (DoS): This is when software robots (bots) bombard a system with spam and fake transactions to bog down and paralyze a network. It's analogous to a crowd of people standing in front of a door to a store preventing real customers from entering the store. Bitcoin's proof-of-work system is designed to make a DoS attack on the Bitcoin network prohibitively expensive for attackers. There has never been a successful DoS attack on Bitcoin. Amazon and other e-commerce platforms have borrowed from Bitcoin to adopt proof-of-work systems to thwart DoS attacks.

Difficulty Adjustment: The Bitcoin protocol requires new blocks to be created (mined) and inserted into the blockchain every ten minutes on average. Miners race to solve a math puzzle generated by the SHA-256 algorithm. The winning miner is rewarded with bitcoins (currently 6.25 bitcoins) plus the privilege of mining the next block and inserting it into the blockchain. As the price of bitcoin increases, more and more miners join the network to compete for the mining reward. So the difficulty of the math puzzle must be adjusted regularly, usually increased in difficulty, to keep Bitcoin on schedule with producing a new block of transactions every ten minutes on average. The difficulty adjustment is made every 2,016 blocks, which is about every two days.

Digital Signature: A digital signature authenticates the identity of the sender. It demonstrates that the sender of bitcoin is the owner of a private key corresponding to the sender's public key, but keeps the private key hidden. In addition, a unique new digital signature is generated by your private key for each transaction to prevent double spending.

Distributed Ledger: This is what Bitcoin is, a ledger built on blockchain technology that's distributed to a worldwide network of computers (nodes and miners) and is updated in real-time as transactions occur. Distributed ledgers don't need to be built on blockchain, don't need to be decentralized, and don't need to be uneditable the way Bitcoin is.

Double-Spend: A double-spend is an attempt to send the same bitcoins or satoshis twice. The Bitcoin system is designed to prevent the dreaded double-spend. Each transaction is unique, safeguarded by cryptographic code. Every transaction must be linked to other transactions. The transaction history is secured by the immutable blockchain. To date, there has never been a double-spend on the Bitcoin network.

Encryption Algorithm: This is a function that transforms a message into a random-seeming string of unreadable code. This code can only be unscrambled and read with a decryption key. Encryption is how private data is sent over the public internet without the public being able to read it.

Ethereum: This is the #2 crypto asset in terms of market cap, about half the size of Bitcoin. Ethereum is attempting to build a decentralized internet as a platform for decentralized applications (DAPPs) by using complex "smart contracts." As of now, there are no applications on the Ethereum platform that are especially appealing. Because the proof-of-work mining protocol that secures the blockchain is too slow for a decentralized internet, Ethereum is attempting to transition to a "proof-of-stake" security system.

Exchange: An exchange is a company that facilitates the buying and selling of assets, such as stocks, commodities, or cryptocurrencies. Coinbase.com is an example of a crypto-asset exchange.

Fiat Currency: A fiat currency is money that is issued by governments, but that is not backed by gold, other commodity, or fixed set of rules. In a fiat money system, the issuance of new money is decided by people making subjective decisions.

Forks: In Bitcoin, there are two primary types of "forks" that can occur in the blockchain. A "hard fork" is a fundamental change in the Bitcoin protocol that creates two paths users can follow – two blockchains. One follows the old protocol. The other is the new version that creates a new currency. The market then decides which blockchain to follow. Bitcoin Cash was an example of a hard fork created by renegade miners and developers in 2017. The main argument was over block size. Bitcoin Cash wanted a faster, cheaper, more scalable version of Bitcoin. The market chose traditional Bitcoin. Bitcoin Cash is less than one percent the size of Bitcoin in terms of market cap. There are also "soft forks" that are approved by the Bitcoin community, such as for software upgrades or minor protocol changes. Upgrades and changes to Bitcoin require 95 percent approval from bitcoin miners and nodes to be adopted. "Soft Forks" do not produce a new currency, just updates to the software or make slight changes to the protocol. Software updates such as Segregated Witness (SegWit) in 2017 and Taproot in 2021 were accomplished with "soft forks." There can also be "accidental forks," which are covered below under "orphaned blocks."

Genesis Block: The Genesis Block in the Bitcoin blockchain is the very first block of the blockchain, generated by the protocol on January 3, 2009.

Halving: Every 2016 blocks, or about every four years, the rate of new bitcoin supply entering the system is cut in half. Currently, 6.25 new bitcoins are created and enter circulation every ten minutes on average. In the Spring of 2024, this rate of new bitcoin supply will drop to 3.125 bitcoins entering circulation every ten minutes with each new block. "Halvings" will continue to occur every 2016 blocks until the 21 millionth bitcoin is issued in the spring of 2040.

Hash and Hashing: A hash in blockchain is cryptographic data that flows in one direction and cannot be undone. It's analogous to putting beef through a meat grinder to create hamburger. The process can't be reversed. Hash functions are a basic tool of cryptography and blockchain management. Each block of transactions includes the cryptographic hash of the previous block in the blockchain, which links the blocks in chronological order. SHA-256 was created by the U.S. military and is the hash technology used by Bitcoin to secure the blockchain. A unique piece of data will always produce the same hash code, similar to how beef is the same meat whether in hamburger or steak form.

Hash Rate: This refers to the computational processing power being used by the Bitcoin network. The higher the hash rate, the more difficult it becomes to conduct a "51 Percent Attack" on the network.

Hyperbitcoinization: This is the tipping point when bitcoin becomes the preferred medium of exchange for the world.

Layer 2: Bitcoin is often criticized as being too slow and cumbersome to work well as a currency for routine daily transactions, such as to buy groceries or a cup of coffee at Starbucks. So systems are being built on top of the Bitcoin base layer to add more speed and functionality. In similar fashion, gold used to be the base layer for the dollar. U.S. paper currency were certificates redeemable in gold. Paper currency was a more functional Layer 2 solution built on top of gold as the base layer to make transactions easier. Following this model, the Lightning Network is being built on top of the Bitcoin base layer to enable cheap, fast micro-transactions. Other Layer 2 and Layer 3 applications are also being built on the Bitcoin base layer to add functionality to the network.

Lightning Network: Lightning is being built on top of the Bitcoin base layer to enable quick cheap microtransactions to be accomplished off the blockchain. Lightning aims to solve Bitcoin's "scalability" issue. Lightning is not a currency. It's a network overlayed on top of the main Bitcoin blockchain that enables users to transact in fractions of a bitcoin (satoshis) for little or no fee. In the Lightning system, a payment channel is opened between users who want to transact with each other. The main chain tracks how much of your bitcoin leaves the chain for the payment channel you open on Lightning, then how much came back to the main chain when you close your Lightning channel. You can keep your Lightning channel open with whoever you are transacting with indefinitely. Lightning is not built on blockchain technology, which is slow. It's a simple ledger system that's tracked by automated scripts. Digital signatures by the parties confirm transactions.

Mempool: This is where pending transactions are held, waiting to be gathered by a bitcoin miner for verification, batching in a block, and then placed into the permanent blockchain.

Miner: Miners guard the Bitcoin network and perform the work of the Bitcoin blockchain. They mine blocks by verifying transactions, group them in blocks, and place them in the blockchain. They are paid for their work with transaction fees plus an extra reward. For each block, miners race to solve a math puzzle generated by the SHA-256 algorithm. The first miner to solve the math puzzle wins the reward, currently 6.25 bitcoins, and the right to mine the next block. This is how new coins enter circulation. A new block of transactions is mined every ten minutes on average. The miner is responsible for the validity of all transactions in the block he's assembling, or he loses his reward. This is part of how the Bitcoin protocol incentivizes security. All nodes and miners are incentivized to protect everyone's bitcoin because, by doing so, protects the value of their own bitcoin.

Mining: This is the process by which miners verify transactions, assemble them in blocks, and add them to the blockchain. The worldwide network miners are competing to mine the next block by solving a cryptographic math problem generated by the SHA-256 algorithm. The winning miner receives a reward, currently 6.25 bitcoins, plus the right to assemble the block of transactions, verify transactions in the block, and insert that block into the blockchain. Mining is also how new bitcoins enter circulation. Mining requires specialized ASIC computers that can only be used for mining Bitcoin, no other purpose.

Mining Pool. Miners often join mining pools to split rewards and transaction fees to keep their cash flow steady for individual miners. The biggest mining pool in the United States is Foundry USA, which has 18 percent of the world's hash rate. Individual miners can redirect their hash power to any mining pool at any time.

Monetary Policy: Rules by which money is created or removed from circulation. In fiat monetary systems, the supply of money is controlled by the government, usually by central banks.

Monetary System: Mechanism or process by which money is created, enters circulation, and is accounted for.

Multisignature: A Bitcoin address can be set up to require more than one signature (multi-sig) to authorize the spending of funds. This increases security for the address.

Node: A node on the Bitcoin network is a computer that participates in the verification of bitcoin transactions. Originally, there was no difference between nodes and miners. As the computing power needed to mine bitcoin grew more intense, some nodes invested in powerful ASIC computers to mine for bitcoin, while other nodes only participated in the validation of transactions, which could be done with a $400 laptop computer. Non-mining nodes oversee the work of the miners. Nodes also vote on Bitcoin upgrade proposals. The Bitcoin ledger is distributed live and in real-time to the worldwide network of nodes and miners. There are also "lightweight nodes" who do not store the complete ledger, but download part of the blockchain. They use Simple Payment Verification (SPV) mode, which is accomplished with cryptographic shortcuts.

Nonce: An abbreviation for "number only used once." The nonce is the number bitcoin miners compete to find in order to receive the mining reward. The nonce number is added to a 32-bit field in the Bitcoin block to show other miners and nodes the number has been found by a miner who will complete the mining of the block while the rest of the miners compete to find the nonce for the next block. Nonces are often used in other internet security applications, such as for multi-factor authentication.

Orphaned Block: Though new blocks are mined every ten minutes on average, sometimes valid blocks arrive at the same time or almost the same time. This creates a temporary of "accidental" fork, two branches of equal length. The true chain is determined by where the miner puts the next block. The true chain is the longer chain because the longer chain represents the most work. This creates an "orphaned block." This block of transactions then falls back into the mempool of pending transactions to be mined again.

Payment Channel: See "Lightning Network" above.

Peer-To-Peer (P2P): This refers to transactions that take place between two people, "peer-to-peer," without a central administrator.

When you shake hands with someone, you just walk up and just shake hands. You don't need a middleman shaking hands for you. This is what Bitcoin enables. With Bitcoin, no one can freeze your account, stop your transactions, or seize your money. You are your own bank. The white paper by the unknown creator of Bitcoin, pseudonymously called Satoshi Nakamoto, is titled "Bitcoin: A Peer-to-Peer Electronic Cash System."

Private and Public Keys: Bitcoin users have a private key and a public key. A public key is analogous to a slot in a vault where money can be deposited, but cannot be accessed without a private key. Your private key authenticates your identity. Private keys also generate digital signatures for transactions that authenticate the transaction without revealing your private key. Private keys actually generate your public key, so are cryptographically linked. Your private key is like a passcode – a 256-bit number, which can be represented in a variety of ways. If a thief were to get a hold of your private key code, he could steal all your bitcoin associated with that key. Also, if you lose your private key, you lose access to your bitcoin. Because the code of a public key is so long, your public address is a hashed (condensed) version of your public key. This gets complicated. You can publish your public address on your website so people can easily pay you bitcoin. This is often done in the form of a QR code.

Proof-of-Stake (PoS): This is an alternative transaction validation consensus protocol to the proof-of-work (PoW) protocol Bitcoin uses. The advantages of proof-of-stake are 1) less energy is used by the network to validate transactions; and 2) transactions are faster. The disadvantages are that the network is less secure and more vulnerable to "51 Percent," "denial of service" (DoS), and other attacks. Instead of solving a complex math puzzle to earn the right to mine and validate blocks and receive the block reward, nodes just vote on the validity of transactions. The number of votes a node can cast is in direct proportion to the amount the node has staked. Nodes that have staked the most have the most votes. Nodes also accumulate block rewards in proportion to the amount they've staked. So the tendency on a PoS blockchain network is toward centralization of power in the hands of the largest stakeholders, who are more like shareholders in a corporation. Ethereum is transitioning from a proof-of-work protocol to proof-of-stake to speed up operations on the blockchain. PoW isn't working for Ethereum because Ethereum is attempting to build a decentralized internet for decentralized applications, decentralized organizations, and decentralized finance. All this requires speed and substantial centralized management by humans, so isn't decentralized.

Proof-of-Work (PoW): Proof-of-Work is a key pillar of Bitcoin's security protocol. PoW was originally developed as a mechanism to block spammers by requiring the sender of a communication to solve a math puzzle. For the email or communication to make it through spam filters, the solution to the math puzzle must be included with the communication. This "proof of work" shows that significant computational power was used to create the communication. The purpose was to increase the cost of spamming. Bitcoin uses a proof-of-work algorithm to block "51 Percent" and denial-of-service (DoS) attackers by making the cost of sustaining an attack prohibitively expensive. As the price of bitcoin increases, the competition among miners to solve the math puzzle and win the reward of 6.25 bitcoins becomes ferocious, increasing the hash rate (computing power). So the math puzzle must increase in difficulty to protect the security of the network. The difficulty of the math puzzle miners must solve is adjusted every 2016 blocks, or about every two days. This is called the "Difficulty Adjustment."

Protocol: The rules of a network or system. Railroad tracks must be the same width for the railroad network to function. The Bitcoin network is governed by a set of rules that can only be adjusted with 95 percent approval from the network of nodes and miners.

Recovery Seed Phrase: Private Bitcoin keys are a long list of numbers and letters that can be represented a number of ways. Bitcoin wallets are typically able to generate a list of unrelated words that can be used to recover your Bitcoin funds in the event you lose your private key code. Seed word phrases can also used to create your Bitcoin wallet (private and public keys).

Satoshi or Sat: Money denomination on the Bitcoin network. One satoshi (sat) equals $1/100,000,000^{th}$ of one bitcoin. And one bitcoin equals 100 million satoshis.

Satoshi Nakamoto: The pseudonymous creator of Bitcoin. The identity of Satoshi remains unknown. Satoshi might be an individual or a group of cryptographers and software engineers who had been working for many years to create a system of incorruptible money that would be governed by mathematical cryptographic algorithms, not people. Satoshi's white paper describing the Bitcoin protocol was published on October 28, 2008. Bitcoin was formally launched on Jan. 3, 2009, with the mining of the first block, the "Genesis Block." One million bitcoins remain in Satoshi's wallet today and have never moved.

Schnorr Signature: This is a type of digital signature system that allows multi-signature functionality for bitcoin transactions and with less data than used for the older "elliptic curve signature scheme" Bitcoin used. This was part of the Taproot upgrade approved 2021 designed to speed up the network. Schnorr signatures streamline verification by using a sum of public keys to match a sum of signatures to verify a sum of transactions in a block, instead of each transaction having to be verified separately. This further speeds up the network by allowing more transactions per block.

Seed Phrase: See "Recovery Seed Phrase."

Segregated Witness (SegWit): An upgrade to the Bitcoin protocol first proposed in 2015 and approved by the network in 2017. The primary upgrade was to increase Bitcoin's maximum block size from 1 MB to 4 MB to allow for speedier transactions, while still protecting decentralization. For more information, see the "block size" entry above. The SegWit upgrade also moved signatures outside the transaction data. This reduced the amount of space needed for transaction storage, thus allowing more transactions in a block and speeding up the network.

Self-Custody: The means you possess your own private Bitcoin key or keys on hardware wallets, disconnected from the internet. You are not trusting an exchange or third-party custodian with your keys. You are your own bank. This is the only way you can secure your bitcoin from being seized by government, a court order, or hackers.

SHA-256: SHA stands for "secure hash algorithms 256 bit" and was first developed by the U.S. National Security Agency (NSA) in 1993 to secure applications and protocols. Bitcoin uses SHA-256 to verify transactions and calculate proof-of-work math puzzles. The National Security Agency's permitted its SHA algorithms to be published in 2001. The Bitcoin network is secured by military-grade cryptography.

Signature: A digital signature in Bitcoin is proof that you own the private key without having to reveal your private key. Your signature allows you to send funds. It also ensures that no one can modify the transaction. Private keys generate unique signatures for each transaction so there can be no double-spending.

Smart Contracts: This is a computer program that executes multiple operations autonomously in accordance with the protocol, or set of rules. For example, if A is accomplished, then B can be accomplished. Escrow functions can be set up using "smart contracts." The Lightning Network incorporates "smart contracts." Ethereum is trying to build a decentralized internet for decentralized applications (DAPPs) using more complex "smart contracts" – so far without much success. The jury is still out on whether complex decentralized "smart contracts" built on blockchain technology governing complex human interactions is possible.

Stablecoins: These are crypto tokens that attempt to peg their price to a fiat currency, such as the dollar or euro. The biggest ones are Tether USDT, USDC, and Binance USD – all pegged to the dollar. MakerDao's *Dai* token, built on the Ethereum platform, is attempting to be a decentralized stablecoin governed by "smart contracts." The best use cases for stablecoins are to transmit value across borders without having to use a currency exchange, a bank wire transfer, or a service like Western Union – services that are slow and incur substantial fees.

Taproot: Approved in 2021, this was the second major upgrade in Bitcoin's history. This primarily involved batching multiple signatures and transactions together to allow for more transactions per block, thus speeding up the network. Before Taproot, each digital signature had to be validated against a public key. See the "**Schnorr Signatures**" entry above for more detail.

Testnet: Bitcoin Testnet is used by developers to test potential upgrades and improvements to the Bitcoin software and protocol. Transactions on Testnet have no monetary value. Upgrades and changes to Bitcoin require 95 percent of nodes and miners to approve before a change is adopted.

United States Federal Reserve System – "The Fed": This is the central bank of the United States. The Federal Reserve System was created by Congress and President Woodrow Wilson in 1913 with the Federal Reserve Act, ostensibly to create more economic stability. Often called "The Fed," the U.S. Federal Reserve is headquartered in Washington, DC. There are also 12 regional Federal Reserve Banks, each of which has 24 Federal Reserve bank branches. The Fed's seven-member Board of Governors is appointed by the President of the United States. Each governor is appointed to a 14-year term. The Fed manages the money supply by creating (printing) new money, sets interest rates, and regulates banks. Bitcoin was created as an alternative to fiat money printing.

UTXO (Unspent Transaction Output): This is the unspent bitcoin in your digital vault – or address.

UTXO Set: The collection of all addresses on the Bitcoin network with unspent transaction outputs (UTXOs) associated with each address. All bitcoin on the network is accounted for at all times. This allows nodes to verify the unspent outputs for each address to prevent double spending.

Wallet: A wallet holds your private Bitcoin key or keys. It can take a number of forms. "Hot Wallets" refer to any Bitcoin wallet that is connected to the internet. "Cold Storage" is a hardware wallet that is not connected to the internet, usually a USB drive device that is password protected. Veteran Bitcoiners hold multiple hardware "cold storage" wallets for redundancy. For wallet options, see chapter in this book on how "How to Start: Resources."

51 Percent Attack: A 51 percent consensus of nodes and miners is required to validate transactions. This means if a large entity, perhaps China, were to deploy computing power amounting to more than 51 percent of the combined computing power of the entire network, the attacker could conceivably overpower the network and prevent the network from functioning, might even be able to rewrite the blockchain history. No successful "51 Percent" attack has ever been launched against Bitcoin, though there have been successful "51 Percent" attacks on smaller blockchains. The Bitcoin protocol contains multiple countermeasures to reverse a "51 Percent" attack even if one were to temporarily succeed. The larger the Bitcoin network grows, the more computing hash power is needed to mount a successful "51 Percent" attack. The proof-of-work security algorithm and protocol is aimed specifically at preventing "51 Percent," denial-of-service (DoS) and similar attacks.

Index

Index

Index

Index

Index

About Benjamin Hart

B en has been in the advertising business for more than 30 years. His letters, ads and websites have generated more than $1 billion for his clients. Ben has written a number of books, including:

- *How to Write Blockbuster Sales Letters* (2006)
- *Fund Your Cause: Secrets of Successful Direct Mail Fundraising* (2005)
- *Faith & Freedom: The Christian Roots of American Liberty* (1988)
- *Poisoned Ivy: The War on Freedom of Thought by America's Elite Colleges.* (1984)

Ben is a freedom "maximalist." He graduated in 1982 from Dartmouth College where he helped found America's most famous pro-freedom student newspaper *The Dartmouth Review* in 1980, and which continues to publish.

Ben's first book *Poisoned Ivy*, which he wrote during his senior year at Dartmouth, chronicles the founding of *The Dartmouth Review* and was the first book to describe the odd "woke" ideology (which Ben called "The Ethos") that was taking hold in the faculty lounges of America's elite colleges and that aims to end freedom of thought. *Poisoned Ivy* was a national bestseller. Ben and his wife Wanda have six children.

About Ben's Wife, Wanda
and why she likes Bitcoin

Wanda at age 15

Life was good in Laos until suddenly it wasn't. The Communists conquered her country in 1975. Wanda says it was much like the movie *The Killing Fields*.

In 1979, Wanda, at age 13, escaped with her mom through the jungle. Wanda's mom had a small amount of gold, which she sewed into the threads of Wanda's dress where thieves would not notice it.

They left all their other possessions behind, including two houses.

They managed to cross the mighty Mekong river to Thailand in the dead of night. They walked for many days and nights, and eventually found their way to a refugee camp. They spent nearly two years there before they were able to board a boat to America.

Wanda arrived in America at age 15 with two dresses and one pair of sandals. Wanda really understands the value of Bitcoin.

Civilization is fragile. It can collapse at any moment, and usually happens when you least expect it. Bitcoin is your insurance against economic and political system collapse.

Stay in Touch with Ben & Wanda!
Sign up for Ben's <u>FREE</u> *Bitcoin Weekly Report* at

BitcoinInstitute.Net